A BIG WHALE HUNT
Whalers from the Roych Fleet strike it rich. (From a contemporary painting in the New Bedford Whaling Museum)

THE BARK *GREYHOUND*
This was the last sailing ship Captain Joe served on.

Captain Joe

Whaleman From New Bedford

by

CAPTAIN JOSEPH GOMES

as told to

DON SEVRENS

VANTAGE PRESS   NEW YORK   WASHINGTON   HOLLYWOOD

FIRST EDITION

All rights reserved, including the right of reproduction in whole or in part in any form

Copyright, 1960, by Joseph Gomes and Don Sevrens

Published by Vantage Press, Inc.
120 West 31st Street, New York 1, N. Y.

Manufactured in the United States of America

Library of Congress Catalog Card Number: 59-14290

To the late

CAPTAIN ANTONIO C. CORVELLO,
who started me on my career as a whaleman
and taught me the rudiments of navigation;
and
WILLIAM H. TRIPP, former Curator of the
New Bedford Whaling Museum, who often encouraged me to climb the ladder to the title of
Master Mariner

PREFACE

Joseph Gomes was born on one of the Azores islands.

As a boy he saw the native islanders go out in their thirty-foot whaleboats and chase and kill many sperm whales. The dead whales were towed ashore, and on inclined stagings they were stripped of their blubber.

Brick try-works had been constructed nearby. The blubber was boiled in the big iron pots and rendered into the valuable sperm oil. With this shore whaling young Gomes became quite familiar.

What fascinated him the most were the big whaleships which from time to time visited his island. These vessels came from New Bedford and other whaling ports, and stopped there to get supplies, and to sign on the islanders as crew members.

One of these whaling vessels was the schooner *Pedro Varella*, whose master was Captain Antonio Corvello. Young Joe shipped on the schooner as cabin boy and seaman.

Captain Corvello's next voyage was as master of the bark *Greyhound*. He had taken an interest in young Gomes, so he shipped him as a boat steerer.

While Gomes was making good progress as a whaleman, the business was dying out. He was advised by whaling captains and others to give up whaling, and to try to get into steamboating.

Mr. Gomes acted on this suggestion and soon became an assistant pilot on the steamships *Maine* and *New Hampshire* of a line of passenger vessels running daily from New Bedford to New York. These were overnight trips. Being very ambitious and eager to advance, while the steamship was docked at New York during the daytime, he attended a school or college of navigation in Brooklyn, N.Y. In a few years, he graduated with the proud degree of master mariner.

As the years rolled on, he eventually went to the west coast and became a steamship inspector at Los Angeles, California.

In the pages which follow, Captain Gomes tells a most fascinating story of his salty seafaring life.

W.H.T.

June 25, 1959
New Bedford, Mass.

CONTENTS

Chapter		Page
I	Stowaway	9
II	Madam Three Bellies	16
III	Pigs 'n' Chickens for Davy Jones	27
IV	Whaleboats and Whales	31
V	Fajazinha and the Festival	39
VI	Sailor's Return	50
VII	The Fighting Whale	54
VIII	Turtles, Eggs, The Devil's Sister	57
IX	Heaven!	64
X	Another Port, Another Girl	71
XI	Horses Versus Whales	77
XII	Waterlogged	84
XIII	New Ship—New Job	91
XIV	First Whale	97
XV	A Gam and a Stop at Flores	105
XVI	Bedbugs and Cockroaches	109
XVII	Splice the Main Brace!	112
XVIII	Sailor Ashore	116
XIX	Dangerous Harbor	125
XX	The Whistler and the Barbeech	132
XXI	Flying Boat Steerer	139
XXII	Strange Medicine	144
XXIII	Not My Type	148

Chapter		Page
XXIV	Captains' Rendezvous	151
XXV	Going Up!	160
XXVI	Tidal Wave	167
XXVII	Free Show at Sea	173
XXVIII	The Captain's Festival	179
XXIX	Sailor's Holiday	188
XXX	Killing the Schoolmaster	193
XXXI	Nantucket Sleigh Ride	198
XXXII	The Doll of St. Helena	203
XXXIII	Full Ship and Linda's Sister	212
XXXIV	Sudden Blow	220
XXXV	Failing Fortunes	223
XXXVI	New Horizons	227
XXXVII	From Dungarees to Uniforms	230
XXXVIII	Navigation and Knockouts	236
XXXIX	Young Captain	241
XL	Officer or Sailor?	248
XLI	Count Felix Von Luckner	253
XLII	*Aqui Nos Estamos,* Barcelona	255
XLIII	Flower of Madrid	259
XLIV	Empty Ship—Homeward Bound	270

CHAPTER I

STOWAWAY

Mine was a seafaring family. My father was the master and part owner of the bark *Fairhaven*, a three-masted square-rigger, whose home port was New Bedford, Massachusetts. As long as I can remember, it was the only ship on which he ever sailed as master. What ships he was on before I was born, I do not know.

My father was a man of rather stern appearance, with a dignified bearing—straight, lean and tall. He had black, wavy hair, rather kind-looking eyes, and he always wore a big, black moustache. From the moment he arose in the morning until he went to bed at night, he kept a chunk of plug chewing-tobacco, as big as his thumb, in one cheek. He seldom spoke, but when he did his first words were preceded by a well-directed spurt of black fluid, which, I am sure, would have filled a teacup. Then followed a swipe with a big red handkerchief; but to this day I cannot remember ever having seen a drop of tobacco juice on my father's face or chin. He was clean-cut, even-tempered, and loved by everyone. I never heard of his maltreating any man in all his years at sea, nor did I ever hear of his having any trouble with his men.

My mother was a beautiful woman. She first caught my father's eye when she was fifteen. They were married shortly afterward, and from that moment he never let her out of his sight if he could help it.

Their honeymoon was a four-year whaling voyage on the bark

Fairhaven, after which they wintered in New Bedford. In the spring, they embarked on another four-year voyage, during which my older brother and older sister were both born—at sea. My father served as doctor and nurse. My mother seemed none the worse for her experience, for she enjoyed good health throughout all of her long life.

They wintered again in New Bedford, and in the spring my mother insisted on going to sea with my father, as before.

They headed for the western whaling grounds, a large body of water that lies off Newfoundland, with the Azores almost in the center. On the way to meet the mother ship, they stopped to visit my grandmother in the village of Fajazinha, on the Island of Flores in the Azores.

They found my grandmother ill. My father, in spite of his desire to have his wife and family with him, insisted that my mother remain in Flores to care for my grandmother. There was no one else to do it.

From there, my father continued on to the Island of Fayal, about a hundred miles to the eastward, to meet the mother ship, discharge the summer's catch of oil, take on provisions and continue on to the southern or winter whaling grounds in the South Atlantic.

I was born about four months after my mother landed on Flores. My father paid visits occasionally, usually once a year. Sometimes, about every three or four years, he would miss a yearly visit because of having to return to the home port of New Bedford, but on occasion he would spend the winter in Flores instead.

The first twelve years of my life were rather uneventful. After school hours I became very skillful, beginning at the age of seven, at catching eels. I recall one in particular that I captured in a covered culvert where the stream ran under the village square. There was barely room to crawl on my hands and knees and keep my head above water. I caught the eel on a hook, using a rabbit's heart that I had obtained from a neighbor. It was a very large eel and it fought me all the way out of that two-hundred-foot-long tunnel. It wrapped itself around me—around my arms, my legs, my neck—and though I was ten years old at the time, I got out of there completely exhausted. My mother scolded me roundly, saying that I might have drowned and the eel might have bitten me. Well, as for drowning, that never occurred to me, and I assured my mother, with my ten-year-old wisdom, that eels don't bite.

Aside from catching eels, there wasn't much to do other than the usual deviltry which boys of that age can originate. I must have been fairly adept at that, because people whom I have talked to later in life, who knew me then, left me with the impression that I must have been some special kind of stinker. I recall one incident that might have helped to create such a thought.

There was a woman, a widow of about forty, who lived a short distance from our house. She was always very good to us, giving us cookies and things, and we were very fond of her. Being a widow, she always dressed in black, according to the custom among our people. There was also a girl named Leopoldina (four or five years older than I) whom I disliked heartily.

Now, it was the custom for the women of our village to do their washing in a pool just above the spot where the stream entered the long culvert under the village square. They would kneel on the smooth, flat rocks at water level and wash their laundry, piece by piece.

I came to the pool one day, prior to entering the culvert in search of eels, and there was Leopoldina, dressed in white, with her back toward me, busily engaged. I crept up quietly, grabbed her by the stern and shoved her, face downward, into the water. But it wasn't Leopoldina! It was the cooky lady instead. She was the same size as Leopoldina, but that was the only time I ever saw her dressed in white.

I was horrified. I pulled her out and walked home with her, carrying her laundry. I think I cried most of the way.

Frank, another boy, saw the whole thing and promptly told his mother, who in turn told my mother, and she asked the cooky lady about it. Anyone who knows boys would know why we loved the cooky lady. She simply said to my mother, "No, Frank made a mistake."

This still would not have saved Leopoldina if the opportunity had occurred again.

At Fajazinha the sea was the nearest thing to us. Probably because my father and many other relatives were seafaring men, I was determined to follow in their footsteps.

By the time I was fifteen years old, my father had built a large stone house. Also by then, a younger brother, Frank, and two younger sisters, Maria and Louisa, had been born—all the result of my father's occasional visits to Fajazinha.

As I said, I wanted to go to sea and become a captain like my father. Mary, my older sister, had recently become engaged to the captain of the *Pedro Varella,* a two-masted whaling schooner. This looked like an opportunity to me, so I asked Captain Corvello if he would take me sailing with him.

"Oh, no, Joe," he said. "You are too small. You are only a boy. You can't do anything."

"Well, I can peel potatoes."

He agreed to take me on as cabin boy.

One thing stood in the way, however. In the Azores, every native-born boy, regardless of parentage, has a military obligation and is not allowed to leave his island until it is fulfilled. At the age of nineteen or twenty, he is called into military service and must serve two years. After that, he is free to go wherever he likes.

The crews of the whalers at that time were mostly Cape Verdian fellows and West Indians, mostly blacks, but some were mulattoes.

To get on board a whaler, I would have to fool the authorities. I would have to pass as a member of the crew. I had to be black. Furthermore, I would have to embark from Fayal, a neighboring island. And I would have to go there by steamer—which I did, with my mother's consent.

I should explain here that the ships are anchored in the bay at Fayal Harbor, inside the breakwater. One goes from ship to shore in whaleboats, rowed by some of the ship's crew.

Well, I was black all right—a good, shiny black. I had bought a can of shoe polish and covered every visible portion of my skin with it. I mixed in with some fellows who were having a good time ashore, and I told them that I was going aboard the *Pedro Varella.*

"Well, I'm on that ship," one of them told me.

"What is the name of the captain?" I asked.

"Captain Corvello."

"That's right. He is the captain, and he is going to marry my sister."

That, I thought, was a real feather in my cap. Anyway, this fellow, Tony, took me out to the ship and put me on board. I went by the authorities like a breeze. They never gave me a second glance. They never even gave me a first glance—they never found me. Tony hid me in the cargo hold between the casks, which, by that time, were filled with water. We were to sail two days later.

I stayed in that hold for two days and three nights, literally wedged between those casks—wedged in so tightly I could hardly move.

I formed an everlasting abhorrence of cockroaches then. They crawled up my legs, down my neck, into my sleeves. And I could do nothing about it. The only consolation was that they didn't bite. But they tickled. They made me itch. I hated them.

Tony told the captain where he had hidden me.

"Okay, keep him there and feed him. Take fruit to him two or three times a day and leave him some crackers, hardtack and water. Make sure that he gets enough water."

On the day we were to leave, the customs officials and the police came aboard to search the ship for stowaways. They did a thorough job. When they got down among the casks where they could neither see nor reach, they would take a long pointed sword and thrust it into the spaces.

When they got to where I was hidden, my heart almost stopped beating. There was just enough light reflecting down through the hatchway so that I could glimpse that deadly point flashing in and out around me. It passed so close to my face that I swear I could smell the steel; so close to my hand that I felt the rush of the blade. I felt it scratch my clothing. Had it struck me, I should probably have yelled. Of course, that is the effect it was intended to have. But, naturally, I was determined not to make a sound.

After lying there for two days and three nights, I would rather have died than give myself away. But those cockroaches! Those devilish cockroaches—I'll never forget them as long as I live.

The officials left soon afterward, satisfied that there were no stowaways on board. There was a lot of noise. I didn't know what it was. The ship could have been breaking up and sinking, for all I knew. But the noise, I learned later, was from heaving up the chains to take up the anchor, and from hoisting and setting sails, preparatory to getting under way. At the moment, however, I just had to trust to luck. I was still just a little black boy hidden down among the casks, with the cockroaches still crawling over me.

I don't know how long it was—it seemed like an eternity—before Tony came down to get me out of that hole. He had to pull me out by my feet, as I couldn't possibly turn around or get out unassisted. The ship was rolling and pitching, and I was getting seasick. I didn't know then what it was, but it felt like a whole revolution in my stomach.

When Tony brought me out on deck, I was really dizzy. I couldn't walk, or even stand. I could only crawl. When the captain saw me, he let out with the greatest laughter I have ever heard from anyone. He said he had never seen anyone so shiny, and so black.

Then he went to his cabin and returned with his washbasin, soap, and a towel; and I got some of it off. Not too much, I guess, for I was too busy hanging over the rail. I was heaving as hard as I could, and I remained in that condition for eight straight days. On the eighth day, I crawled on my hands and knees and dragged myself to the quarter-deck, where the captain was seated, and begged of him, "Captain, please knock me on the head and throw me overboard. The Lord will forgive you."

He just laughed. "Oh, you don't know what you're talking about. You'll get well after 'while."

"Oh, no. Please, I am so sick. I've got nothing else to throw up. The water stinks, the food stinks, everything stinks. Please! I forgive you, and the Lord will forgive you. Please! Just kill me and throw me overboard!"

He laughed some more, and tried to make me more comfortable. At heart, he was really a rather kind man but, oh boy, he could be, and was, rough on me.

He was rather a young fellow, twenty-nine or thirty, rather Irish-looking, with red hair and red whiskers. He acted much like an Irishman too, and he was a very good, very conscientious sailor and captain.

The mate—chief mate or first mate, but simply called "mate" on the whalers—was a very kind man. He took hold of me and washed my face and hands. I was still pretty black.

At sea, all greenhorns, meaning new sailors, get their clothing—oilskins, boots, dungarees, sou'westers—from what is known as the slopchest. When the slopchest is opened, the old sailors get whatever they need in the way of clothing for the next six months.

So, after I had gotten what I needed from the slopchest, the mate helped me to change my clothes and I felt a little better, but I still couldn't stand on my feet. I was still too sick to care much about anything. I went over to the carpenter's bench and leaned back against the try works, head tilted back and eyes closed, with the sun shining on my face. After a while, I smelled another disagreeable odor and I opened my eyes. Two sailors were putting on their oilskins. I closed my eyes again, and thought no more about them. I was in a lonely world with my horrible *mal de mer*.

I didn't realize that the sunlight had disappeared until I felt raindrops on my face. I felt no disposition to move or to do anything at all. I could have been completely submerged and I would not have cared. The drops thickened into a downpour. I opened my mouth and took in the rushing drops. It laved my eyelids and my face and I sat silently, motionlessly, becoming drenched in the downpour. After a while, the rain subsided but I sat on, hardly noticing the sailors removing their oilskins. I was barely conscious of the freshened breeze and the motion of the ship sailing along under full sail. I was conscious of the fact that the breeze felt good, coming through my wet clothing. Gradually my clothing dried and I was aware that I felt considerably refreshed. For the first time, I began to feel an interest in what was going on around me. Even so, for many days and most of the nights, the carpenter's bench was my private refuge and I usually sat there in that same position, leaning back against the try works, my eyes closed, my mind in a state of semi-awareness, trying to close out the sickness of the sea.

CHAPTER II

MADAM THREE BELLIES

I still couldn't eat, or even drink water. From the time we left Fayal, on the 28th of September, 1910, to the time we arrived at Barbados, West Indies, on the 28th of March, exactly six months later, my stomach never really got settled. The coffee would stink so that I used to hold my coffee cup with my right hand and my nose with my left. The water was foul, and they kept the coffee hot twenty-four hours a day. I tried my best, but the coffee was too strong, and I wasn't a seaman yet.

After about a month, I was able to do my work fairly well. My job was to wash the dishes and the tablecloths, scrub the cabin floors and the officers' cabins, and do whatever the steward, who was the cook's and cabin boy's boss, wanted me to do.

By the time we got to Barbados, I was sixteen. I hadn't gained any weight but I had grown a little. The seasickness had gradually begun to wear off, and as I felt better I began to go about the deck and learn more about the sailors' work on a sailing ship. By the end of that first six months, I was getting fairly good at climbing the masts and getting about in the rigging. One thing helped: I wasn't afraid. I was determined to be a good sailor.

We stayed at Barbados for four or five days. While there, I asked the captain if he would let me go in the fo'c's'le, and let me be a sailor.

"Well," he said, doubtfully, "you are a little too small. You're too young to do that kind of work. That's rough."

"Yes, captain," I argued, "but I can do it. I have been doing it right along. I go up the masthead practically without using the ratlines. I can go from one mast to the other, swing in the stays, and do anything the sailors do, with the exception of rowing. I am not very good at that, but I'll learn, this month while we are ashore. I will learn to row, and I will be a good sailor."

You see, our next stop was Dominica, where we were to meet the supply ship, ("mother ship," to us), discharge oil and take on supplies. We expected to be there about a month.

The captain agreed that if I would show ambition he would let me do it.

After six months at sea, and especially after the violent seasickness I had experienced, plus the prolonged discomfort that followed, my first and most natural desire, when we arrived at Barbados, was to set foot on solid ground. However, though the starboard watch, of which I was a member, was the first to go ashore, I was not permitted to go along. I should explain here that the starboard watch was always the first to go ashore on a two-watch ship.

As there was no work to be done on board ship that first afternoon, the starboard watch promptly took off. I was not only left behind that day, but the next day also. In fact, I never set foot on Barbados at all on that first trip. Neither the mates nor the boat steerers, who ranked as petty officers, nor even the members of the crew, would let me go. This had been my first experience at sea and, God knows, after that first six months, I wanted to set foot on solid ground.

Regardless of what I had in mind, however, the crew had something else. They watched me constantly. Whenever any boat went ashore, for whatever cause, there was someone on my tail.

All day long there were bumboats alongside, selling stuff. Furthermore, the girls were always trying to sell stuff to the sailors and trying to get aboard even though it was against regulations. Of course, if the mates were out of sight, the crew encouraged the girls to come aboard. There was always someone around to see that I didn't get away on one of those bumboats, or even near enough to the girls to talk to them.

I was only sixteen years old then, but those girls looked doggone good to me. After you're out to sea for six months, any girl would look doggone good, and I liked to talk to them. But, by gosh, those guys wouldn't even let me get close enough for that. Anyway, at that age I had no bad thoughts in my head and I just couldn't figure it out.

On the third day, the captain came aboard and told us that he had clearance papers and would set sail that morning. We picked up anchor and sailed out. We didn't need tugboats since we were on the lee side of the island and the trade winds on the lee side of Barbados are always favorable to get out without assistance. All we had to do was to get up the foresail and, I believe, the forestaysail, raise the anchors and get under way.

We set up the rest of the sails on the lee side of Barbados and got out into the open sea in the early afternoon. We coasted around the north end of the Dominica coast—the Island of Dominica—where we were to meet the mother ship and the other whalers, discharge oil and take on water and supplies. We went around the north end of Dominica and, naturally, had to jibe over as we were coming around the northwest corner into the harbor.

As we came around the knoll we could see that some of the whaling ships were already in ahead of us. We could also see the mother ship anchored in the harbor, which is on the lee side of the island and is very sheltered, since the Trade Winds come only from one direction. So we kept on tacking ship.

Tacking ship is maneuvering back and forth to come up to the windward. Angling to right and left is called starboard tack and port tack. It is done in order to come up close to the other ships, or to the anchorage.

We began shortening jibs—outer jibs and topsails—and getting up to the anchorage. Naturally, we lowered the mainsail and the jib, held the ship on the wind, and let go the anchor. That left us with the foresail and forestaysail heading straight into the wind, causing us to drift, as with a steamer or motorboat which is put in reverse so as to slack back on the chain.

When the anchor hits bottom, the chain has to be slacked off so that it can drag enough to catch and hold at an angle, which requires a length of chain three times the depth of the water. This means that with a depth of fifteen fathoms (called one shackle) on the chain, measured from or next to the hawse pipe, two more shackles (thirty more fathoms) must be let out to allow the proper angle for the anchor to catch or dig in, as in sand, and hold.

As soon as we dropped anchor, a boat came from the mother ship—a big four-masted schooner—and the captain and the mate came aboard to greet our captain. Captain Corey of the mother ship was a good friend of Captain Corvello, our captain, and also of my father. He had seen my father before leaving New Bedford, and my father had told him I was on the *Pedro Varella* and asked him to carry a message to me. Consequently, after he had been aboard for a short time, he asked Captain Corvello to send for me. He introduced himself to me and we had the usual greeting, boy to man.

Captain Corey was a man of fifty, I would say, very dignified in appearance. He looked more like a diplomat than the captain of a sailing ship.

My English isn't too good today. At that time it was horrible. I could speak Portuguese, Spanish, and a little French, but the only English I knew was what I had learned from orders spoken on shipboard, which were always given in English. I used my head, my face, my hands. I guess I really talked with my hands. At any rate, Captain Corey seemed to understand me.

My father wanted me to know that he was happy over my determination to become a captain, and in the letter he included a hundred dollars in bills in American money. He thought I might need some in an emergency and, of course, he knew how much, or how little, a cabin boy would get at the end of a voyage. He was always doing things like that. He also encouraged me to keep studying and to learn English.

I had brought a Portuguese-Spanish dictionary with me from Fayal, and was getting on pretty well with it. I had been unable to get an English dictionary, however. I was at a further disadvantage, too. Most of the sailors spoke Portuguese or Spanish and some French. On Dominica, English and French were spoken. On St. Eustatius, a Dutch island which was always called Santastatia by the sailors, they spoke English almost entirely. Our third mate was from there, and had I paid more attention to him, I could have learned more English.

I intended going to the United States and becoming an American citizen. My older brother and sister, having been born aboard an American ship were, by law, American citizens. I realized the fact that if I were to become an American citizen I would have to learn English. So I asked Captain Corey if he would get me a Portuguese-English dictionary. He got me one from the bark *Bertha,* which came in about a week later.

I set myself to the practice of studying about five hours a day, and by the middle of the summer I had practically memorized that dictionary. All the time, I kept before me the goal of becoming an American citizen and sailing an American ship, as my father had done before me.

But to return to our arrival in Dominica: after the formalities were over and the doctor and customs officials had boarded the ship, we received boats from the other ships and from the crews that were already ashore. The other captains came aboard to shake hands with our captain and to exchange news and gossip and compare individual catches of oil. After all, oil was our business, and it was the only reason we were there.

After we had the sails furled and everything shipshape, we were ready—the starboard watch, that is—to go ashore.

Since we were anchored about a half mile from the pier, we had to have a boat. Consequently, we did the customary thing on such an occasion. We removed all the gear from the second mate's boat and used it for transportation.

So far as I was concerned, there was an entirely different attitude about my going ashore this time. Whereas previously everyone had watched me like a hawk at Barbados, to keep me from going ashore, now they were interested in getting me there as quickly as possible. However, the steward, who was my boss, wouldn't let me go until he could go also, so the crew got busy and helped him get ready. We had a whole boatload ready to take off with that starboard watch.

The village has only two streets. They might both be called Main Street, although I don't know whether they even had names. I would call the first street Front Street. We landed at the pier and started up Front Street. That crew stuck with me, surrounded me as though I were a magnet of some kind, and they favored me as if I were a **tin god.**

I wanted to know what was going on. "What the heck? What is this all about?"

"Wait. You'll see. Come on. You'll see." That was all they would tell me. We kept walking. We passed two or three barrooms. Some of the men wanted to go in, but the others wouldn't let them. There were women and girls there, outside the houses and especially the barrooms, calling to us to come in. But that gang stuck together like a flock of chickens, with me in the center. No one was allowed to deviate from the course we were taking up the street, and I didn't like it one bit. As we were walking along, we were collecting a crowd of sailors from other ships, as they came out of the barrooms. They knew they had a pigeon in their midst, but I didn't know what was going on. We finally got to a place where they called to a woman by a name that I learned later was known to all the whalers at sea.

"Three Bellies. Hey, Three Bellies. Come over here. We got a pigeon for you!" I still didn't know what it was all about; but she came over and crooned, "Sonny Boy. Oh, you are tender. How old are you?"

"Sixteen," I said, trying to get away.

"Oh, Sonny Boy, what a treat Mama Three Bellies is going to have with you."

I squirmed loose and ran. I still didn't know what it was all about, and I was a little bit scared, too. But it wasn't much use. Those guys caught up with me immediately and brought me back. Mama Three Bellies started running her hands over my face and was really making me blush, and I'm not the blushing kind either.

I began to do a little thinking then. I remembered hearing certain remarks on board the ship: "We're heading for Three Bellies' country"; "We'll see Three Bellies pretty soon"; "We've got a pigeon on this trip." This was strictly a frame-up, a put-up job. All the watchfulness at Barbados—and *now!*

I was locked in Three Bellies' house. Every door and window was checked, and I wasn't let out until about two hours later. After they let me out, they went in a body down the street with me on their shoulders, chanting, "Three Bellies has done it again!"

I had been initiated in the full tradition of a novice, of a kid like me, as a sailor on a whaling ship. I was a full-fledged sailor in anybody's language.

All I ever learned about Three Bellies was that she was the most famous prostitute in the West Indies. Every sailor who ever walked down the street with her referred to her as "Your Majesty." Prestige seems to be a peculiar thing. It depends on where, who, and what you are, according to the local customs.

During that stay on Dominica, Three Bellies' house was mine. If anyone was there when I came to the door, he left immediately. While I was there, no one was allowed to enter. That was the unwritten law—the custom.

It was customary for the captain to sleep ashore and let the mates take care of the ship. The captain would come aboard at about the middle of the day.

Now that I was initiated as a sailor, I couldn't understand why I could not be one. I met the captain when he came aboard. He asked me how I felt about the incident of the day before. I felt my face turn kind of red, and then he asked me what I wanted to see him about. I told him that the crew had called me a full-fledged sailor, and that I wanted to be one; that I didn't want to be a cabin boy any longer. I had talked to the chief mate and he had agreed to keep me on the shore boat as one of the oarsmen, so that I could learn to row, if the captain would allow it.

I told this to the captain and he laughed and said, "Okay, Joe. Now that you're a man and a sailor, I'll have to let you try it." So the captain told the mate to take me on deck; that I was to become a sailor. He also told the steward that I wasn't working for him any longer.

The bay at Dominica is very smooth, being on the lee side of the island. It is quite large—eight or ten miles across at the mouth—with rocks at the sides, at the entrance, and close to the beaches, but as it goes in toward the village and the river's mouth, there are beaches of beautiful, fine sand. We were anchored a mile and a half or two miles out, and our principal task was, in sailor's language, "making water." We would fill the oil casks with water at the river and tow them to the ship.

I was put on the starboard watch. I worked very hard, and after the second mate saw me handle the oars a few times, he knew that I meant business and that he could do something with me.

I wasn't big, but I was tough, and I could fight my way through wildcats.

The captain was always getting after me because of my getting into fights. I would jump any sailor on the ship. Whether I beat him or got beaten didn't make too much difference to me. One day while in Dominica, I got into a fight with one of the boat steerers, a petty officer.

It was customary for the women of the village to do washings, particularly for the sailors, there at the river where we were making water. Having no means of transportation, they would walk from the village, about a mile away. I don't believe I ever saw a horse and wagon there; only a saddle horse now and then. The women would wash a bundle of sailor's clothing for a shilling. Some sailors would make a contract with a woman and bring her several bundles from their fellow sailors.

The rocks were smooth, and each woman had her place for washing clothes.

Well, I was talking to a young woman who was between eighteen and twenty years old, when this boat steerer—I remember his name, Jack Carr, a fellow from Trinidad—came by. The girl was pleasant and nice and I was enjoying talking with her and watching her wash clothes. I guess she was attracted to me a little too. Anyway, there was no malice in my thoughts, but Jack started to give me the dickens. He said, "While you are here in Dominica this trip, you have to be true to Three Bellies, and whether we are here two weeks or six, she's your woman and you have to be true to her. Any time you go up to her house, regardless of who she's got in the house she's got to put him out and take you in. That's the regulation. Everybody knows that, so you stop talkin' to this woman."

I tried to tell him that I was just having innocent conversation. He grabbed me and choked me and dragged me away from her. He was bigger and older than I, and a petty officer. But, after all, I was ashore. I popped him in the eye. They told me afterwards that before he knew what had happened I hit him five times, two rights and three lefts, or vice versa. Only I didn't know enough then to keep away from him, and he caught me and really gave me a whaling.

Anyway, he had a black eye and a cut lip. During the rest of that trip, while in Dominica I stayed away from anything that wore skirts. I just kept on with the job we were on—making water.

When the mother ship arrived, she dumped empty casks overboard for the various ships. Ours had the letters "P.V." stenciled on the sides. Normally we would have had two reserve water-casks on board, which would be partially empty by the time we came into port. We would refill these also, while waiting for our turn to discharge the oil casks and take on supplies.

On the *Pedro Varella,* which was a small schooner, we naturally carried a lot less water than does a bigger ship with more space in the hold. The *Pedro Varella* had been a gunboat in the Civil War. She was a ninety-three-foot vessel of ninety-one tons, and when I went on her she was sixty-seven years old. A larger whaler carried only a slightly larger crew: one additional whaleboat with a crew of six men, plus two more men as ship's keepers while the boats were out whaling.

All casks had to be filled, regardless. Otherwise they would dry out. The difference was that there was a lot less water per man on a small ship than on a larger one. Also, if we had good luck in filling up with oil at the beginning of the season and then had poor luck later on, we could run awfully short of water. A lot of that precious water would have to be dumped to make room for the oil.

Finally came our turn alongside the mother ship. To get alongside, we lowered two of our own whaleboats with their crews. The rest of the crew stayed aboard to heave up the anchor to the hawse pipe. The two boats then towed us to the mother ship. One boat could have towed it very easily, but I believe the captain didn't want to lower the dignity of the ship, since all the other whalers required two. The *Pedro Varella* was the smallest whaler in the fleet.

When we got close to the mother ship, we put lines out, and tied up alongside, with the fenders on the mother ship between, to act as bumpers and help to slide alongside easily.

The name of the mother ship was the *Richard W. Clark,* and she hailed from New Bedford, Massachusetts. To me, at that time, she was very large and very nice. Today, of course, after years on big steamers, she seems very small. But I was looking at her then through the eyes of a sixteen-year-old boy, and comparing her size with that of our small schooner. She was a large four-master, and when we tied up alongside her, it was like a cow with a newborn calf. There was that much difference. I climbed up the masthead to get the full effect.

After all, she had to take on the oil from seventeen whalers and, as I said before, ours was the smallest of the lot.

We stayed alongside for two days, taking the oil casks out with the boom from the mother ship. To stow away well on our small ship, we had to use smaller casks running in size from five to twelve barrels each. The smaller casks afforded better stowage on the forward end and wings, with the larger casks placed amidships. Our barrel capacity was something over five hundred barrels. Since cow whales are comparatively small, that represented a lot of whales. A very large cow would yield up to thirty barrels. One day we had seven cows alongside, but got only a little more than a hundred barrels from the lot. Our cargo represented between forty and sixty whales for the season, unless we were lucky enough to get some good bulls.

When the oil was unloaded the operation was reversed. We took on a brand-new cask filled with clothes, boots, dungarees, and so on. Hardtack came in casks. Molasses and corned beef came in barrels.

When the job was finished, we got two boats ready to tow the *Pedro Varella* back to our anchorage where we had left our filled water casks tied together and anchored with a cage anchor. It was always good policy to use two boats to pull away, one at the bow and one at the stern so that one ship couldn't sweep into another.

At our old anchorage we dropped anchor, pulled the casks alongside, took up the cage anchor, and took on the job of precisely stowing the casks. The small casks we pulled up by hand with rope and tackle. For the larger ones we rigged a derrick, using the forepeak boom. That's the big piece of wood on top of the foresail, used to keep the foresail spread. We would disconnect the part of the windlass that engages the anchor chains, lead a line to the windlass, and just use the capstans to haul in such heavy material.

Stowing the casks in the hold is a job requiring precision. They had to be stowed so they would not roll in the slightest degree, and every little space counted. They were then chocked up with special chocks of soft wood that we were able to get right there in Dominica, by the river. Presumably the wood belonged to the King or Queen, or perhaps to no one at all. We just went and cut it, split it and sawed it into pieces so that we could lay the casks one on top of the other, three deep and four across, athwartships.

When we started to use the water we would begin at the forward end. As each cask became empty, we swabbed out any remaining water that could not be siphoned out. The swab was wrung or squeezed out so that not a drop of water was wasted if we could help it. The only time we wasted water was when we would run out of empty casks for oil. Then it had to be dumped overboard. Ordinarily, the casks would have been empty long enough to be fairly dry so that there was no danger of mixing any water with the oil. When we did have to dump water overboard to make room for oil, it always made us feel pretty bad. Of course, we were lucky to get the oil. That's what we were there for.

We were at Dominica about five weeks. The day of departure brought up something I didn't know about. No one had told me. The crew lowered a boat and two men escorted me ashore and up to Three Bellies' house. I had to bid her farewell. Those crazy sailors called it a divorce. I didn't want to go, but I was forced to go ashore. The captain knew about it and didn't interfere. He saw me leave with the two sailors and knew perfectly well what it was all about. Anyway, Three Bellies was no longer obligated to me, nor I to her. When I came aboard, the crew all gave me the "Hip-hip-hooray, Joe's got his divorce," followed by a big "Ha, ha, ha." The tradition of the sailors and the sea had been served.

The customs officers came aboard, gave us our clearance papers. We picked up anchor and put out to sea.

CHAPTER III

PIGS 'N' CHICKENS FOR DAVY JONES

With sails set we left Dominica for Santastatia and the Western Grounds, sailing down between the islands of the West Indies—smooth sailing and fast—with the wind behind us, off our starboard quarter. Leaving Dominica about noon we sailed that night, the next day and night, and were hove to the following morning. That is, we had to shorten sail and wait for daylight and drop anchor off Santastatia, one of three Dutch islands. We used to buy yams and potatoes there, since Dominica produced very little of any kind of produce—only a little fruit—and had practically no cultivation of any kind. At Barbados we had taken on only enough fresh produce to last until we reached Santastatia.

The officials came aboard as usual, and while the produce was being brought aboard and the ship's business getting settled, we set about getting everything shipshape—sewing canvas, splicing lines—everything that needed to be done prior to the summer season on the Western Grounds. This was our last port of call and we had to take advantage of it.

The morning after the captain came aboard with his clearance papers, we weighed anchor, set sail, and went around the lee side of the island. We soon came around it and sailed off into the blue yonder.

With a pretty stiff trade-winds breeze, we made good time until we got into the calms of the Sargasso Sea, five or six hundred miles from Santastatia. We were also getting the counter-current which recurs around the Atlantic and, after several days of very little progress, we could see that we were running into a storm.

Before going to bed the captain advised the second mate, who was then on watch, not to take any chances on the topsails; to take in the topsails and the flying jibs. Of course I wasn't much of a sailor yet, and the second mate made me stay on deck. He sent experienced sailors to the masthead and out on the flying jib boom; first to furl the topsails and then the flying jib.

The ship was already rolling and pitching very heavily. Every little while the flying jib boom would dive into the waves. It was ten o'clock by then, and very dark. The men finished the job of furling the flying jib. By then we were on the port tack and the vessel was heeling 'way over. The second mate wanted to raise the boats on the port side as high on the davits as they would go, to keep them from getting smashed. But Michael, one of the boat steerers, a nephew of the chief mate's and an old sailor, suggested that it would be better to do it on the starboard tack, as the bulwarks on the port or lee side were very well under water.

The mate thought we could do it without incident, so we hoisted up the second mate's boat, which was on the starboard quarter. Then we tacked ship, which brought the port side around into the weather, with the boats high above the water. We raised the number one boat—the chief mate's boat—but the mate was afraid to try to raise the number three boat without more manpower. The third mate's boat—number three boat—was farther up on the bow about midships, abreast of the foremast, and in a much more dangerous position.

There, when the ship plunged into a wave, the men hoisting up the boat could be swept back against the rigging or washed overboard. The mate, fearing trouble, called up the port watch a halfhour early. The weather was getting heavier by the minute, and as soon as the port watch came up we started to shorten sails.

By now we were going through the waves so fast that we almost lost the third mate's boat. We were just tying up the sheets and tackles when the ship dived into a wave and went right through it, not having time enough to rise with it at the speed we were going.

We had all of our fresh meat on deck, still alive, consisting of two pigs, one calf, and several chickens. All were swept overboard and I almost went with them, along with three other fellows. They hit the galley and hung on. I wasn't so lucky. I was swept toward midships, hit the skylight, and was thrown against the rigging, hanging onto it with both arms until I could breathe again and get on my feet.

We held the vessel to the wind to slow it down; got the mainsail and jib topsail in; furled the mainsail and put up the main trysail (a small, three-cornered sail); and went back on course.

The captain had come on deck when we hit the big wave. Some little time later he suggested that the wind was too heavy and we had better take in the foresail.

The port watch had taken over and I had gone to the fo'c's'le by then, but hearing the commotion on deck, I came up. As soon as the foresail came down, I went back down to my bunk to get some sleep, knowing that in three-and-a-half hours I would be called out again.

In those days all hands were four and four—four hours below and four hours on deck. There were two watches only, port watch and starboard watch.

When I came back on deck at four o'clock in the morning, we were running on the fore and main trysail and forestaysail only. The staysail is a small jib on the forward part of the foremast, with the forward end fastened right where the flying jib boom leaves the bow. There were no sails over the sides. We were snug and all set for a heavy storm. In fact, we were in it, with the wind between seventy and eighty miles per hour. The seas were very heavy. When we went down between a couple of waves, we couldn't see a thing. We passed a steamer, or rather a steamer passed us, for we were making very little headway. She was only about a mile away but when we went down between the waves we couldn't see her at all, the waves were so huge. She wasn't making much headway either, probably only two or three knots per hour. The water was blowing from the crests of the waves. The air was full of sea water. It was really a heavy storm.

The storm lasted all that day. Just before dark, the captain said he thought that we would get out of it sooner if we went on the starboard tack, working out of a semicircle. I knew the meaning of this navigational term by then, since the captain had been teaching me navigation, and I was already familiar with the use of the quadrant which he had given me. In fact, he had started to teach me navigation the day after we left Santastatia. When he presented me with the instrument, he made one of his few speeches. "Joe," he said, "you are not here to be a sailor. You are not here to be a mate. You are here to be a captain, and the sooner I can make a captain out of you, the better it is for the family. Your father made a captain out of me and I am going to make a captain out of you."

He then set about showing me how to make the different adjustments: how to use the shade glasses, and how to shoot the sun. In short, he taught me how to work navigation, step by step.

At the same time, the steward, who had procured a third-grade English reader while we were in Barbados, was teaching me English. He was instructing me in forming English words and verbs and putting them together. Remember that I was also standing deck watches—four and four—and learning the deck work. I have said that after I was fifteen years of age I never had a day of formal schooling. That is correct. On the other hand, I doubt whether many boys my age ever set themselves as rigorous a learning program as I adopted for myself, or stuck to it so unremittingly, month after month—yes, and year after year. I was a very busy boy.

We ran out of the storm the next forenoon. The winds began to subside and we started to tack back again. When we were back on the port tack, we hoisted the jib. And then, when the captain saw that the ship could take it, we took down the foretrysail and hoisted the foresail. By afternoon, we were sailing with the lower sails out, that is, jib topsail, jib, forestaysail, foresail and mainsail. The waves were very high but the breeze was light. Not light enough to let the sails jar, but enough not to let the ship roll. We were just jumping along the waves, going from one to another. By next morning we were completely out of the storm and the big waves, so we put up the topsails. The sea was getting smooth and we were making good progress toward the Western Grounds. As we entered the outer portion of it, we knew that luck was with us. We sighted a school of whales.

CHAPTER IV

WHALEBOATS AND WHALERS

Now came my first experience in a whaleboat. To give the reader a little better understanding of the event, and to share a little of its thrilling adventure, I shall try to present a word picture of the boat and the action.

The whaleboat was a rather fragile craft, light in weight and built for speed and maneuverability. Four men could carry it, while empty, two at the bow and two at the stern. Its length was twenty-eight feet, give or take a few inches either way. The length was pretty well standardized because of the gear that carried it aboard ship and hoisted and lowered it to and from the water. It was approximately six feet wide amidships, and was sharp at bow and stern for quick reversal of direction and to make it capable of being rowed with as much speed backward as forward. It was framed of the best quality oak. The gunwales were also oak, but its hull was of cedar strips about half an inch thick and six inches wide, butted against each other, steamed and molded to follow and to hold the contour of the frame. It could be rowed with oars, paddled like a canoe, or sailed like a small sailing-boat. Its rudder could be shipped instantaneously, in which case a steering oar was substituted. And its light but strong mast could be dismounted in seconds, thus clearing the way for speedy action. It had a loggerhead at the stern so that, once fast to a whale, it could be towed at whatever speed the doomed whale could muster. It was painted white, and its hull was as smooth as glass.

Every item of its gear was dictated by necessity and so situated that it was ready for split-second use. Every member of its crew of six had a job to do and knew how to do it. The slightest failure in man or gear could mean sudden disaster and death to every man aboard.

The gear consisted of the following: paddles, one at each thwart where the man sat to row; spare oarlocks, one right next to each one in actual use; five oars, each in its proper place, and a steering oar at the stern; two warps of one-inch manila rope, each forty to fifty feet long, one at the bow and one at the stern, so coiled as to be perfectly in the clear at all times (these ropes were used to tie up the boat, or used as tow lines); three lance warps of best grade 15-thread manila, about one-quarter inch, each about seventy-five feet long, coiled separately under the bow box where it could be kept dry; a spare one-inch emergency line about fifty feet long, also coiled and stowed under the stern platform beyond the foot or base of the loggerhead; two tubs, one larger, which fitted exactly between two thwarts, forward of the after-thwart, and a smaller one forward of the second after-thwart. The larger tub would have the equivalent of two coils of one-inch special manila, and the smaller tub would have one coil, each line instantly available for attaching to a harpoon or ready to be connected to the other with a harpoon knot. On each platform, bow and stern, was a knife sheathed in heavy canvas or leather, the sheath being securely tacked down; two bailers and one bucket. The bucket was used to douse water on the line in the tub in case of fire from friction on the loggerhead. All three items were fastened under the thwarts. There were also the following items: One fresh-water keg which held about fifteen gallons, lashed to the thwarts forward of the small tub; a waterproof metal-container filled with a ten- or fifteen-day supply of hard tack; two buoyant "drugs" lashed under the thwarts; two hatchets, one at the bow and one at the stern, sheathed and sharpened like razors; the mast, properly rigged with shrouds and mainsail and jib halyards; a mainsail quite large for the size of the boat, attached to boom and peak (both made of bamboo or light wood) with two reefs and reef lines in case of bad weather, and the jib; a spare mainsail halyard and a spare jib halyard; three lances on wooden staffs, razor sharp and sheathed, ready for instant use, rigged with fifteen-thread manila for the lance warp to be bent onto; five harpoons; two bow harpoons, called live irons, and three spares, also razor-sharp and sheathed, each fitted into a wooden staff about six or seven feet long and fitted with one-inch special manila, also ready for instant use; a jack for the live irons, a compass, a lantern, and two short warps the same size as the whale line.

Finally, a shoulder gun and a darting gun with dynamite and caps were ready for quick kills when necessary or for killing bulls. And a sharp spade with a wooden shaft, and three red flags on wooden staffs also were included.

The lines in the tubs were always ready for immediate attachment to the harpoons—to be "bent" on. The top end was straight. The bottom end had a spliced eye ready to receive the end of another line and made fast with a harpoon knot, or ready for a second harpoon, as the case might be, or to have a "drug" attached to it, also with a harpoon knot. The "drug" served as a buoy on the end of the line, for use in emergencies. There were two "drugs," number A and number B, each different. Number A was like a small keg encased in a manila network so that it could not get loose. It had a forty-foot line that could be instantly fastened to the bottom or eyelet end of a line.

Number B "drug" was a strong square frame about eighteen inches across, fitted with balsa wood for buoyancy and a line from each corner long enough so that it could be joined to form an eye. A short line was spliced through this eye, with the other end left free and ready for attachment. The square "drug" was used as a spare.

The reason for the "drugs" was a most practical one. Assuming that a cow whale had been fastened but was not yet dead, and a bull which was much more valuable, appeared, the line on the cow was slacked off, the bull harpooned, and the chort line bent to the harpoon, and "drug" A bent to the line, whence line and "drug" were cast over the side, clear of the boat and men. Then we would finish killing the cow and take off after the bull which had the "drug" in tow.

We had been sailing with full sails in a northeasterly direction. We already had men at masthead. Always one mate, one boat steerer, and one sailor, with a sailor on the foremast, and the boat steerer and the mate on watch on the mainmast. Right after breakfast my watch was due on deck. We relieved the port watch at eight o'clock. The second mate and boat steerer would go on masthead, and one of the sailors would go up on foremast.

I saw Mr. Manuel, the first mate, picking up a pair of binoculars. He walked toward the forward deck, went up the rigging and joined the sailor on the foremast. He hadn't been there ten minutes when the mainmast yelled, "There she blows!" To a whaler that sound is just like a letter from home. It means that someone has sighted a spout. The captain jumped up and yelled, "Whereaways?"

"Off the port beam!" was the answer. It couldn't have been in a better direction.

We immediately put the wheel up and headed toward the spouts with the sails full and by. In about fifteen minutes we could see from the deck that the whales were spouting in all directions. The ocean, up beyond the lee bow, was full of spouts. We could see it was a school of females, or cow whales.

The captain yelled, "Stand by to lower!" By this time we had taken in the fore and main topsail and the flying jib to slow the vessel down. As we approached the whales we slacked the jib topsail down to the flying jib boom, but didn't furl anything.

The captain ordered the main peak to be slackened so as to slow the ship, preparatory to the lowering of the boats. He ordered the wheel down, to head into the wind, which naturally stopped the ship. We were hustling like beavers, getting the whaleboats ready to lower, and in about three minutes we were in the water. The first mate's boat was first. His blocks have to be heard before the second and third mates' boats can be started. Then it is: God help everybody!

In three minutes we were on the whales, and every boat was fast to a whale right close to the ship. There was great commotion —whales everywhere! Some were swimming right under the boats. Fortunately for us, they were good-natured. They didn't kick, but they were swimming in all directions. The whale we were fastened to was so tame, so good-natured, that she didn't even take one quarter of the line in the big tub.

Naturally we took in the oars preparatory to putting them over the side immediately, and the boat steerers and the mate exchanged positions, with the boat steerer going to the steering oar and the mate going to the bow to get his lance and start lancing the whale.

The whales we had fastened to were swimming right along with the school at approximately four or five knots. While we were pulling in the line, the mate grabbed the lance and made it fast to the lance warp. Then he made the lance warp fast to the boat, so we wouldn't lose it. Taking in the line as we were doing, we gained rapidly on the whale without using the oars at all. At the same time, the boat steerer was taking in the line around the loggerhead, while the sailor at the after end of the boat, next to him, coiled it back in the space between the afterthwart and the stern sheets.

The line must never be taken off the loggerhead because there is no way of knowing when or where the beastie is going to go. Once she goes, there is no time to put the line on the loggerhead. It would burn the hands. So the boat steerer always keeps at least one turn around the loggerhead and keeps feeding the line to the after man who keeps coiling it, ready for it to run without getting tangled if the whale starts off again.

My position was at the bow, next to the mate—first of the three men pulling in the line. As we got close to the whale, I was so excited I couldn't sit down any more. I stood up. I couldn't help it. We pulled up past the tail, and I felt so happy I could have kissed it.

The mate was a lean, wiry, powerful man, six-feet-four in height. Standing on the bow with the lance in his hand, he was ready to start killing the whale. He yelled at me, "Goddam it. Sit down!" But I was so excited I couldn't sit down. We pulled and pulled and got right on top of the whale. I was pulling for all I was worth, and the instant the bow came right against the whale I clinched the line under the edge of the bow platform and held it there. The mate let her have it. I don't believe he threw that lance more than three or four times before that whale started to spout blood. He praised me afterward, saying that the reason he had been able to do it so quickly was because I held the boat right on top of the whale.

When the whale starts to spout blood it means that she has been hit in the heart or lungs, because being lanced three or four times in the intestines wouldn't do it. This time the harpoon had fastened well forward, up near the neck. By pulling up on top of the whale as we had, that powerful mate could reach the vital area of the heart and lungs, and deal a fatal blow.

The boat steerer was already back at the steering oar, pulling the boat away from the tail of the whale. The man who had been coiling the line was tending the loggerhead. The mate knew the whale was already dying and that it was time to get away from there fast. He shouted back, "All oars, stern all! Stern all!"

We put the oars out and sterned—rowed to the stern—to start the boat backwards, and were away from there in no time. The whale was now obviously in the throes of death. She took a few turns around, thrashed about, turned her fin up—and was dead.

We came up to her, and the second mate ordered us to get him a red flag. We always carried three or four in the boat. The flag is attached to a staff six to eight feet long. At the foot of the staff are two or three notches, so it won't pull out.

We pulled up on the line again until we were right alongside. The mate made a hole with the spade, sank the flagstaff into it, and cut the line loose. Off we went again to get another whale.

The school by this time was about a half-mile away. The ship was probably a mile and a half off, and coming toward us. The first mate had killed a whale by this time, and had put up a flag. The third mate's whale was dying.

Back on the ship, we could see that the captain had put the third mate's flag back on the foremast. This meant that the third mate was to go back to the ship which, otherwise, would be short-handed with three whales to take in tow. With three whales so close together, there was no room for maneuvering the ship, so each whale had to be pulled alongside, where the captain could put another harpoon into it, put a line on it, and put it in tow.

The weather was good. The sea was smooth. Under such conditions, a whaleboat could be rowed at a maximum speed of ten knots an hour. In almost no time we were upon the whales again.

After a whale is killed, the boat steerer's first job is to get another harpoon ready. Three spare harpoons, mounted on poles and ready for a line, are always carried on the boat. Two harpoons are always struck into the whale, if possible, both bent to the same line. If there isn't time to strike with both harpoons, the second is immediately cast overboard, still attached to the line.

Getting the harpoons ready was, of course, hard work, and was the first thing to do after killing the whale.

It cannot be emphasized too strongly that the first and last law on a whaleboat is to have everything constantly in readiness down to the last, most minute detail. Therein alone lies the secret of success and safety.

In a school of whales one naturally tries for the largest. These whales were so tame, and the sea so smooth, that we went partly around and then cut across, right into them. Four or five hit the boat as we were coming in. They just sort of bumped it a little, but didn't do any damage. Just as we were going by the whales, the boat steerer struck one with both harpoons.

To the amazement of all of us, one of the harpoons struck the whale squarely in the heart. She sounded, right then. Down she went, straight down, with the line sizzling and smoking and setting the loggerhead afire. The boat immediately began to tilt, bow down, from the tremendous pressure and speed, even with four or five turns around the loggerhead. The after sailor passed the hand guards to the mate, who was still at the stern and handling the line. They are called nippers, and are made like potholders, out of heavy canvas sewed double thickness. These nippers protected his hands from the smoking rope. At the same time, he seized the bucket to douse the line in the tub with water. The stern of the boat continued to rise until the boat stood at an angle of seventy-five degrees to the surface of the water. The line continued to streak out and didn't stop until the big tub-line was almost used up. There couldn't have been more than one or two turns of the coil left in the bottom.

I had seen this happen in the previous season, looking through glasses from the deck of the ship. But to have it happen to the boat I was on was quite a sensation.

The mate slacked off on the line and the boat settled back on the water. In heavy seas this would have been a ticklish and dangerous operation. In such a case, if the line were slacked off too fast, the boat could, and almost certainly would, capsize.

We had to pull in the line—the line and the whale. She didn't come up very easily. We had to pull, and keep on pulling. By and by, she came out spouting blood. I heard the mate tell the boat steerer, "Good job, boy. Look at the spout!" They exchanged ends again, with the boat steerer going aft and the mate coming forward, where he picked up the lance, ready to finish killing the whale.

By the time this was accomplished, the ship was alongside. With the third mate and his crew back on board, there were enough men to handle the sails and get the three previously killed whales in tow.

We now had two more whales to tie up. The first mate had also killed another one. We threw the line over the bow and soon all five whales were secured by chains through the hawse pipe. Of course, the third mate had no chance of getting a second whale, because he had been called back to the ship.

A few days later, we ran into a school of tame whales again. They behaved so similarly to the first school that we all thought it must be the same school.

On the first day, we got nine cows. We hadn't finished getting the blubber aboard when they came over to us again. So we lowered just two boats and went out and got two more cows each. It was just like having our own private yard, where we could pick them up as we pleased.

We were not due in Fayal, the Azores, until some time in September. By the second week in June we had all the casks full. The captain said, "We're filled up. We might as well go to Fayal, take off a hundred barrels and go out and get some more." The Western Grounds, at that time, are pretty calm—light breezes mostly—so a sailing ship can't make very good time.

We were probably a thousand miles out. About the second week in July we sighted Pico Island, which lies about ten miles southeast of Fayal.

Pico is a good-sized island with a mountain about seven thousand feet high right in the middle of it.

We put about two hundred barrels ashore, then put out to sea to get more whales. We cruised around over toward Flores, the island where I was born. I went to the captain and asked him if we were going ashore.

"Oh, we will sometime. Right now we're going to get some more whales."

We went off toward the northwest and got a bull, a good-sized one, eighty-odd barrels or so. Then we cruised around until the middle of August.

One day, the captain sent for me. I thought he was joking when he asked, "Would you like to go ashore?"

I answered, "Oh, sure, any place."

"Oh, no, not any place," he said. "In Flores?"

"Would I!" I exclaimed.

"Well," he said, "we'll be there in a couple of days. We are heading right there now. We'll go ashore at Fajangrand."

CHAPTER V

FAJAZINHA AND THE FESTIVAL

Fajazinha, the village where I was born, was only an hour's walk from Fajangrand. I say "walk" because that was the only form of transportation. Very few people had horses there, although on the seaport islands of Fayal, Terceira, and San Miguel there was a good deal of commerce and consequently some horses. There were no automobiles at that time.

In Flores the transporting of cargo and the cultivation of fields were all done by oxen. No horses were available. If you wanted to go anywhere, you walked.

Two days later, we lowered the boat outside of Fajangrand. There's a nice harbor there—small but nice—just big enough for a few whaleboats or small boats. There was a cove with a few cement steps (for getting ashore) along the rocks and it was just large enough for the boats to turn around in. The villages on Flores are all situated along the coast. The ship could be seen from Fajazinha, but we couldn't land there because of the long, sandy beach and the rough water off shore.

The ship stays outside. It doesn't even drop anchor—it just cruises around. In this case the captain and I were the only two natives of Flores, so only we two were put ashore.

The ship had orders to cruise around until time to pick us up. In this case I had one full, glorious week to spend with my mother, brother, and sisters. The captain had a personal interest, too. He was then engaged to my older sister, Mary. We were all set for a very good time.

I was looking forward, too, with a good deal of anticipation, to my visit. I had left as a boy of fifteen-and-a-half, the year before. I was a year older now—a full-fledged sailor—a man of sixteen-and-a-half. I was never any bigger, any more of a man, or as important at any other time in my life, as on that day when I returned to my native village.

Then there was my little sweetheart, Lucy. Ever since I had been eleven, we had been pretty sweet on each other. That last year before I shipped we were very close friends.

In going from Fajangrand to Fajazinha, the very first house we came to was her father's house. Practically the whole town was on the way to meet us.

I embraced and kissed my sweetheart right there in front of everybody—my sisters, too, of course. They were all close friends. That was the happiest day of my life up to that time, and when she kissed me right in front of her father, mother, and sisters, I was more than pleased. Her mother kissed me, too. So did her sisters.

From there we could see part of my father's house, a two-story stone building that stood up above the other houses. From where we were, to the village square, which is right in front of my father's house, is only a few minutes' walk. The way we were walking, however, it took us about a half-hour. About halfway between the two was the girls' school. The teacher knew me and she brought all the girls out. I hugged and kissed every last one of them. Five hundred feet farther on was the boys' school. Their old schoolmaster had been my teacher, and when we came by he brought all the boys out to meet us. He and all the boys greeted me, too, and believe me, did I feel like a celebrity!

We were now in full view of my father's house, and my mother was already with the crowd. Everybody was there except my grandmother, who was close to eighty, and a few old neighbors who were unable to get around very well. Most of the older people were in the village square waiting for us.

How good that village square looked to me! It is quite large for a village that size. It has trees, and the ground is graveled. There are stone seats under the trees, and in plain view across the square, and a couple of hundred feet up the big, wide street beyond, is the village church.

The church really is too large for the village. It is very large and very tall, with two large bell-towers. How, why, and when that huge stone building was built, I do not know. There is an enormous door at the front with a very large door at each side. It has large doors on both sides of the building, with rows of windows made up of small panes of glass. The base of the windows is probably forty feet from the ground and, as I remember them, the windows must have been twenty-five feet high. It is much like the European cathedrals, huge, tall, stately and beautiful. I used to compare it to the main body of the Notre Dame Cathedral in Paris.

Like the European cathedrals, it stands on a raised portion of ground. The street is of cobblestone, worn smooth by long use; and roundabout the church and surrounding the village square are stone houses. The church overlooks the village. It is a very pleasant, picturesque and, to a native who has been away, a very homely scene.

The church is, of course, the center of the religious life of the village. Connected with it, in a spiritual sense only, is the Holy Ghost house, which is the recreational center. Financially, however, it is entirely separate.

My native village of Fajazinha is unique in many respects. It has a population of somewhat less than eight hundred. It has never had more than that. Every family owns its own home and garden—a little plot of cultivated ground. The houses are all of native stone. There are no wooden ones. Only the doors and window frames and casings and the furniture were made of wood. Wood was just too expensive and too hard to get.

Everyone knew everyone else in his own village, and often even in the neighboring villages. In fact, nearly every family on the island had relatives in every village and had lived in the same locality for many generations. When there was a Holy Ghost festival the entire village attended. We had one of those a few days after I arrived, which I shall describe later on.

My father's house was a two-story building facing the village square. The family lived on the second floor. Two steps led up from the street. Then there was a little recess with eight more steps going up to the balcony on the second floor. Each step was a foot high, made of stone, covered with cement. The balcony had a stone wall all along the front, and two doors, one opening into the front room and one into the dining room.

The front room was quite large, with three windows and another door opening into the dining room, which had one window. The upper half of the door was glass—Dutch type.

The kitchen was next to the dining room and had two windows looking out on the balcony. The back door of the kitchen opened onto a platform with a toilet to the left, and steps to the right going down to the ground, which, on this side of the house, was only three or four feet below. The three bedrooms were also at the back of the house. All the rooms were fairly large. They would compare very favorably with those in an American home.

Being the captain of an American ship, my father had built the house with American money, and I would say that the plan of it was similar to American houses in many ways. The outside and inside walls of the house were covered with a smooth white plaster. The doors and window casing were painted green. It was a good-looking house.

We had a bathroom, too, but no running water. The tub was of wood, and not very large. In fact I never saw one large enough to sit in. Some were square and some were round. One stood up and took a sponge bath.

As little children we used it very seldom, however. Since the weather is very mild and there was a creek right in front of the house with a little pool close by, we would take our soap—boys and girls—and wash each other there. The older girls and women, of course, would take their baths in the house. The men, however, would go in a group—seven, eight, or maybe ten—on Sunday morning, to the main creek, where there was a large pool, and there they would spend an hour or two swimming around and having a good time. Not in the winter time, though. While it didn't get very cold, and I don't remember ever seeing any snow, it was still too cool for comfortable bathing. I can't remember the temperature ever getting below thirty-five or forty degrees. Of course, as we boys got older we would go to a pool farther out that was hidden by the trees.

The life on the island is simple and honest. There is no jail. There are no courts, no police, no judges. There is one official—a clerk—who serves as sheriff, chief of police, and mayor, and whose salary is paid by the government.

In each village there were men who operated their own fishing boats. In my village there were three boats, one of which was owned by my father. That meant that if six men operated the boat my father owned, then he, as owner (or my mother) got two shares. The boats were small sailing-boats which were kept in a small natural harbor about an eighth of a mile from Fajangrand, toward Fajazinha. When the men took them out they would stay overnight so as to get a good catch. Then they would bring in the catch and salt it down for the winter.

There were only two stores. One merchant sold tobacco from a little room in his home. The other sold clothing, salt, sugar and a few spices. The people raised their own vegetables, including corn, which was ground locally by water power. Each family had its own cow and pigs.

There was no electricity, nor were there any autos, horses or wagons. Few people wore shoes. The life in the village very closely resembled pioneer life in America, in earlier times.

It was Thursday when I got home. I remember the day because, on that evening, my girl friend and her family and some of the other boys and girls in the village came over to visit. We were playing games with the grown-ups in the dining room. My mother had moved the dining table over into one corner and we had all the floor for games of all kinds, simple games for the children, of course.

By and by, Lucy whispered in my ear, "Hey, Joe, let's skip." So we did. We went out through the kitchen to the field back of the house. We had quite a large corn field there. I don't remember who started it, but we got very chummy. We were quite a bit in love, and I did enjoy it. After all, she was a beautiful girl. It was moonlight; not a full moon, but quite bright. I could see her lovely face. She was very light-complexioned—not dark like most of the Portuguese—not dark like me. She looked more like an Irish girl. Her mouth was like a partially opened rosebud, sweet and red. And she was so tender, so sweet and so loving, I thought I was in Paradise.

After a while the kids missed us and started looking for us. They figured out where we were and started looking through the corn field, spreading out clear across it. Of course, we could hear them coming, so when they got to us we were just holding hands and putting on an act. We all went back together to the house and, by that time, the older folks were ready to go home and put the kids to bed.

It was only nine or ten o'clock, but as all the folk were farmers with their land to tend, they went to bed early. Anyway there was to be a Holy Ghost festival in the Holy Ghost house on Saturday, and preparations were to begin the next day.

Every village on the island has its recreation hall. Some have two. A city, of course, has more. The hall, called a Holy Ghost house, is also the place where religious feasts and festivals are held and, consequently, is indirectly connected with the church.

In Fajazinha there was a Holy Ghost house facing right on the public square. Like all others, it was a building about fifty feet wide and probably two hundred and fifty feet long, with a little altar with a crown on it. The community dances and other festivities are held there. Of all the activities, most important are Holy Ghost feasts, a dozen or fifteen of which are held every summer. There was going to be one this very Saturday.

Next morning my sister, Mary, said that the cattle for the festival were to be killed that morning. I was going to go. In fact I had every intention of going but, after a year at sea, just home one night, with a lovely little sweetheart coming by with her sisters on an errand into the country, and asking me to go along—well, what else could I do? We had a very good time. All three girls were very attractive. By the time we returned, some men were coming in with the cattle, skinned, dressed, and quartered. The meat is hung up in one end of the Holy Ghost house until the next morning, at which time a half dozen men will come in with butchers' tools and cut the meat up into small portions. Part of it is set aside for the Sunday dinner. The remainder is cut up in pieces of various sizes to be distributed that same day to the individual homes in the village. This is a ceremonial affair.

By ten o'clock the meat was cut up and the four Holy Crown musicians had arrived. One of these carried a big drum similar to the old-fashioned war drums, suspended by a sort of ribbon around his neck. Another carried cymbals, and the third had an instrument called a *pandeiro*. The fourth member of the group carried the silk Holy Ghost flag. This flag was quite large, and I believe it came from Italy.

Someone is then sent to fetch the priest. The musicians go to meet him, playing Holy Ghost hymns as they go. They sing as they march and if the priest is a young man, as this one was, he joins in the singing with gusto.

Bread in round loaves, resembling the French bread sold here in the United States, which had been baked the night before in the homes grouped about the village square, had been brought in. Together with the meat, it was ready to receive the priest's blessing.

The priest says a little prayer to the Holy Ghost before the little altar with the Holy Ghost Crown upon it. The blessing completed, the Crown Carrier is appointed. The priest's function is finished, but the Crown Carrier's function is just beginning. He now takes charge.

Ten or twelve big baskets are filled with loaves, and others with pieces of meat of varying size. Two strong young fellows carry the baskets of meat between them, suspended from poles on their shoulders. Two younger boys carry the bread in the same manner. And a group of young girls, between ten and seventeen years of age, all beautifully dressed in white lace, are ready. Forming a ceremonial procession, with the musicians and the Crown Carrier in the lead, followed by the girls in their lovely dresses and the boys with the bread and meat on their shoulders, the group proceeds to the knoll beside the church, where they begin on an established route through the village.

The Crown Carrier enters the first house. He is followed by two girls, one carrying a platter of bread and the other carrying a platter containing chunks of meat. The girls never touch the bread or the meat.

The proper quantity of bread and portion of meat to fit the individual family has been placed on each platter by an experienced young man especially appointed for the task.

Each family in the village is, of course, prepared for the occasion. All members of the household are grouped in the front room by a table with two platters on it. The Crown Carrier enters and goes to each member of the family gathered there, and gives each member the opportunity to kiss the Crown. If a person is ill in bed, or an older bedridden person is in the home, the Crown Carrier goes to that person also. The girls come in following the Crown Carrier and put bread and meat on the platters which are on the table. As the Crown Carrier departs, he says, "May the Holy Ghost remain in this house with you," or words to that effect.

The same procedure is followed at each house. The only difference in the procedure is that two girls are waiting at each subsequent house for the Crown Carrier to enter. When the baskets are emptied, additional ones are ready and waiting to be distributed. This ceremony takes about four hours, and goes on until every house in the village has been visited.

By the time the group returns to the Holy Ghost house, everyone is a bit tired. There is little time to rest, however, for musicians are already there with banjos and accordions, and everyone dances for an hour or two before going home for dinner.

In the evening, nearly everyone in the village comes to the Holy Ghost house. That is when the fun begins. Everyone dances, and everyone knows how; boys and girls from ten or eleven, on up to eighty or ninety years of age. Everyone who can dance is welcome to join in. The dances are square dances, folk dances—old Portuguese dances, very like the dances of the pioneers in America.

Naturally, the older people get enough of dancing before very long. Then they sit around on benches and tell stories. Everyone stays. Everyone is friendly. There are no enemies in the village.

One wonders why! Is it because they are so simple, so untouched by the outside world? That can hardly be true.

Of all the married men in that village, only one, to my knowledge, had not come from the United States, or off an American ship. That is, some of the men had gone to the United States, made some money, and returned and married. Later on some had returned to the United States and either stayed or gone back to the island. Some married in the United States and returned to the island to live, build a home and have a family. God knows, one could never come from a whaling ship and be untouched by the rest of the world.

About ten o'clock, the old folk began to think about going home. About midnight, the younger people began doing tricks and playing games. There is no gambling, though, in the Holy Ghost house. If anyone mention the word "gamble," he is dishonored for life. It's all clean games and clean fun.

About twelve o'clock, my Lucy and I sneaked out and went over to my father's house, which was only half a block away. We went into the basement where the tools and farm implements, potatoes and hay, were kept. It was a nice clean room, dark and quiet. We climbed up on the hay and made love for a while, then we returned to the Holy Ghost house where the party and games were going on.

Shortly afterward, the captain and Mary left and went to my father's house. At least that is where they were, talking in the front room, when I got home. I bade them goodnight, and went to bed. I slept with my younger brother. Being only eleven and not interested in girls, he was already in bed.

The next morning, Sunday, all the women in the homes surrounding the church and the village square were up early to begin cooking the meat for the festival dinner. Every home had large iron-kettles, different sizes. The larger ones would hold between twenty and fifty gallons. Some of the families also had extra-large ovens for baking the festival bread. The meat for the festival dinner was distributed to the homes with the large kettles so the women could begin cooking it early in the morning. They would make a broth with it, which was used to pour over the bread served at the festival.

All the families on the island have chores to be done. The chickens, cows, and pigs have to be taken care of. The priest has designated a time for the Mass, usually between nine and ten o'clock, when everyone can attend except the women who are cooking the meat. Then a second Mass is held for these women, who are relieved by others, usually their daughters, because the cooking of the meat must go on.

No one goes home after the second Mass. All stay around the village square, visiting and telling stories.

Then, a little after noon, the meat and broth are brought in from the homes in large pans, and a soup called *sopa,* is made. The sopa is made with special spices and has a tang to the taste. It is not hot like Mexican food but is especially spicy and really very good. I liked it but I never learned how to make it. I don't know anyone who knows. Anyway, I'm no cook.

The men and women, little boys and girls, sit at the tables. The older girls, married and single, between eighteen and thirty, serve the tables. Everyone is dressed in his or her best. The girls wear lacy white aprons over their dresses and they look elegant indeed. They keep on serving and people keep on eating and it seems as if there is to be no end. The waitresses don't serve themselves until everyone else has had enough. Then they sit at a table reserved for them under the trees, or the married ones may join their husbands.

Every family brings its own dishes. If the weather is good the people stay on until it is time to do the chores again. Those who have no particular duties at home stay on, dancing and singing together until they are ready to call it a day and go on home to bed.

I still had Monday, Tuesday, and Wednesday left, to enjoy myself ashore. On Thursday the ship was to come back to Fajangrand, lower a boat and pick us up at noon.

On Monday I walked down to Lucy's house and spent most of the morning with her mother. We were very good friends. I also visited with her father, who was the postmaster, and with the rest of the children. They had twin boys and three girls. They were all light-complexioned, more like an Irish family than Portuguese. We walked over to my house before dinner, but we didn't go right up to the second floor. We stayed in the basement for a half hour, in the hay, making a little love. After all, we hadn't been alone all day.

I could hear the dishes rattling in the dining room and I knew my mother and sisters were setting the table. We went upstairs to have dinner. Of course, being engaged to my sister, the captain was there. He told a few jokes. My mother kept right up with him, in English too.

My mother was very well read and she had an exceptionally good mind. Born in New Bedford, she learned English as her native tongue, of course. She was studying to be a teacher when she married my father and went to sea with him. After settling down at home in Fajazinha, she had a reading club and gave lectures. Women from all the surrounding villages came to her for counsel and advice. One thing I remember particularly was that we never sat down to a meal without someone saying grace, and no one was ever excused from the dinner table in the evening until the Rosary was said.

Tuesday and Wednesday were much the same. My girl and I were practically inseparable. Of course, in the evening she would go home or I would go home, depending upon where we were.

Thursday came—time to part. More than a hundred people walked over to Fajangrand with the captain and me. My little sweetheart cried, and I felt very, very sad indeed; for the romance I had found ashore was much more appealing in a personal sense than any romance of the sea. Only a sense of duty, of filling a man's job and becoming a captain like my father, made me turn and go resolutely away. But I brushed off a few tears as I went.

The people went with us as far as the water, taking up the space from the custom house right down to the end of the breakwater. We shook hands with all the men and kissed the women and girls. I liked that part of it, but one special kiss lasted longer than all the rest, I can tell you.

We bade everyone good-by. The whaleboat picked us up and took us over to the ship. We were soon aboard and headed for Fayal, for the rendezvous with the mother ship. Thence off for the winter season in the South Atlantic.

We left Flores and its memories behind and headed for Fayal.

On the second morning, we picked up the crown of Pico Island, which is southerly from Fayal, and sailed in between the two islands where the harbor and breakwater are situated, with the city of Horta in view.

CHAPTER VI

SAILOR'S RETURN

The mother ship and two or three other whalers were already in ahead of us. We came in, dropped anchor, and the port officials came aboard to clear us. After that, the usual greetings were in order. The captain and mates from the other ships came aboard, all friends of Captain Corvello.

Shore merchants, hungry for business, soon arrived and along with them came the bumboats with produce and merchandise.

It was customary, after we had everything shipshape, to get ready for dinner aboard ship, and after that to go ashore. It was also customary to break watches, leaving a watchman aboard, whose duty it was to see that the bumboats didn't come by and relieve us of any gear or supplies. It was also his duty to keep the two kerosene anchor lamps burning—one at the bow and one at the stern. The watchman was relieved at midnight by another, who stayed on until morning.

This was my first time in Fayal since I had left there as a black, seasick cabin-boy a year before. This time I went ashore with my head held high, for now I was a white sailor on an American ship, which was just as good as being an American citizen so far as my presence here was concerned, and the authorities couldn't touch me.

We had to go the whole length of the city of Horta before we got to Rua Velha (which means Old Street) where the sailors hang out. There are four or five such streets with barrooms and prostitutes, and by the time the sailors from all the whalers get together there it is a pretty rowdy place. There was a lot of dancing with the girls, both in the barrooms and on the streets.

The sailors tried to teach me to drink and smoke but I would have none of it, although I became a pretty steady smoker in later years. I didn't go for the dancing or the fighting in the streets. So I left rather early and walked back toward the dock.

There was an old man there, old to me at that time, of forty-five or fifty, who had a little general-store. He sold a little of everything. His family—a wife and two daughters—helped tend the store. I had become acquainted with them the year before. In fact I had bought from them the shoe black that had changed me into a black boy and set me out on my seafaring career.

One of the sisters, Josephine, who was about a year older than I, was really beautiful. Naturally, I wouldn't stay with the sailors when there was someone like that around.

They were very glad to see me. "Where was I going? Where had I been?" I hadn't told them of my plans the year before, fearing they might report me to the authorities. They gave me such a friendly reception that going to see them became my regular habit every evening. I would go to the back of the shop and visit with the girls and their mother, and help by doing things around the place. Josephine and I became very friendly. She was such a beautiful girl that I think I actually sometimes blushed when I would find myself staring at her.

Anyway, we became very friendly. We would go on long walks all day Sunday, after church. It wasn't long until we started making love, and she enjoyed it as much as I did. My intentions were all very good, and we kind of got engaged. I guess you would call it that. She told her mother and her mother said, "That's nice."

I think everybody took it for granted that when we finished growing up I would come back and we would be married, or something like that. Of course, I told her I was going to be on whalers and that we would be together every year except once in a while when the ship went home to New Bedford.

I didn't know it then but I think Captain Corvello knew that a steamer was coming in that day. I ran into him on deck and he questioned me, "Joe, are you going ashore today?"

"Yes sir. I think so, sir." On shipboard everything was "Yes sir, no sir," for that is part of the discipline. I believe the discipline is more rigid than in the military. "It's my watch ashore and I think I'll go ashore, sir."

"Well, no. I don't think you should. I think you should wait. The steamer will be here in an hour or so and I think you should wait to see who is aboard."

"Oh, wait a minute," I said. "I don't care who is coming. I've got a date with my girl, sir." I tacked the "Sir" on the end of the sentence, realizing I was a bit sassy. You see, I would take advantage of the captain pretty often, knowing he was engaged to my sister.

"No. You stay aboard. That's orders."

Well, orders are orders and, coming from the captain, they had to be obeyed, regardless.

In a little while the steamer came in and dropped anchor and Captain Corvello went ashore. Soon he returned with a woman and a girl. At a distance I couldn't make out who they were. But when they came closer I could see my sister Mary, the captain's fiancée, and my nine-year-old sister, Maria, who had come along as sort of chaperone. I was very surprised and happy. By the time they got to us, the captain had already told Mary that I was infatuated with the storekeeper's daughter. She didn't like it a bit. She said I was too young to get mixed up with girls, and right then and there she gave me orders to stay away from that store and that girl.

I respected my sister, who was about five years older than I. When we were younger, my mother had been very strict with us, and when I needed a whaling, if she was not able to give it to me, Mary would take over and do a thorough job of it. I always obeyed orders from her.

This was a little different. I told myself that grownups didn't know everything. I sneaked away. Of course, I knew better than to be seen around the store. So I would go in the back with the girls or their mother. I guess I didn't fool anybody too much.

Three or four days later, the captain and my two sisters came to the store and asked for me. Josephine's father knew I was there, so he called me out. Naturally I didn't like it a bit. Mary became angry and asked to see the girls. It wasn't girls. It was just girl, because Josephine was the only one back there. Her sister was out somewhere with their mother.

Josephine came out, and when Mary saw her she simply said in a very surprised voice, "Oh, Joe. I don't blame you. She *is* beautiful!" The way she said it caused Josephine to blush, and I blushed too. So Mary didn't object any more to my seeing Josephine.

Mary talked to Josephine's father, and soon her mother returned and joined them. Mary liked them all very much. She bought quite a few things from them to take back to Flores. My parents were not rich, but my father had done well. They could buy what they wanted. They had a lot of land, too, that had been inherited from my forefather. You see, my great-great-grandfather had been a bishop, and I don't know how it happened but he had several sons and daughters, and that is how we came to have so much land. So because of the income from the land, together with my father's earnings from the whaling industry, we were able to buy what we wanted. Mary was a very sensible girl where money was concerned and she did not spend it foolishly.

Anyway, I could now go to the store without disobeying any orders. In fact, the captain and Mary seemed pretty happy to have me go. She would often have me come by the hotel and take little Maria with me. She said it was so nice that Josephine's younger sister was just the right age for Maria to play with!

I had one watch on and one off, every other day, which meant, of course, that I could go ashore only every other day. I soon discovered, however, that I could hire a sailor to take my watch. Then I could go ashore every day.

I had the hundred dollars in American money that my father had given me and, with the rate of exchange at five-to-one in favor of the American money, I could hire someone to take my watch for twenty-five cents a day.

I would rather spend my time with Josephine anyway, even though there were no movies to go to. We had plenty of good times together. In fact the whole family did.

The store was just back of Front Street, right near the docks, and when all the whalers were in, there were a lot of people coming and going, so Josephine's father would keep the store open until about nine o'clock. Then he would get his banjo and play it while we all danced and sang. I taught both girls a number of dances. Mrs. Souza knew a lot of songs, which she taught to the rest of us. She would take a man's part and she and I would exchange with the girls. So, altogether, we spent some very enjoyable evenings.

We were soon ready to go to sea again, but the captain held over for a couple of days, waiting for the steamer that stopped at a lot of the island ports on its way from Europe. When it arrived we went aboard with my sisters and wished them well on their trip back to Flores. The steamer left in the late afternoon and we made ready to put to sea the next day.

At Fayal, in those days there were no tugboats. We had to do our own maneuvering to get out of the harbor and around the breakwater. It was quite a trick, but the captain was a good sailor. We shortened chains, set sails, set jibs, raised the anchor, and the captain took us out very nicely. We went out around the northwest end of Pico and set sail for the Cape Verde Islands.

CHAPTER VII

THE FIGHTING WHALE

Two of the mates, the boat steerers, and a lot of the crew were from the Cape Verde Islands, so the captain used to give liberty there. He had many friends on the islands and liked to visit there, himself. We were out of Fayal a couple of days on the way there when we picked up a whaler. It was the brig *Sullivan,* under Captain Hagerty. He and his wife and family (three boys and a girl) aboard. At the moment he had set signal flags to "mate." On a whaler, that was a signal for help in catching a whale, in which even the two whalers would share and share alike if they were successful.

We could see that two boats were fastened to the whale and the other two were trying to get close, but could not. Our schooner could go closer on the wind than the brig *Sullivan*—four points on the wind, compared to eight for the *Sullivan*.

The captain took the ship close in to the whale and gave the order to stand by and lower away. We were in the water immediately and then the fun began. We rowed around and tried to get past the whale. We got close, but we were still almost a boat-length away. Mr. Cruz, the second mate, was a big man, six-feet-four, and tremendously powerful. He could throw a harpoon like no other man I have ever known. He could throw it farther than the length of the whale boat, and he never missed. One has to see it done to appreciate it really. The line attached to the harpoon is about an inch and a half in circumference. It is heavy, and a lot heavier when wet. The length of the line has to be figured in split-second timing, and the harpoon must be thrown so that the line will not drag. Otherwise, the harpoon will land too flat and will not penetrate the blubber.

Well, Mr. Cruz exchanged places with the boat steerer and got up on the bow of the boat. He threw that harpoon from a distance of more than thirty feet and made us fast with a perfect hit.

Another of the *Sullivan*'s boats got fast a moment before we did, and now that whale took off again. He was wild. He took those four boats through the water so fast that every one just hit the crest of the waves. The other boats were rowing like mad, trying to catch up with us.

Finally the whale slowed down and the *Varella*'s first mate's boat got fast. That, too, was an exhibition maneuver. The harpooner was a small guy, half blind, who could throw a harpoon up into an arc, trailing the line, and make it come straight down into the whale's back. No one else I ever saw could do it that way. I asked his uncle, Mr. Manuel, who was the first mate, how he did it. The only explanation I got was, "I don't know. It's just a gift from God."

The harpoon struck so that the whale spouted blood, just a tint of it however, and the whale kept going.

Mr. Cruz was also one of the best lancers I have ever known. He tried again and again, but he couldn't get up past the whale's hump to where he could get at the whale's belly. He used the darting gun. The whale kicked and dodged. No one, with lance or gun, succeeded in making an effective hit. The whale turned and started back toward the *Sullivan*. This gave the fourth mate from the *Sullivan* a chance and he threw a lance. The whale kicked and cut the bow of the boat clean away right where the fourth mate stood. The fourth mate went into the water.

We were going to cut our line and pick him up but Mr. Manuel told Mr. Cruz, "No, there is another *Sullivan* boat behind us to pick him up."

The crew in the stricken boat then used a maneuver known to whalers to keep their boat from capsizing. I didn't see them do it then, as we were having our own troubles, but I've seen it done since.

They took the mast-and-sail and placed it athwart ships at the middle of the boat and lashed it to the midship thwart. The boat was water-logged. If they were not too far away and the sea was not too rough, they could eventually get back to the ship themselves, but they waited for the boat from the *Sullivan* to tow them back to the ship.

We fought that whale from a little after ten o'clock in the morning until after dark that night. It had eight harpoons stuck in it, and had towed four whaleboats for most of the afternoon—five, until the fourth mate's boat had been stove in. The whale had been shot I don't know how many times, but either the dynamite failed to explode or it went right through, or it missed.

After dark, the *Sullivan* and the *Pedro Varella* put up two white lights—the signal to call us back to the ships. We all cut loose and turned about, but it was after ten o'clock when we got up to the *Pedro Varella,* which had made better time following us than the *Sullivan*. We were exhausted. I never dared say so, but I was glad we didn't finally succeed in killing the whale. I don't believe I could have done a bit of work the next day.

All the mates and the crews talked about that whale after we got back on board. They all agreed that they had never seen a whale as wild as that one, or one that just wouldn't slow down or die. It was ridiculous, but it was true. And it wasn't a very big whale, either. The mate figured that it was only about fifty or sixty barrels in size.

CHAPTER VIII

TURTLES, EGGS, THE DEVIL'S SISTER, AND LINDA

About two and a half weeks later, we reached São Nicolão Island in the Cape Verdes. This island is commonly known as St. Nicholas. It is about a thousand miles north of the Equator. We let off the mates and sailors who lived there, and cruised around. Because of the current and changing winds, the captain wouldn't consider dropping anchor there. The steamer that stops there occasionally would drop anchor, but it didn't have to depend upon the whimsical winds for its safety.

The captain usually allowed the men four or five days ashore to visit with relatives. Most of their own families—wives and children—lived in New Bedford, but they would have brothers or sisters or parents on St. Nicholas.

After four or five days we set sail for the South Atlantic to go down below the Equator. We were pretty unfortunate. We got into the calms of the Equator and for two weeks, with full sails set, I believe we actually went backwards. The sails flapped back and forth twenty-four hours a day. It was awful.

I was learning navigation then. I took sights every morning, noon, and night, whether I was on watch or not. I stayed right at the captain's side. That was orders, anyway. He was teaching me how to handle the telescope and the shade glasses, and how to read the scales and the quadrant.

Finally we got to the whaling grounds. Our luck was good and we filled the ship. In January we sighted a barren island in the middle of the South Atlantic. It had a little vegetation but it was mostly rock, with many turtles and turtles' eggs and seagulls' eggs.

We picked up the largest turtles and baked them for fresh meat. We turned some over on their backs so they would be available in the same place when we left. We filled cardboard boxes with eggs and put them aboard, and we had a few meals of "fresh" eggs. They smelled a little bit, rather a fishy odor, and about half of them were rotten. The steward was pretty efficient at culling them out. He broke them open at the rail. If they were rotten, he opened his fingers and they fell into the ocean. If they were good, a quick shift dropped them into a pan.

We had been at sea for more than three months. The fresh turtle meat and the "fresh" eggs were a welcome change in what had been a very restricted diet of hardtack, corned beef, salt pork, beans, dried-pea soup, and bread baked on board about every third day.

Our menu didn't vary much. For breakfast we generally had skouse, a stew made of broken pieces of hardtack, with small pieces of corned beef, pepper and spices. I didn't care much for that, so about an hour or two after breakfast I would make a can of camoka. This was made by grinding four or five pieces of hardtack. To grind the hardtack I would put it in a small sack and pound it with a block of wood until it was like coarse flour. Then I added a few drops of vinegar in a cup, and a little molasses. It's better with sugar, but we had only molasses. I usually preferred camoka to the pea or bean soup that we usually had for lunch.

The bread was pretty good. We never had toast. I didn't even know what toast was, at that time. For dinner we would have hash —hardtack mixed with small pieces of chopped corned-beef. There was no way to grind it, so the steward chopped it for the cabin (officers) and the cook chopped it for the crew. Coffee was on twenty-four hours a day, strong and black—awfully strong. The pot was washed only once during the day. When the pot got low, in the middle of the afternoon, in went a bucket of water and a few more measures of coffee.

Well, those eggs and turtles were okay. We had a turtle about every third day as long as they lasted, and we ate eggs until there were no more. Then back to the corned beef and hardtack.

Our ship was filled just in time to head back for Barbados, West Indies. We arrived there about the middle of March. This time I was not forbidden to go ashore. Barbados is a large city, the largest I'd ever seen, with many stores, good streets, and a mixed population with a good percentage of Europeans. It was a pretty clean city, too, and I enjoyed it very much. There were buggies and wagons with horses, but no autos at that time.

One thing impressed me strongly. There was a coal steamer being unloaded at the dock there one day—unloaded by men and women carrying baskets on their heads. They were colored people of all ages, traveling like a stream of ants, out of the hold, over the decks, onto the plank and onto the dock, with another line going back onto the ship and into the hold. It was pretty hot, and that impressed me as an awfully hard way to earn a living. But Barbados was a beautiful city with a beautiful bay dotted with many ships, small schooners and several steamers loading and unloading cargo.

We had already taken on fresh meat, potatoes, yams and some vegetables. Some of it the captain had sent aboard and some had been bought from the bumboats that were continually coming alongside with things to sell, including girls. The whole thing is a regular business with them.

By the third day, the captain had his clearance papers so we set sail for Dominica to unload the oil and take on supplies and provisions for the next season. We went around the lee side of Barbados and as we mounted around the northwest corner of Dominica we could see seven whalers in addition to the mother ship, the *Richard W. Clark,* anchored there ahead of us.

It was early forenoon. There was a good stiff breeze blowing and the captain took our little schooner in very handily. We anchored in between the other whalers. The officers came aboard, and the captain of the *Richard W. Clark* and the captains of the other whalers also came aboard to exchange greetings with Captain Corvello.

We were in a safe harbor. Soon everything was shipshape. Being on the starboard watch, I could go ashore that night with no fuss about Three Bellies because I had been initiated. I had nothing to do with her any more. I was "divorced"—free to go as I pleased and, believe me, I did.

The first Sunday we were ashore I went to church. I don't know what kind of church it was, only that it wasn't Catholic, because I didn't understand any of the service, but I stayed anyway. After the service I bought three or four bananas and had lunch. Then another fellow from the ship went with me for a walk, and we climbed the hill overlooking the bay. We were sitting there eating the rest of the bananas when I looked down suddenly to see a big snake crawling over my legs. It was as thick through as my arm and I couldn't see either end of it. Both ends were hidden in the grass and leaves. I let out a yell and made a beeline for the town, about two miles away. I never stopped until I got to the dock. I was really exhausted. When the fellow who had been with me arrived a little while later, he said he didn't know what it was all about. Anyway, I guess I was still scared. Some of my shipmates and some of the fellows from other ships said I was white as a sheet. I was out of breath and covered with sweat. Somebody said to me, "What the hell is it? Have you seen the devil?"

"No, but I saw his sister."

"What do you mean?"

"Well, I saw a snake. It was right on top of me. I never saw one before but I've heard about them and it was as big as my arm!"

"Where were you?" They all wanted to know.

"I was up on that hill." And I pointed to it.

That was one of the few things that ever scared me, and to this day I am afraid of snakes. I've seen some since, in side shows. Some of them aren't bad, I guess, but that one time was enough for me. I didn't see a head. I didn't see a tail. I just saw the middle of it, and I didn't stop running until I reached the water's edge.

Some of the fellows took me into a bar for a drink. I had some ginger ale, and it was good and refreshing. After a little while we came out and walked along Front Street. I said, "Let's walk up toward Three Bellies' house. I want to see what I got tangled up with last year."

When I saw her again I didn't want any part of her. I half walked, half ran, back to the dock. Captain Corvello and a cousin of mine, the captain of the bark *Wanderer,* were there. I hadn't seen this cousin before. He shook hands with me and said, "Oh, Joe. Were you the one who saw the snake and ran all the way down the hill, awhile ago?"

"My goodness, yes. But how did you hear about it?"

"Oh, the word travels fast. I heard all about it."

He asked me what color the snake had been. I couldn't even tell him that. But he took me into a bar and I had a soft drink. No wine or hard liquor for me. I liked the taste of wine but I wouldn't touch it. I just didn't want to learn to drink and get the habit.

Some of the fellows went back to the ship for supper, but I went to a little restaurant. They didn't even serve the dinner on plates. They used a sort of wooden platter, and they had fish and some potatoes that were neither white nor sweet. Later, when I learned more English, I called them "morphodite" potatoes. There was some fresh fruit, too. It was pretty good and I went back for a second helping, but I could eat only about a third of it.

There weren't any tables. The customers ate standing at the counter or took their food out into the yard. There were two good-looking girls who did the serving. They were both a little older than I. I think I took a second helping more as an excuse to stay than because I was hungry.

Anyway, we were talking, and the older girl helped me finish the food. My English was poor but she could speak a little French and so could I. So between the two and the use of hands, we got along pretty well. She said she was going home a little after dark, so I hung around until she was ready to go.

I asked her if I could walk her home. She replied, "Yes, come on." On the way we passed a little drinking-counter. Here we would call it a soft drink stand. We stopped and each had a couple of soft drinks. We were getting pretty well acquainted so I walked on home with her.

I was trying to get close to her but she was too wise. I put my arm around her but she objected, saying, "Oh, no. We are only kids, and my mother never allowed me to do such things. Anyway, I don't even know you."

"All right. Are you going to work there tomorrow?" I asked.

"I work there every afternoon."

"You don't work there in the morning?"

"No. I go to school in the morning."

"I can't meet you there tomorrow. I can only go ashore every other night," I said.

"Well, when you go ashore, come on in."

Well, I liked that. I stayed aboard the next day, Monday. I thought I would let her think about it. I kind of liked her. She was fairly good looking, plump but not fat, and a very agreeable sort. We had dinner at four o'clock, so Tuesday night after dinner I took the first boat ashore, which was at four-thirty.

Naturally I went straight to the little restaurant where the girl worked, and she was very glad to see me, which pleased me quite a bit. She waited on me and I had some more of those potatoes and fish. She asked me if I wanted some bread.

"Heck, no. I can get that every day on the ship."

She gave me a drink that was delicious. It was pineapple juice mixed with banana, a homemade drink that her mother had prepared. The girl had some too. It was so good that pineapple has been my favorite fruit ever since.

I waited until she got through work. Then we went out and down to the river. We didn't stay there very long. She had something else in mind. We walked over to the beach on the north side of the village. I thought she was liking me a lot better. There were crabs all over the place. I had never seen crabs so large. They were walking and snapping their jaws—two pairs of nippers. Good Lord, they looked vicious! I urged her, "Let's get out of here. I don't like those things."

"They aren't harmful. They'll run away from you. They run away from us because people catch them to eat."

"People eat that stuff?" I asked.

"Oh yes. They're delicious."

She wanted to cross to the other side of the beach, but I still wasn't convinced that those huge, evil-looking crabs could be trusted. I urged her to go. Apparently she knew what it was all about, but I didn't like those things snapping at my legs. She started to cross but I coaxed her back, and we came back to town. We had another soft drink and then went the full length of the town, where there were a lot of little shacks along the beach. One of them was owned by her uncle so we stopped and she talked to her relatives. They were a young couple with a baby, and I asked them to come to town and have a drink with us.

The fellow must have misunderstood me, for he acted as though I had insulted him. I was only trying to be nice to them, so I held my temper. The girl didn't like it either, so we left and crossed over to the next back-street. When we got there, she put her arms around my neck and kissed me. Boy, was I surprised! I knew then that we were going to be very good friends because, well, that came so suddenly and I had only spent a few pennies in American money on her. Of course, those people are very poor and they live very simply. Their food consists mostly of fruit, yams, some kinds of roots, and those "morphodite" potatoes and fish.

Their mainstay was fish which was procured with a community net. The net was about a thousand feet long. The fishing ground would be baited and a group of people would stay at each end of the net, on shore, while the middle would be carried out with skiffs. It was weighted on the bottom edge so it was let down, and everybody would join in pulling the fish up on the beach.

I never saw one patch of cultivated ground while I was there. Even around the houses there would be no more than a strip a few inches wide and five or six feet long that had any plantings of any kind. I never saw people like those anywhere. I guess they just didn't like to work. Many of the men were half-naked—no clothes from the waist up. But the women were decently dressed. I don't know how they managed to live, but they appeared to be well nourished. Some were even plump or fat.

The girl was on the plump side. Her mother, I discovered, was the belle of the town—the entertainer. She sang her native songs and some that were in Spanish and French. I understood the French words, but they didn't make any sense. None of it made any sense. She did a sort of dance, mostly jumping up and down and opening and closing her legs, rather like an African jungle-dance.

CHAPTER IX

HEAVEN

We completed our rendezvous with the mother ship, picked up our water casks and headed for Santastatia. It took about the usual time because there you can always depend on the weather. The wind is always from the same direction and doesn't vary much. We dropped anchor and proceeded to take on more provisions, including yams, for the coming season. About the latter part of April we moved out and headed for the Western Grounds.

We were very fortunate that season. We began to catch whales in good number, including bulls. One of the bulls was very large and produced a hundred and ten barrels. The others each produced as much oil as several cows.

We filled early, so about the middle of July we set sail for the home port—New Bedford. The captain said we were almost six weeks ahead of schedule. This pleased everyone. The captain was particularly happy. He could get back to Flores that much sooner, to marry Mary. As for me, well, New Bedford was the center of all my dreams.

We were very short of water. With the heavy catch that we had on board, we had had to pump water overboard to make room for the oil. We had only enough water to take us home in average weather. What we had was for drinking and cooking only. On a small schooner like the *Pedro Varella*, there was never any surplus. Every possible means had to be used to conserve water.

Clothes had to be washed. Working in the grease, blubber, blood and slime as we did, it took a strong solvent to get them clean because salt-water alone is useless. One practice, though by no means nice, was to set up a barrel with holes of various sizes bored through the head of it. A few inches from the bottom was a spigot. Everyone contributed to this barrel so that the barrel was always partially full of urine. When one had to wash clothing, he drew off the amount needed into a bucket, drenched the grease and slime out of the garments, and then rinsed them by trailing them over the side of the ship in the ocean. I always tied mine in a bundle and held onto the line so as to draw them in quickly when sharks appeared. A couple of passes by a shark and there wouldn't be much left to wear.

Just before we got out of the whaling grounds we got into calm weather. We lost several days, so the captain cautioned us about the water. We went into voluntary rationing, using no more than absolutely necessary. We washed our faces in salt-water using only a small cupful of fresh water for rinsing. Although there was a bucket of water at all times at the back of the galley, I don't believe anyone ever tried to take advantage of it.

After a few days, we picked up a slight breeze and began to make headway. The ocean currents had put us considerably eastward off our course, so we had to sail northwesterly.

When we got near the New England coast we hit a good breeze and made progress on the fourteenth and fifteenth of August. It was on August sixteenth that I first laid eyes on the coast of Massachusetts. The breeze was good and we drew in rapidly, passing Gay Head Lighthouse on the starboard, and Hens and Chickens Lightship on the port side. We went on into Buzzards Bay to the anchorage which is just outside the dredged canal, four or five miles outside of New Bedford Harbor.

The harbor is a very sheltered, good, closed harbor, and from where we were I could see New Bedford. The city rises from the waterfront to a considerable height, and I could see the clean, painted, bright-looking houses, and the streets laid out in front of them. There were lots of cotton mills there then—red-brick buildings with tall chimneys, giving it a lot of color and a picturesque look that made it really beautiful.

After twenty-three months of sailing, and the anticipation of seeing it, New Bedford was heaven to me. And the next day I was going to be there! Tears of joy ran down my cheeks. I can feel them now, again, as I relive that moment. I still feel that way about it. I know that if every native-born American, or every naturalized American, could realize what a heaven on earth we have here, no one in civil or political life could ever bring himself to do anything to jeopardize the security of this, our country. To all who may read this—boys and girls, men and women—this country is heaven!

We shortened sails as we came in, dropped anchor and took in the rest of the sails. The captain ordered the flag up for the tugboat. In a very short while a small tug, the *Sherman,* came out by the lighthouse at the other end of the dredged channel at the entrance to New Bedford Harbor.

The tug didn't touch us. It just came alongside and gave us a tow line. We picked up anchor and the *Sherman* towed us into New Bedford Harbor. We dropped anchor in the center of the harbor; the tug left us and soon we saw the boat coming with the doctor and the immigration officers.

The doctor gave us some kind of shot, at least those who were here for the first time. After he satisfied himself that there was no disease aboard, he called the immigration officers aboard. There were a number of fellows who had never been in the United States before, all older than I. When the officers reached my name, one of them said to me, "Oh, I remember your father telling me you were aboard; that he had a son on the *Pedro Varella.* I think a lot of your father. We have been friends a good many years. He is a good man."

I felt good all over to receive such a friendly greeting and to be in the U.S.A.

We were soon cleared and at liberty to go ashore. I was looking across toward the other side—toward Fairhaven—when the tug again came alongside. This time it didn't tow us. It just tied lines to us, fore and aft, and put us up to Merrill's Wharf where we were to discharge the oil.

I had lost no time in getting my seabag ready to go ashore, and was just waiting for the word when the captain sent for me.

"Joe, you wait. Don't go ashore yet. I will go with you so I can show you where your aunt's house is. She runs a boarding house, as I told you before, and I'm sure she's got room for you. If she hasn't, she'll make it."

I asked if it was safe to leave my seabag in the fo'c's'le.

"Oh, no. Bring it aft. We will lock it in the cabin." I did so. He locked the cabin, and we left with a retired whaling-captain who was the agent for the ship. The captain introduced me, and we walked up Union Street—beautiful Union Street—and I was amazed to see those big buildings, three and four stories high, side by side, on both sides of the street. There were stores on the street level. Every building had stores, all of different sizes and forms. We passed two or three barrooms and several restaurants before we got to the corner of Union Street and Acushnet Avenue.

"Well, we'll cross over to that corner and wait for the streetcar," the captain directed. There was a streetcar going north, one block away on Pleasant Street.

"What's that thing?" I asked excitedly.

"That is a streetcar. We'll get on one in a minute."

"My goodness. Are we going aboard that thing?"

"Oh, yes. That's the only way to get around over here."

"Oh, that's good," I exclaimed.

We crossed Acushnet Avenue and waited for the next streetcar going south.

The first car was the wrong one. It was going to the south end of New Bedford, over to Dartmouth. I had already started for it when the captain grabbed at me and yelled. "No, we don't take this one. We have to take the one that reads 'Fort Rodman.'"

Good enough. Soon, along came that great big thing screeching on the rails and clanging bells. I thought it was the most beautiful thing I had ever seen—running on iron rails, with a great big officer in uniform up there running it.

The officer opened the door and we went aboard, climbing up two steps. The captain said, "Come on in." He gave the officer some money. I didn't have any American money in small change, anyway. Then I noticed that the officer's uniform was kind of dirty, and I didn't like him very much. I never could stand dirty clothes and I didn't like people who wore them.

We sat down, and that thing started going. Pretty soon it was zooming by those beautiful houses. There aren't many stores on Acushnet Avenue. We were soon passing apartment houses. Mostly three-story buildings.

I didn't know what they were so I asked the captain. He explained, "That's where people live, one family on each floor. Don't you see the curtains at the windows? Whenever you see curtains you know that women live there. American women, or other women after they live in America awhile, get pride, and put up white curtains at the windows and doors, if there are glass doors."

I was really amazed. For the first time the captain was talking like a human being. He wasn't using that rigid voice. He was trying to smile. He even managed to grin a little. All at once he wasn't the captain any more. He was an entirely different man.

In a little while he asked the conductor how far we were from Grinnell Street. Just then we came to a brick building on the left, and the captain said, "Oh, I know. It's the next block."

The conductor slowed the car down and we got off. I paid particular attention to the pole there, and memorized the name of the cross street—Grinnell Street. We crossed the street and went down to my aunt's house, which was a three-story building. We didn't ring the bell but went around to the back and knocked at the door.

I saw an old lady come to the door, and my first impression was that I didn't like her. She was pleasant, but she had dirt on the front of her dress, and I liked things and people to be clean.

She recognized the captain, "Oh, Tony boy. Come on in. Who is this kid with you?" He told her who I was and she embraced me and kissed me. I didn't like that either, because she had something black on her upper lip.

We sat down and she gave us coffee—good fresh coffee, and some homemade cake. I think that was the first really good cup of coffee I'd ever had, and to this day I love homemade cake.

I began to like her a little better, in spite of the dirt on her dress. Her apron was black and white with ruffles around it, and it was kind of spotted with something that looked like dirt. She pulled something out of her apron pocket, took off the cover, put some of the stuff in her nose and inhaled.

"What's that, Aunt Emily?"

"This is snuff. Would you like some?"

"Oh, no, thank you," and I pushed her hand away. Then I saw that the stuff on her upper lip and on her dress was snuff and I decided, having already disposed of the coffee and cake, that I was going to like her much better.

She left, to go and wake up her husband. He was a fisherman and owned a boat that ran in and out of New Bedford. He had come in earlier in the morning and was still asleep.

"Captain, why does she smell that stuff?" I whispered, as she went out the door.

"Well, she likes it. It's the same as with people who smoke and chew. It's a habit." Again I was surprised that the captain had given me a direct answer. On the ship he always had been very strict. He never carried on a conversation. He wouldn't grin and he wouldn't smile. He was pretty tough. He had changed on the way up to Aunt Emily's, and he was still acting civilized and almost human.

My uncle got up, and was he big! He was over six feet tall, big shoulders and chest, and no tummy. He must have weighed over two hundred and fifty pounds. He was built like a wrestler. (At that time I didn't know what a wrestler was.) What a man! And when he shook my hand he squeezed it so hard without ever realizing it, that I bent over. After we talked a little while, the conversation lagged. But, well, he was a fisherman.

My aunt asked me what I was going to do; was I going to stay in New Bedford, or was I going back to Flores?

"Flores? Hell, no!" I didn't know any other expressive English words. "I am going to stay right here in heaven."

She smiled and said, questioningly, "Heaven?"

"Yes, isn't this heaven? Isn't this beautiful?"

She stated, in a matter-of-fact voice, "Well, I've got a room on the second floor that I can spare."

All of Aunt Emily's boarders worked in the cotton mills near by. Most of them roomed there too, but since she had a full table and a spare room and not much chance for more roomers, I felt I wouldn't be imposing. So I said that it would be just fine. She asked me where my clothes were.

"On the ship. I'll get them tomorrow," I told her.

"I'll get a horse and buggy and we'll bring them up here," the captain said.

"Well, where are you going to go?" my aunt asked him.

"Oh, I'm going with Captain Santos. I'm only staying here until we settle up the voyage and pay the crew, and then I'm going back to Flores and get married."

"Yes, Joe's mother wrote to me about it," she said. He left a few minutes later and I went out with him to the street because I was so fascinated with the streetcars. The car looked just as big as it had before. The conductor looked just as impressive, and I was fascinated by the noise the wheels made on the tracks. It sounded like music. I watched it until it disappeared down the street. I went back into the house.

"When you need to go to the toilet, Joe, it's out there," and Aunt Emily pointed to a little house painted white, out in the middle of the back yard under a grape vine. Then she took me in and showed me the bathroom—a little room with a tub in it and what looked to me like the spigot on the urine barrel on the ship.

"What's that thing?" I asked expressing a good deal of wonderment, for I had never seen a porcelain tub before.

"Why, that's a bath tub and here are the faucets where you turn the water on. See, the water comes out here," and she turned what I thought was the spigot.

"Where does it come from?" I wanted to know.

"Oh, it comes from the city," she explained. She turned the other faucet. "Feel it." I put my finger under it and the water was warm. "Oh, my God. It's almost hot. This really is heaven. I'm sure of it now."

"Look. Haven't you ever taken a bath in a tub before?"

"Why, I've never even seen one."

"Well, you are going to take one right now. I'll go and get you a towel and soap. It's almost four o'clock. The boarders will be coming in at five. You can take a bath while I'm getting supper ready."

"How many boarders do you have, Aunt Emily?"

"I have ten, and you make eleven." She started the water running and told me to turn it off when it got to be about a foot deep. "Now I've got to go, so you take your bath."

I've been in a lot of tubs in many places since then, but I never enjoyed a bath as I did that one. Just imagine having a bath in warm water! Good gracious! Believe it or not, I cried. Nobody could tell me this wasn't heaven. At that moment I was convinced beyond any doubt.

I got out and went to my aunt, who was setting the table.

"Look, Auntie, I had a bath in warm water. This is heaven and you can't tell me differently because I won't believe it."

She laughed and called Uncle Joe and told him about it. He laughed too. They had had such things for so long that they just took them for granted, as we do now.

CHAPTER X

ANOTHER PORT, ANOTHER GIRL

Soon the boarders came in. My aunt introduced me to all of them, men and girls, and when we sat down at the table she was kind enough to seat me between two girls. It was a long table and this was the first time I had eaten at a table since I left Flores, almost a year ago. I soon got acquainted enough to joke and talk with the others at the table. Most of them spoke more Portuguese than English, so I felt pretty much at ease.

After dinner I told Aunt Emily I wanted to go to town and asked her for her address in case I should lose myself. I decided to walk as I didn't trust myself alone on the streetcars. I walked to Acushnet Avenue and down it, toward the city. I noticed a big brick-building about a block down and then I saw the name on it, Montepiel. I kept on until I got to Union Street. I really enjoyed the beauty of the center. I walked one block to the left, to the corner of Union and Purchase streets. On one corner was a bank. Across the street was a great big building facing Union and Purchase streets, and it was one of the tallest buildings I'd ever seen—four stories high, with a clothing display behind huge windows.

On one corner was a cigar store. Across from it on the opposite corner was a shoeshine parlor. I stood on each of the corners acquainting myself with the streets and buildings, and then I went back to Acushnet Avenue and on south, back to Aunt Emily's.

One of the girls met me at the gate and asked me where I'd been. I told her I had been down to the center and that I had walked both ways since I didn't trust myself on the streetcars.

"Oh, no," she exclaimed. "Come on. What are you going to do now? Are you tired?"

"No. It wasn't very far."

"Well, come on. We'll take a ride away up to the north end. The streetcar goes all the way. We'll go to the end of the line so you can see the city."

We did just that, and stopped at the center on the way back and decided to get off and walk around a bit and then walk the rest of the way home. It must have been about nine o'clock. We didn't know exactly, as neither of us had a watch. Rose took me up Union Street as far as the theater. It was the largest I'd ever seen. That entrance was beautiful.

"My goodness. I'd like to go in."

"Oh, it's getting late. We'd be awfully late getting out. What do you say we come back tomorrow and go to the show?"

"It's a date," I agreed.

We came down Pleasant Street to Acushnet Avenue and went to a lunch counter. We had coffee and a treat—apple pie—the first apple pie I'd ever tasted. Then we walked down Acushnet a few blocks, and took the streetcar the rest of the way home.

"Look," said Rose, "what do you say, let's go to the south end tomorrow, before we go to the show?"

"Perfect," I agreed.

We stopped and sat on the front steps awhile and talked about this and that as we cooled off, for it was a pretty warm evening. She went to her room on the third floor, and I went to mine, which was on the second floor, and went to bed. Thus ended my first day in New Bedford—a day filled with new and very pleasant experiences.

Next morning I was up early. I couldn't have slept late had I wanted to. I went down to the galley—I mean kitchen. My aunt was just coming in. I talked to her for a while as she prepared breakfast. The boarders came in, one by one, and we sat down to a breakfast of ham and eggs. It was, I thought, fit for a king, and I ate like a pig.

After breakfast the boarders left and went to the mill. A little later I heard whistles blowing and I wanted to know what they were. "Those are the different mill-whistles. They blow when it is time for people to start work," Aunt Emily explained.

I decided to go back to the ship, thinking that I'd probably meet Captain Corvello and be able to get my seabag down. I walked down Acushnet Avenue to Union, turned right toward the water front, and had gone only a block when I heard, "Look who's coming."

It was Captain Corvello, standing with two other men just outside a whaler's outfitting store.

"Joe, are you lost?"

"No, I'm not lost. I thought I'd find you down around the dock and I could go down to the ship and get my seabag."

"Well, come over here." He introduced me to the two captains who were with him, and to a couple more who were standing close by, and then to Mr. Harwitz, the owner of the store. Mr. Harwitz then took me in and introduced me to his son, David, who was a little older than I.

David showed me around the store. It was large and there was everything there that a whaler could use or need. Tables were piled high with shirts, dungarees, boots, oilskins, and underwear. At the back of the store were chairs and tables in a clear space. Here was where the whaling captains, especially the retired ones, would meet in the afternoons and tell stories. Over at one side was a similar place for the mates. There was one old-timer there, Captain Mandley, who was eighty-three years old and getting pretty feeble.

Captain Corvello was waiting for me, ready to go back to the ship. "We might as well get a horse and buggy. There is a stable down here on First Street, and I'll take you and your seabag up to the house. I'll take mine over to Captain Santos because I've got to get ready. I've already got my steamer ticket."

He explained that the ship was to sail from New York one day during the following week, going via Boston, and then to San Miguel, in the Azores. At San Miguel, he would take the inter-island steamer to Flores.

We got the horse and buggy. I enjoyed riding in it even though it was pretty rough. The street at Merrill's Wharf was never very smooth and we crossed a lot of railroad tracks before we got alongside the ship. The boat steerer got the captain's stuff and put it in the buggy, and I got my seabag.

Some of the mates and the crew were there. I remember the captain told them they would be paid off the next Friday. The accountants were settling up the voyage, which was quite a job. There were the various shiploads of oil for the three years, with different prices and different quantities. Then there were the individual drawings of the sailors at various ports, and the percentages, called "lay," that each member of the crew received. My pay, when I got it, was twenty-three dollars and forty-seven cents for the twenty-three months that I had been on the *Pedro Varella,* from the time I'd left Flores to my arrival in New Bedford.

We left Merrill's Wharf with the horse and buggy and our bags of clothes, going up Union Street to Water Street, where we turned left.

This was quite a contrast to the New Bedford I'd already seen. This was a poorer residential-district. The houses were badly in need of repair. The kids were pretty ragged, with dirty faces. There were lots of second-hand stores, several hockshops and three or four old, rather dirty, barber shops, with just one barber chair. We kept on until we got to Grinnell Street, where we turned right to Acushnet and on over to Aunt Emily's. I got off with my bag and the captain continued on to Captain Santos' place.

Aunt Emily was getting dinner. "Joe," she ordered, "empty your seabag. You are in the United States now and you can't go around with wrinkled clothes."

"United States? You mean heaven, Aunt Emily."

"Well, okay. But empty it out here on the floor and we'll decide which goes to the laundry and which to the cleaner's. They'll be here tomorrow to pick it up."

I helped her a little with the dishes and with setting the table. After dinner, Rose asked me if I was ready. "You haven't changed your mind about going to the show, have you?" she asked.

"Oh, my goodness, no."

"Well, all right. I'll be ready in a minute."

She wasn't a beautiful girl, but she had personality. She was just a little bit of all right. She was of medium stature and nice-looking. She was about eighteen, I think. She came down in a minute and we took the car at the corner of Grinnell and Acushnet Avenue, going south to Fort Rodman.

After we had ridden for a few minutes, the car turned left onto Rivet Street, down to Water, and then right. Lo, and behold, there was another center.

"How did we get here so fast?" I asked, thinking it was the same center I had seen.

"This is the south-end center on Water Street. It's entirely different. This is another business center," she told me.

There were jewelry stores, clothing stores—all kinds of stores, big and small. And many people were on the streets.

We ran out of that section a little farther on, and the car turned off onto the biggest, widest street I had yet seen. We came to the top of a knoll and I could see water. She explained that Fort Rodman was on a point of land with water on both sides, and that we were looking at the bay. Soon we would be able to see where we had come in on the ship.

In a moment there was Buzzards Bay before us. The car stopped for a few minutes and then started back to New Bedford, toward the center.

I thought we were going to get off at Union Street, but we went on a block to William Street. "I want you to see the center real well. Up at Union and Purchase is a beautiful corner," she told me. From the four sidewalk-corners we had a fine view of all the streets. We went up Pleasant Street, which is very wide. There are the courthouse and other government buildings, the mayor's office, and a nice little park and one or two statues. I thought it was elegant.

"Which show would you like to go to?" she wanted to know.

"Why don't we go to the theater we saw last night?"

"All right." She led the way up William about three blocks and turned left, and there it was, right at the corner of Union and Sixth.

I thought the picture was tremendously funny. There was no

story. Just a lot of funny antics, but it was the first movie I'd ever seen. Rose didn't care much for it and, of course, I wouldn't now, but at that time it was marvelous. I would have stayed to see it again but she said, "Well, we've seen it." And we went out.

Walking down Pleasant Street, we came upon a restaurant and I suggested that we have coffee and apple pie. I thought she might like something else but, then as now, like all women she was watching her figure.

"Figure?" I said. "What's that?" I had never heard that expression before.

"I have to watch out that I don't get too plump—too fat. Girls have to do that. Boys don't have to bother." This was something entirely new to me.

We went home and sat on the front steps. I put my arm around her and kissed her. She liked that. Then she returned the favor. And from such a nice girl I really enjoyed it. Then I went up to her room to look at her family album. I never enjoyed family pictures as much as I enjoyed those. You see, we didn't light the lamp.

Every evening we got together and went to a show after supper, until the day I got paid off. The captain told me the day before so that I could go down and get my pay. He was going to leave immediately afterward, go to Boston by train and visit some friends, and then take the steamer to the Azores to marry my sister.

I mentioned before that my pay was twenty-three dollars and forty-seven cents. I had made no drawing anywhere, and the clothing I had bought from the slopchest, including underwear, shirts, dungarees, oilskins, boots and sou'wester, was part of my pay. It was the owners who made the money on whaling ships.

The captain explained that he would stay overnight in Boston, with the friends he had told me about, and leave on the steamer the following day. So he wouldn't be seeing me again until he got back from the Azores.

"Now wait a minute," said I. "Before you go I want to get something for my mother and sisters."

"I haven't got room to take anything," he objected.

"Well, how about some jewelry? Trinkets and such?" We went

to a jewelry store and I spent the whole twenty-three dollars and forty-seven cents, in addition to ten dollars of the money that my father had given me. Of that I had only spent a few dollars, plus eight dollars for a suit that Rose insisted I buy to go to the movies. And, oh, yes, I bought a jackknife for the captain to take to my father who was wintering in Flores, and another for my younger brother. We bade one another good-by, and I sent regards to all my folks and friends. His parting question was, "Can you find your way home?"

"Oh, yes. I can even take the streetcar now. I've been out every evening with one of the girls at Aunt Emily's."

"Of course. You would!" And he left to catch his train.

CHAPTER XI

HORSES VERSUS WHALES

I went back to the boarding house. There was a man waiting there, a cousin of Aunt Emily's. She introduced me to him and he asked me if I was working.

"No. I just got off a whaler," I told him.

"Have you got plenty of money?" he wanted to know.

"No, I haven't, because I spent all of my pay and ten dollars besides, for presents to send to my mother, father, sisters and brother. I still have a few dollars, though, that my father sent me."

Mr. Lewis was a farmer who delivered milk from door to door in New Bedford. I was a little skeptical about working on a farm, but a job was a job, so I agreed to try it. We arranged to meet at four o'clock next day when he would come by after finishing his milk route.

I was ready when he arrived but I had picked out only a few clothes to take along. My aunt gave us coffee and some cake, and I warned her not to rent my room to anyone until I knew whether or not I would keep the job. After all, I had never been on a farm.

I would come back and settle with her in a few days, anyhow.

The farm was near South Dartmouth, in the same county. We started off. The sun was beating down and it was hot. I didn't like the smell of that horse, but I figured that I could stand it if Mr. Lewis could. We made several stops, where Mr. Lewis would chat with friends. The country was beautiful and I was enjoying myself. The streets were nice, with a few black dirt-roads.

Finally he turned in at a gate on the right. There was a neat-looking house, painted white, and a good barn, one story high, painted red. It was really a nice place. I heard quite a commotion and saw several dogs, ducks and chickens. Two children ran out of the house to greet the wagon. Mr. Lewis didn't ask for his wife. In fact he didn't ask the kids anything, and I was rather surprised. I began to wonder if he lived alone with the children.

"Come along, Joe. Come to the barn," he said, as he unhitched the horse. I stayed at a respectful distance. When we got to the barn I could hear a sort of squishing noise. I discovered it was his wife and daughter, milking the cows. I had never been close to cows before. In Flores our farming was done on shares, by another family. I was pretty skeptical about going into the barn. I was afraid they would run me against the wall, or some doggone thing.

Mr. Lewis saw me hesitate, and urged me on. "Come on, Joe. They're nice and tame. They won't hurt you. They aren't whales. They won't kick you."

I went in, and he introduced me to his wife and daughter. The daughter was a nice, plump kid of sixteen with rosy cheeks, nice teeth and very bright eyes. She kept right on milking her cow until she had finished. Then she poured the milk into a large can and started on another cow—the last one. I counted eight cows.

When she finished milking, she went to feed three cute little calves, giving milk from a bucket. I went with her. Then she said, "Come on, Joe. You might as well learn the business," and went to feed the hogs. One was large and one was small. She explained, "This large hog we are going to kill for meat this winter. The small one is for next summer."

Then we all went into the kitchen. The table was set and the food ready. We had roast beef, several vegetables, salad, milk and coffee. It was a strong table.

After we had eaten I asked if we might walk around. The girl said, "If you will wait until I wash the dishes, I'll go with you."

"All right. I'll help you," I said.

She gave me a towel, and as she washed the dishes and handed them to me I dried them. She would tell me where to put them, and soon we had them finished.

We walked out and crossed a big, bare field; an enormous one, I thought. "What's the matter with this field? There's nothing on it."

"Oh, we just harvested the crop and my father is going to plow it tomorrow."

"How are you going to plow it? I haven't seen any oxen."

"Oxen?" she questioned, surprised. "Oh, no. We plow with horses." With this, she grabbed my hand and led me to another field, a pasture where there were three horses. They were enormous. "My goodness. I never saw horses that big before!"

Apparently they were very gentle, for she called them by name and went up and patted each one. She asked me to come and pet them, too, but I was afraid of them.

"See," she said, "they are just like kittens."

"Oh, no. They are too big. I'm not getting near those things."

We walked around some more and then returned to the house. The two small children had been put to bed, but Mr. and Mrs. Lewis were still talking. We sat down with them and they said they were going to start plowing the next day.

"Yes," I said, "your daughter showed me the biggest horses I ever saw in my life."

"I have three fine horses," Mr. Lewis informed me.

"Do you use one horse on the plow?"

"No. We use two horses on the plow."

"Then the horses are not as strong as oxen because we use only one ox on a plow in the old country."

"Yes, I know. But this is a different plow. I can do as much work in one hour as one ox and a wooden plow would do in one day."

"That I'll have to see," I remarked.

"You will, tomorrow."

In the morning, Mrs. Lewis and the girl went to milk. But I'm ahead of my story. First of all, while it was still pitch-black dark I heard dishes rattling in the kitchen. I knew someone was up so I got up, too. Mrs. Lewis was in the kitchen.

"What are you doing up so early?" I asked. "It is still dark outside."

"I'm getting breakfast," she answered. "As soon as we have had breakfast my husband harnesses the horses and gets ready to start plowing while we do the milking."

In a few minutes I heard a stomp, stomp, stomp. It was Mr. Lewis coming in, wearing heavy shoes. We had a breakfast of cooked oats, or something, and bacon and eggs.

"After breakfast," he said, "we will go and hitch up the horses."

"Oh, no, not me. I'm afraid of horses."

"After you get used to them you won't be afraid," he told me.

"They look awfully big," I said.

"They're not as big as whales and, from what I've heard about you, you're not afraid of whales. You don't need to be afraid of horses, either. Not when you know how tame and gentle they are."

He went to get the horses. They came to the gate, slow and sure. He gave them some grain—corn or oats—in canvas bags which he hung over the horses' heads, with the mouth in the bag. He harnessed the horses while they were eating, and hitched them to the plow. The plow amazed me. It was all iron. I wanted to see how the thing worked, and asked if I might go along. He had already taken the feeders off the horses' heads.

"Sure," he said. "You've got to come anyway. You gotta learn. You're going to drive those horses. I'm going to turn them over to you, in a little while."

"Oh, no, you won't." I was getting a little worried.

"Oh, come along," he said.

I went alongside and he showed me the different things to do. "When you want them to go left, you say 'Hoy'. When you want them to go right you say 'Gee', and when you want them to stop you say 'Ho'." At least that is what I thought he said, and I wondered if he had ever been a sailor, and how come they said "Ho" to a horse. He said "Giddap" when he wanted them to go. Anyway, those four words seemed to be enough.

We got around that field in a surprisingly short time, and there was a wide band of freshly-turned ground behind us. The ground turned all one way, smooth as could be—not rough as it would be with a woden plow which turns the ground both ways because there is no way to turn the ground over actually. It really looked beautiful to me.

"Come on, Joe. You take it." I was sort of dreaming along and the words came almost as a shock to me.

"Oh, no. I can't do it." But Mr. Lewis insisted and, lo and behold, I was amazed to see how easy it was. Once in a while I got mixed up with "gee" and "hoy" but I soon learned that the word was "haw" and not "hoy". But it didn't seem to make any difference to the horses.

"Anyway, the horses know what to do better than you do, so don't worry about it," Mr. Lewis told me. He made one turn around the field with me and when we got in front of the house he said, "God bless you, Joe. The horses will take care of you." So we kept on going.

I think it was about seven o'clock in the morning when he left me alone. It was rapidly getting warm and soon I had to shed my outside shirt, and I kept on plowing. The girl came out before she went to school. She said, "Whoa," and the horses stopped. "I'm going to school now, Joe. I'll see you when I come back. You're doing a nice job. You're doing it like an old hand."

"Oh, don't you believe it," I said, rather pleased.

"Yes, you are. You're doing all right. My father has been watching you and he says you are doing all right. You are going to make a good farmer."

"I doubt it. I'd rather be a sailor. These horses are beginning to stink."

"Oh, no. You don't mind." She left and I continued plowing that field, going round and round. It got to be about eleven o'clock and I tell you that sun was beating down pretty hard. Stinking horses, no breeze, lots of dust, my face dripping with sweat, and my white undershirt turned black and soggy. Still I kept going round and round the field.

I took off my hat. Mrs. Lewis called me and told me to put it back on, but I couldn't understand what she was saying. However, I put my hat back on, and later she told me: "Joe, remember this.

Never take your hat off in the sun because, even though you have a lot of hair, you can still get a sunstroke. So keep your hat on."

I was well drilled in taking orders from anybody who was in the position of being an officer, and I figured her husband was the same as captain, and I rated her as mate. So I said, "Yes, sir." She said, "You don't say 'Yes, sir' to a woman. You say 'Yes ma'am'." I thanked her and kept on going until lunch time.

The lunch was very good but it was too hot to eat. Mrs. Lewis insisted that I drink cold milk which she kept in a tank of water— the only means of refrigeration they had. Some of the townspeople had ice boxes, but none of the farmers had them.

By three o'clock the sun and heat were almost unbearable. I was sweating as never before, and I was black with dust. One thing I had decided: I was not going to be a farmer.

About five o'clock Mr. Lewis came around and told me I was doing a wonderful job. Of course that pleased me like everything, but I was getting awfully tired. I admitted I was. "My arms are tired. I've held them in this position all day handling the plow, and working on this uneven ground doesn't do me any good. But I can take it. How long do you think the horses can take it? They have been sweating all day and they are tired."

"Yes, they are tired," he said, "and we will quit right now. Anyway, I've got something else on my mind, about tomorrow."

Well, I thought to myself, he could keep his horses. I had something on my mind and it wasn't farming and it wasn't horses.

While he unhitched, I kept my distance. Even though I had been plowing, the plow had been between me and the horses, and I wasn't going to get too close to those feet. I didn't trust them, no matter how tame they were supposed to be. They might not kick but they really had the equipment for it.

The horses were fed and put out to pasture. Mrs. Lewis wanted to break me in on the milking, but I said, "I'd rather watch you and Elvina do it." I had made up my mind I wasn't going to stay, so why learn something I wasn't going to do? Mr. Lewis came and helped, so it didn't take very long. Then I helped Elvina feed the ducks, chickens, and geese as well as the calves and pigs.

By the time we arrived at the house, Mrs. Lewis had dinner on the table. After we had eaten, Elvina asked me if I had ever washed dishes. "You bet I have," I answered. So I washed them and she dried them. Then she wanted to go for a walk, but I had had enough walking for one day. We just sat on a bench by the barn and talked for a while, and about nine o'clock we walked back to the house.

The children were already in bed. At least they weren't around. Mr. Lewis said to me, "Well, Joe, another two days and you will finish that field." I sort of grunted, and went off to bed.

I awoke some time later. I had no idea what time it was but, as tired as I was, I might have slept quite awhile. I dressed very quietly and got together the few clothes I had brought. I went out quietly and started down the road toward New Bedford. After about an hour I heard a noise behind me. It was a horse and wagon pulling up alongside me. "Hey, boy. Where you goin'?"

"I'm going to New Bedford," I answered.

"Well, climb in. Where are you coming from?"

"Oh, that's a long story. Where in the world are you going at this hour?" I asked him.

"Oh, I'm taking milk into New Bedford. I've got a wagon full of milk. By the way, where do you come from?"

"Well, I was working at Mr. Lewis' place, but I didn't have the face to tell him I was quitting, so I just walked off. He'll understand when he finds I'm not there in the morning. He'll know I just left." Then the man said, "If he doesn't, I'll tell him on the way back. I have to stop there to leave his empty cans."

"What do you mean?"

"Oh, I've got his milk with me. I pick up his milk also. We take turns delivering our milk every other day."

When we came to New Bedford he asked me where I lived, and I told him it was near the corner of Grinnell Street and Acushnet Avenue. "I'm staying with my Aunt Emily."

"Oh, Emily is your Aunt? If you stay on the wagon I'll be there after 'while. I leave milk at her house." So I rode along with him and at about daylight we arrived at Aunt Emily's. I went to my room and a few minutes later heard her stirring about in the kitchen. I came right down and she was rather surprised to see me.

"What are you doing here, Joe?" I told her the story. She laughed and remarked, "Well I could have told you when you left that you wouldn't stay. That's a rough job. Did you milk any cows?"

"No. But I plowed all day and Mr. Lewis said I did a good job. I know he was pleased because he said so."

Thus ended my first experience as a farmer. Rose and I took up where we left off, and she helped me a great deal with my English.

CHAPTER XII

WATERLOGGED

I went down and hung around the water front for a couple of days and spent a lot of time at Harwitz' whaler's outfitting store on Second and Union streets. But there was no shipping out of New Bedford and I was advised to go to Boston. It was the same there. They gave me the cold shoulder because of my age and size.

Rather discouraged, I went back to New Bedford. When I arrived home, I told my aunt about it and asked her what I should do. "I could send to my father for some money but I don't want to do that," I told her.

I took to walking through the center and around, and a day or two later as I was walking up Water Street in front of Robinson's Whale Oil Works, one of the men recognized me. "Aren't you the boy who was walking up Union Street a few days ago with Captain Corvello?"

"Yes," I said.

"Weren't you on the *Pedro Varella* with him?"

"That's right."

"What are you doing now?"

"Nothing. I can't find a job. I went up to Boston yesterday but they wouldn't take me because I am too young."

"Wait a minute. We've got a job here."

"You have? What is it?"

"Oh, you can do it. You can do this job. Just wait a minute and I'll get the boss."

He went inside, then came back through the open gate and took me in with him. The boss asked me where I worked and I told him I'd never worked ashore; that I had just come off the *Pedro Varella*.

"Oh you did, eh? Captain Corvello?"

"Yes," I said.

"I used to ship with him when we were boys. I used to go to sea on whalers also. What is your name?"

"Gomes. Joe Gomes."

"Captain Gomes' son? Captain Gomes on the bark *Fairhaven?*"

"That's right."

"Good! I've got a job here. It doesn't pay much, but it will keep the wolf from the door."

"Wolf? What's that?" I'd never heard the expression before.

"It pays ten dollars a week. It will keep you alive. You won't get rich, but you won't starve. That's just a way to express it."

"Ten dollars a week. That's plenty of money. That's more than I can use."

"Oh, no. I don't think so."

"I pay only four dollars a week, board and room, so I'll have six dollars to spare."

"You have clothes and laundry."

"But I wash my own clothes."

"You can, but I doubt it. Anyway, if you want it, the job is yours."

"Yes, I should say I do want it," and I went to work right then and there.

I liked the job. There was nothing hard about it. I did odd jobs like sweeping, handling boxes and cans. Everybody was my boss, but that was all right. I kept right on with the job until about the middle of January. On Sundays—we didn't work Sundays—after coming out of church, I would walk uptown. On one particular day, I went to see if the whaler's outfitting store was open, and to my surprise it was. There were several men there, sitting around talking. David, the owner's son, was tending store.

"Well, Joe. We haven't seen you since you started to work for Robinson's," he said.

"Oh, no. I work all day, and I didn't know you were open on Sundays."

He explained that the store was always open. Either he or his father or his brother-in-law would keep the store open. A ship might come in at any time and want to be outfitted in a hurry. Then he inquired, "Are you going back to sea?"

"Oh, yes. As soon as Captain Corvello gets back."

"Why wait? Would you like to take a trip to the Gulf?"

"What Gulf?"

"The Gulf of Mexico."

"Of course, but how?"

"There's a four-masted schooner out here right now. The captain is back there in the store. He wants to ship a man."

"That's the trouble. They call me a boy. That's why I couldn't get a job in Boston. They thought I was too young and couldn't handle a job."

"Oh, come on. I'm sure he'll take you." So he took me to the captain, who asked me a few questions and then assured me that the job was made to order. I would be an extra man. He always shipped an extra man in the winter. I was to be on deck all day but wouldn't have to stand night watches. I would be on call at any time, day or night, to set sails or take them in.

I assured him right then and there that I would go. I didn't even ask about the pay. He told me where the ship was. It was right down next to Merrill's Wharf. I would be sailing at noon the next day and should be on board in the morning. I immediately went back to Aunt Emily's and told her about it.

"Joe," she said, "it's winter. It's a rough job. You shouldn't take it. Besides, you've got a job, a good job, even if you don't want to work ashore, and you're not killing yourself either."

"But I'm not learning anything. I'm not even learning English very fast. Rose has been teaching me but she has a steady boyfriend, now, and she won't be going around with me much any more. Almost everyone else speaks Portuguese. I might as well go. The captain says I can handle the job."

I packed my clothes, and the next morning I went down to the ship. I was going to get a horse and buggy to take my seabag down, but it was less than a mile so I threw it over my shoulder and packed it down on my back.

The ship was a four-masted schooner, not exceptionally large. It was a little more than medium size. At one o'clock she was ready to go. The tug came alongside and towed us outside the dredged channel. We began setting sails, and soon we were out on the open sea. We had a pretty good breeze off Cape Hatteras, but made poor headway getting to the Gulf Stream. Toward the Bahamas we got a pretty good breeze, mostly behind us, and from then on we made very good time. We got into the Gulf of Mexico and sailed up into Mobile. A tug took us to the dock and we started loading.

The ship had come down after a load of railroad ties. We worked steadily for two weeks. When we were finally loaded, the holds were chock-full of ties and the deck was heavily loaded besides, and the deck cargo was well lashed down with chains.

We then set sail for Boston. We had pretty calm weather in the Gulf. After we got out toward Dry Tortugas, those islands off the Florida Keys, we got a little breeze. There, of course, the Gulf Stream began to help us and we went between Florida and the Bahamas pretty fast.

About a day and a half after we passed Cape Hatteras we got into a heavy storm. We were about two hundred miles northeast of Cape Hatteras when the ship began to list very badly. We manned the pumps but the water gained steadily and we had to give it up. The captain ordered the sails taken in. The stress on the riggings and masts was too heavy. We were water-logged and the decks were awash. The captain was afraid of capsizing.

We had only two trysails out, and with a little help from what we had of the Gulf Stream, we were making about a mile or so an hour. But the vessel was steering very badly. The captain ordered the third trysail out and that steadied the ship and she steered better.

While these adjustments were being made the captain ordered the motor boat made ready with extra water and provisions, in case we had to abandon ship. He had extra gasoline stowed away wherever there was room for it, and had the mast, sails, and gear checked to be sure it was all in good condition.

Since there was nothing but wood aboard, it was impossible for the ship to sink. All that added buoyancy would keep her afloat even though the decks were awash. But, of course, she had no stability. Her center of gravity, the captain announced, was too high, and if the vessel rolled over too far she would never come back to an even keel. We had to be ready constantly to abandon ship on an instant's notice. Everything was in top readiness. We could be on the water in the motorboat, and clear of the ship, in thirty seconds.

We settled down, if one can settle down under such conditions, to what soon became a routine of complete wretchedness. All food was cold. Nothing could be cooked or heated. The weather was cold. We were wet practically all of the time. We were able to have a little coffee now and then. The cook had brought a large tin out of the cabin. He smashed it down to a double thickness and built a very small fire out of splinters from some ties. There was no place to get out of the wind except in a small corner of the quarter-deck which we had made into a sort of shelter with a piece of canvas.

There were eleven men in the crew, including the captain, two mates, the cook, six regular sailors, and myself. Every one used the shelter in the best way he could. I would curl up in a corner and take little cat-naps at any time of day when I was not too wet. The rest of the time, particularly at night, I would keep moving, slapping my hands to keep from getting badly chilled.

The morning of the third day, we saw a steamer on the horizon, and the captain ordered the distress flags put up. The steamer drew toward us and when she got close I could see that she was the *Count Van something or other*—from an Italian line. When the two ships were close enough for the two captains to shout to one another through megaphones, the captain shouted to our captain to abandon ship. Our captain did not want to do that. We had remained topside for two days. The sea was smooth enough that there was no immediate danger and, naturally, the captain wanted to save his ship and cargo.

After considerable haranguing back and forth, the captain of the steamer agreed to tow us toward the Nantucket Lightship for a fee of one thousand dollars. He was to wire Boston to send a tug out to meet us, and when the tug took over he would be free to resume his course to Europe.

So we unshackled our port anchor and gave him the chain to tow us. On the second day we sighted the Nantucket Lightship and passed it, about two miles off. The captain of the steamer tried to Morse back to us but nobody understood the code, so he gave it up. In the afternoon we sighted a tug. We didn't know it was ours, but the crew of the steamer did.

In a little while the tug came alongside. The steamer slowed down and the tug went to pick up our anchor chain. For some reason the captain of the tug changed his mind. He told us to heave in our anchor chain and he gave us his tow hawser which we tied to the forward bitts. We proceeded toward Boston and got into Boston Harbor on the afternoon of the second day. The tug took us right up to the dock. Since we hadn't been in a foreign country, there was no quarantine. We needed no entries, or any medical inspection, so we all went ashore.

We had been in wet clothes for seven days and six nights. The entire crew was sick and the captain was in worse shape than anyone. He had taken the same fare and treatment as the crew. The first mate was suffering almost as badly. I guess I was the least affected, perhaps because I was younger, and because I never let myself get really chilled through. After all, the first week in March on the Atlantic still has a lot of winter left in it. We had felt every minute of it.

The ship's owners were waiting for us at the dock and immediately took every one of us to the hospital. The captain had pneumonia. The mate and the cook were close to it.

We were all given a thorough examination. The doctor pronounced my heart and lungs to be in good shape and said there was nothing wrong with me that a good sleep, dry clothes, and a good hot meal wouldn't cure. That made me very happy. I wouldn't have to stay in the hospital, and I could think of more interesting things to do.

The ship's agent, Mr. Phelps, took me to a hotel for dinner. He ordered steaks. Nothing could have suited me better, after seven days of cold canned corned-beef and hardtack. That juicy steak and mashed potatoes tasted pretty good. After that meal I felt as well-fed and satisfied as a whaling ship bedbug.

I went to bed and slept soundly until morning. I got up early and went down to eat, hungry as a wolf. I had a few paper dollars in my pocket but they had become water-soaked for so long that I didn't know whether anyone would accept them. When I showed them to the waitress, she called a man to come over. He remarked, "Oh, you are the boy from that submerged ship they towed in yesterday. I heard you were here at the hotel."

"Yes, that's right."

"The money is good, all right, but you aren't going to pay for your breakfast. It's on the house. Order anything you want."

I didn't know what to order so the waitress asked if she might order for me. "Yes, please do." She was a blonde girl, and very nice. She ordered ham and eggs and fried potatoes and toast. Coffee, too, of course.

I had just about finished with breakfast when the agent came in. He offered me a cigarette but I told him I was too young to smoke. Then he asked if I was ready to go to the office. When we got there he introduced me to a big, fat gentleman who explained that they were going to pay for the clothes we had lost on the ship.

"Would a hundred dollars be enough?"

"Oh yes, that would more than cover it."

"You're satisfied with a hundred dollars?"

"Yes," I answered.

"Well, your wages came to a little over fifty dollars. Here is the whole amount."

I hadn't drawn any money in Mobile, and I felt pretty good with all that money in my pocket. I asked Mr. Phelps how far we were from a station where trains left for New Bedford.

"I tell you what I'll do," he said. "I'll take you to the station and help you get your ticket." Out on the street, he called for a horse and buggy, and in about fifteen minutes we were there. There was a train leaving in about twenty minutes. He showed me where to get the ticket and bade me good-by. He wished me luck, and no more journeys in water-logged ships. I got on the train thinking that Mr. Phelps was about the finest gentleman I had ever met.

CHAPTER XIII

NEW SHIP—NEW JOB

I went to Aunt Emily's immediately upon arriving in New Bedford. I didn't intend to look for another job. Captain Corvello was due to arrive in a week. He had bought an interest in the bark *Greyhound* and had been assigned to her as captain. Naturally, I would ship with him. Anyway, he was now my brother-in-law so I decided that I would just wait around. I had heard an American expression and now, with well over a hundred and fifty dollars in my pocket, I was sure I understood it. I was a "rich bitch."

Rose, with whom I'd had so many good times, was going to be married and wouldn't go out with me any more. But Aunt Emily's husband's niece was now boarding at the house. She looked like the Mona Lisa: rather serious, with a creamy-white complexion. She was not really pretty, but she was fairly nice and we became good friends. She was a few years older than I, and a little taller.

We went to dances once or twice but she didn't like that too well, on account of being taller, so we usually went to shows.

I was killing time until Captain Corvello got back, and the best way to kill time was with a girl.

When Captain Corvello arrived he was alone. The first thing he told me was that my father would arrive in about a month. He was going to pick up Mary later, when we went into the Western Grounds where we would start whaling on the *Greyhound*. The cabin on the *Greyhound* was very good; good enough for a captain's wife and family, although there was quite a lot of carpentry to be done. The captain was very good at that sort of thing so he planned to start in immediately.

I told him the story of my trip to the Gulf and that I had decided to wait for him rather than to look for a short-time job. He said I might as well work with him. Then he asked Aunt Emily if she had a spare room.

"You aren't going to live here!" I exclaimed. I couldn't picture the captain as willing to be on an equal footing with the rest of us, but he surprised me.

"Why not? I'm not any better than the rest of you. I'm just human. I'm a man. We're all equals." I began to wonder if getting married affected everyone so quickly. After all, he had been pretty tough with me but I decided that he was now quite a guy, regardless. Of course, I didn't see much of him after working hours because then he would be visiting with other captains and his seafaring friends.

We went uptown next morning, taking the streetcar to Union Street, and then we walked over to Second Street to the outfitting store. He introduced me to old Captain Smith who was agent for, and half owner of, the *Greyhound*. Captain Corvello owned one-eighth, my father owned one-eighth, and someone else owned a quarter. This *Greyhound* was an old bark, considerably larger than the schooner, *Pedro Varella*, that we had been on, and could carry about twice as much cargo. Her bow was round, just like a tub. I've never seen another ship just like her.

We all walked down to the *Greyhound* and I went down into the steerage, which is for the boat steerers and the steward—one room with five bunks. The captain had just told me that I was going on as boat steerer—my first real promotion, for now I was ranked as petty officer.

I felt pretty important. I was only eighteen and I was responsible for one of the whaleboats and for every item of gear on it. It was my duty to see that the whaleboat, its masts, sails and rigging were in top shape, ready for instant use; that every lance, harpoon, knife and hatchet were razor sharp, properly fitted and correctly placed; that the lines were in perfect condition, with no flaws or broken strands, and all properly spliced. Everything must be perfect, and I was soon going to harpoon my first whale!

I felt my responsibility, and I was glad. I knew that if I made one mistake, I'd never live it down. But I wasn't afraid of whales and the captain knew it. He was a good captain, a skillful sailor, and he knew his business. He had placed trust in me and I knew I was going to make good.

It is with a great feeling of pride that I look back on those years of whaling on the *Greyhound,* and recall that my boat was never found wanting in any respect. My crew never failed nor did any member of it ever meet with serious injury. Only once, out of the dozens of whales that I struck, did my harpoon ever fail to hold.

We went to work on the *Greyhound*. We worked hard, but we didn't push ourselves. We'd start about eight in the morning, knock off for a half-hour or an hour at noon, and quit at about four in the afternoon. The captain would send me home then, so I'd be in time for dinner. He always ate dinner somewhere else. He had only his breakfast at the boarding house, although he paid full room-rent and board, four dollars per week. Aunt Emily wanted to put up a lunch for us, but he said, "No, we always knock off so we can go to a restaurant and have hot coffee."

We worked that way for the first two weeks. Most of the time was spent in rebuilding the try works. On a whaling ship the try works is the heart of the operation. It consists of a brick-and-cement base built in the form of a shallow rectangular tank, with a brick-and-cement cover, or deck. Between the two layers is a space of about one-foot depth. This was kept filled with water, to protect the ship's deck from the terrific heat of the fire under the rendering pots. The brick structure containing the water is called the caboose.

On the cover or deck of the caboose were built two fireplaces of brick, to contain the fire under the two huge pots, each of which had a capacity of from one-hundred fifty to one-hundred eighty gallons. They were shaped just like an old-fashioned, pot-bellied kitchen kettle. A sliding iron door contained the fire within each fireplace and shielded the men who were working in front of it.

Sperm whales produce two kinds of oil—the regular oil from the blubber, and the oil taken from a reservoir in the whale's head. The reservoir is called the case, and the oil from it is called case oil. This was considered to be the highest in grade. Consequently, when the rendering reached the casing operation, all units of the processing were completely emptied, ready to process the casing head separately and store it in separate casks, if possible. The case oil in its original state is like grease and is baled out of the case.

We went on with the work, obtaining the services of two experts on the fireplaces and the more difficult part of the construction. After two weeks, the captain put on shipfitters and started them caulking over the side, along the water lines, around the stern and around the bow, and amidships on the waist. Also on the starboard side, where the whales are tied alongside, for that is the portion that gets the wear and tear. To do the caulking on one side, the ship would be heeled over, and the operation repeated for the other side. The caulking took about two weeks, and then we began to ship the crew.

I heard that Frank Frates was going as chief mate. I knew him by sight. He was an old friend of my father's and mother's. I knew too that Mr. Manuel, who had been the mate on the *Pedro Varella,* was a very good friend of his. Mr. Cruz, who had been second mate on the *Pedro Varella,* was being shipped as second mate on the *Greyhound.*

I was immensely pleased. I knew Mr. Cruz well and he knew me, and Mr. Manuel would tell Mr. Frates about me, too. Since the *Greyhound* carried four whaling boats, there would be a third and fourth mate also, which meant that the second mate would not stand watch. The third mate would stand the port watch and the fourth mate the starboard watch.

Shanghai Joe was responsible for filling out the crew. He was getting along very slowly, which might have delayed us. The *New Bedford Standard* announced on Saturday that the *Greyhound* would be going to sea the following week and that the Salvation Army would be on board the vessel, playing hymns and singing— sort of giving the vessel a good-luck blessing on Sunday afternoon.

On Sunday the ship was ready and open for inspection. Merrill's Wharf and the ship were packed with people. The Salvation Army was on deck with a unit from each of the three centers. People crowded the cabins, the fo'c's'le and the decks, and the festivities lasted all afternoon.

On Monday morning the vessel was towed out into the stream, or harbor. Shanghai Joe was going through all the small towns and communities, looking for young fellows to go to sea. He was still short nine men on Monday afternoon. He told us we could plan on Tuesday afternoon or Wednesday, because he knew where he could get the necessary nine men.

Then he left. The captain ordered the sailors aboard before they changed their minds, and ordered everyone else to be on hand at ten o'clock Tuesday morning. The captain had a ship's keeper who stayed with the vessel.

I arrived at Merrill's Wharf at about nine on Tuesday morning. I was told that Shanghai Joe was already aboard with the nine men. So we all went out to the ship in a motorboat, with the exception of the captain. He went in a tug.

By the time the tug appeared, we had the anchor chain heaved up short, with no slack. As the tug pulled alongside, we heaved up the anchor, gave the tug a line, and went out through the dredged channel.

As soon as we were out, we set sails for Hen and Chickens Lightship, out of Buzzards Bay. As yet, no watches had been set. All the boat steerers knew which watch they belonged on, so I asked the mate if he would put me on the starboard watch, which was the one I had always been on. He said, "Okay. You will be on starboard watch."

As we approached the lightship, I asked Mr. Cruz, the second mate, which boat I would be steerer on. He smiled and said, "I am not going to tell you yet."

"Am I going to be steerer on your boat?"

"Just keep guessin'," is all that he would say.

The last nine men that Shanghai Joe had brought aboard started to crawl up on deck. What a sight! Shanghai Joe had gotten them drunk and kept them that way for a couple of days. One was a young fellow who had just passed the Bar examination. They were all from Gloucester, Massachusetts. Shanghai Joe had lived up to his name.

Watches were set and I got my wish. I was on starboard watch. As I went on watch, Mr. Frates called me. "Joe, you're going to steer my boat."

"What!"

"That's right. You're going to be steerer on my boat. My boat steerer. The captain didn't like the idea because you are a greenhorn, but I heard enough from Mr. Cruz and Mr. Manuel to know that you will be all right."

"Mr. Frates, nothing could please me more. I won't disappoint you. I'll do my best. I'll try to meet all requirements." I was so surprised that I was sort of groping for words. I had never expected to go as boat steerer on the chief-mate's boat. He was one of the very best. "I—thank you from the bottom of my heart," was all I could say.

We were soon out of sight of land, and by the next day we were getting things shipshape. We had full sails set, stays'ls and all. We absolutely meant business. The boat steerers began to get their boats in perfect shape. We knew that the captain was going to start masthead watches the next day.

The boat crews had to be picked. This was left to the boat steerers. Since I was on the first-mate's boat, I was to have first pick. Then each boat steerer picks in rotation until each has four sailors for his boat. The three who are left are called the ship's keepers. They stay on the ship when the boats are out after the whales. Together with the captain, the steward, and the cook, they help to handle the sails. The last man I picked was the young lawyer. I didn't keep him long enough, for he got very sick. Not seasick, but he gradually became worse until finally he couldn't get out of bed. I will say that the captain was very good to him. He catered to him, possibly because he was a lawyer. I wouldn't know. Anyhow, as soon as we reached Fayal, the captain took him to the hospital. There he was given the best treatment available. In fact, the captain couldn't have done more for his own brother. But this is getting ahead of my story.

We set masthead watches the next day and took a southeasterly course. We were out about a week when the cry came from the masthead, "There she blows!" It was one whale alone, which indicated it was a bull whale. I was tingling all over with anticipation and excitement. As I said before, the first mate's boat is the first boat down. That meant that if all went well, the first mate's boat would be the first on top of the whale and I would have my first strike with the harpoon. This was a bull whale, too!

About the easiest way to compare a whaleboat to a whale—a sperm whale—is to think of the boat as a chip and the whale as a small island that could turn into an earthquake or a volcano almost instantly. A bull could pick up the twenty-eight-foot boat and crush it in its jaws as though it were an eggshell, as well as swallow the crew with one gulp. Likewise, a bull whale striking the *Greyhound* head-on could shatter the hull and sink it, just as had happened to the *Ann Alexander* years before.

In fact the sperm whale had long had a reputation, honestly attained, as a fighting whale. The credit for learning how to attack it goes to the Nantucket whalers and their fast, light whaleboats. In Starbuck's list of voyages may be found typical accounts of many tragedies: "Lost second and third mates, and nine men"; "Captain Harris and boat's crew lost, fast to a whale." And there are many more such entries.

CHAPTER XIV

FIRST WHALE, TRY WORKS AND BLUBBER

The whale was to the windward, which meant that we couldn't get any nearer to it with the ship. A schooner could have sailed almost into the wind, within four points at least, but a ship like the bark *Greyhound* could go no closer to the wind than eight points. The newer barks, being sharper and longer, could do better.

The captain ordered, "Stand by to lower," and then added, "Get the boats ready because the *Greyhound* is kind of sluggish."

We had the boat on the water very quickly. We set the sails and picked up on the whale pretty fast. Mr. Frates had the whale dead ahead. Of course, we were all looking at it. I was standing on the thwart, alongside the mast, with one hand on the shrouds. I suddenly saw the whale turn flukes and sound. That means that the whale had done the usual spouting and gone down.

Mr. Frates called me back to sit near him in the after end of the boat. "Joe, did you pay attention how those flukes went down?"

"Yes. She fluked and went down."

"No. That isn't what I mean. Did you pay attention to how the flukes were pointing? North or south?"

"Yes—no. I didn't. I thought I did, but I didn't."

"Well, the flukes pointed north and south. The last spout she had, she was headin' to the eastward. Do you know what that means?"

"No."

"That means, if she comes up in half an hour, she will be about a mile to the eastward because she is travelin' slow." (A whale is usually spoken of as "she.") "If she stays over half an hour it will be about two miles. Now you can go forward. I wanted to tell you this so you can start to learn the business. By-and-by, you are going to be mate yourself or have a boat of your own."

I said, "Thank you," and went forward again.

We held all the boats on the wind and close to each other—fifty to a hundred feet apart. We couldn't talk, we could only signal, for the whale might be right under the boat.

Mr. Frates watched the time and the speed. We didn't dare get ahead of the whale. It might see the shadow of the boat. In about forty minutes, "there she blows," just a little off our port bow, not over a thousand feet away.

Mr. Frates, taking into consideration that I was on the light side in age, weight and size, knew exactly what to do. In fact, he had anticipated a little difficulty because of my lack of height, and had built a slightly-raised platform in the bottom of the boat for me to stand on so that I would be in a proper position to brace my right foot against the thwart, and my left thigh against the bow platform. He knew also that I didn't have the strength to throw the harpoon far; that he would have to come close enough alongside that I could add my whole weight to the weight of the harpoon in order to penetrate the blubber and get into the whale where the harpoon would hold.

All I could think of was getting into action on that beautiful bull, and he had a hump. He had a hump bigger than the bow of our boat. Now, anywhere in front of the hump and in back of the head—the head being equal to about one-half of the entire length of the whale—is soft blubber that the harpoon can penetrate. The entire head is so tough that the harpoon will do no more than make a scratch. We went in at an angle of about forty-five degrees and, as we came abreast of the whale, Mr. Frates put the rudder over and the boat came right in, just about halfway between the neck and the hump. We were right on top. I drove the first harpoon in with every ounce of strength I possessed, and grabbed the second harpoon as I straightened back into position.

Mr. Frates had hauled in the sheet and pulled in the rudder, in the split second that I regained my balance. The boat was already starting to pull away when I hit with the second harpoon, just a little forward of the hump. We got away fast, to keep out of the way of that huge, lashing fluke. There was a terrific commotion with the white water boiling all around, for a few minutes. In seconds the mast was down, the sails stowed, the oars out and ready, and the line around the loggerhead for whatever was to happen next.

As the action slowed down a little, Mr. Frates shouted, "Good boy, Joe, you did it! A nice job."

The mate and I exchanged ends. One thing I haven't mentioned before, is that on a whaleboat no one is allowed to wear shoes or boots. A sharp blow from a heel could make a break in the thin cedar shell of the hull. Everyone is in socks or barefoot.

He went to the bow and I went aft to pick up my steering oar. Mr. Frates looked back and asked, "Are we ready?"

"Shipshape. Perfect. Ready for action."

The whale was running about as usual and had taken out about half a tub of line. The whale kept going and we kept on pulling. The third mate's boat was then gaining on the whale and they got a harpoon in and got fast. The second mate's boat got fast a minute or so later, and all three mates started lancing the whale. Together they made short work of it—didn't have to use a darting gun. As soon as they were sure that the lancing job was adequate, we slacked off the lines. The whale started dying, thrashing and rolling, turning flukes up, and it was all over. My first whale was dead.

I thought the whale would go sixty barrels, but the mate said, "No. Seventy. She's a pretty good-sized one."

The mate ordered the fourth mate, who had not got fast, to go back to the ship with his crew and help handle the ship, for it was pretty well off to leeward. The other boats also cut their lines. Our line was put around the flukes and we began towing, one boat behind the other, toward the ship now only five or six miles away.

When we got alongside, we put a chain on the flukes and brought the chain through the starboard hawse pipe and made it fast to the bitts. We hoisted our boat and got ready for cutting, so that we could get a good start the next day.

In ordinary weather we begin at daylight with all sails furled except the jib, forestaysail, lower and upper topsail, lower and upper main topsail and spanker. The wheel is tied up amidships. These are the only sails kept set while cutting—just enough to keep a little headway, slipping leeward. This keeps the whale in the proper position alongside and under the staging. Out behind streams an oil slick with the water stained red from the blood which oozes from the slowly-turning carcass. The water roundabout is in a turmoil. Sharks of all sizes, by the score, from all directions, rush through the water, attracted by the scent of blood, striking at any piece of refuse floating on the water as well as cutting chunks of meat the size of a large cabbage from all parts of the whale's carcass except, of course, the head.

The first job was to get the big, heavy lower cutting blocks from the hold and get them in place. The upper blocks which are double-sheaved, about a foot and a half in diameter and very heavy, had already been put in place while the ship was in port. Two sets of double-sheaved blocks are fastened up around the top of the lower mainmast. The bottom blocks are single-sheaved, each with a chain strap and sister hook. A line is then woven through the blocks, connecting them with the long, free end of the line leading to the windlass from the upper block. The line is woven through each drum, from port and starboard block. The windlass is now ready to take in the line in the same way it is used to pull in the anchor chain.

FIRST WHALE

The next step in preparing for the cutting is the rigging of the staging. This usually can be done simultaneously with the rigging of the blocks and falls. It is set up at the waist of the ship which is opened up just like a door that opens down to the main deck. The main deck around the rail is covered with copper, to protect the wood. The staging is set up like a catwalk, forming a square with an open center over the whale, with rails to keep the workmen from falling into the water. The staging, the outer-deck portion of it, can be raised or lowered. The inner ends of the two sides are stationary against the ship.

The captain, mate, second mate and fourth mate are the regular crew that work on the staging. The third mate supervises the action on board. Then, with everything set, the cutting begins.

The cutting operation is started just back of the fin located at the beginning of the neck, next to the head. A hole is cut in to receive the blubber-hook and a semicircular cut is made to start it. The officers start cutting spirally around the whale with a spade, a flat, triangular blade with a flat bottom edge which is very sharp, and the point of the triangle perpendicular to the blade terminating in the handle. The blubber hook is set. At the signal to heave, the windlass turns. The blanket piece, a strip of blubber four to six feet wide, starts to lift. The mates keep cutting. The carcass of the whale begins to roll as the strip of blubber is peeled off, spirally, round and round. At the same time, the captain starts cutting at the base of the head, eventually to sever it from the body as the whale continues turning, while the blanket piece unwinds like a spiral bandage.

On deck the third mate watches the blanket piece rise, up and up, like a great thick ribbon, to the top of the lower mainmast. When the upper and lower blocks are only inches apart, the mate yells, "Board Ho!" and, momentarily, all action stops. The third mate cuts two holes in the blanket piece, near deck level. The tail end of the free block is woven through the two holes and brought back to the sister hook. At the order to "Heave on port and surge on starboard," the slack is taken up on the port block and the mate cuts the blanket piece off, one or two feet above it. The first blanket piece is now free. The four boat steerers, each with a hook on a long handle, hold the free end of the first blanket piece as the mate yells to the men at the windlass, "Heave on port. Lower away on starboard." The first blanket piece settles down, flat on deck. The second begins to rise.

The entire crew is now engaged in the cutting. All sailors are on the forward deck. Two are on the fall lines at the windlass. The rest are on the windlass, continuously and rhythmically turning. That is, all but one. He is the chantey.

From a position on top of the try works or on the windlass, he sings out, as long as the cutting goes on, "Blow, blow, blow the man down," verse after verse, often making them up as he chants.

The third mate and boat steerers are taking care of the blanket pieces until just before the cutting is complete, when the boat steerers have a special job to do—one that no one else wanted. Since I was first-mate's boat steerer and had first chance at all the good jobs, I insisted on being first on this one, and nobody objected. The job was to put a chain through the side of the head into the case. The holes for this had been previously cut by the captain or one of the mates.

I put a life-line (which we of the *Greyhound* referred to as a monkey rope) around my chest and yelled, "Here goes nothing!" I jumped overboard onto the whale's head, which by now needed only one more cut to sever it from the body. The mates and the captain stood around on the staging, striking at the sharks to keep me protected. I saw the mate's spade lay open the belly of a shark so that its intestines came out. Another shark started eating on the wounded shark, which acted as though nothing had happened and kept right on after the whale.

One of the boat steerers passed down a curved rod with one end formed into an eye and the other end rounded so that it would not catch. A line was spliced into the eye and attached to a chain. I passed the rod, which was about five feet long, into the hole and out through the cut end of the head and back up to the boat steerer. The chain was pulled through and back up to a thimble or eye, forming a loop through the side of the whale's head.

The head was now completely severed from the body, which was cast adrift. The chain was pulled in by hand, then the starboard cutting block was brought over, putting the sister hooks in the chain as far down as could be reached from the deck, and heaved up so that the nose was down and the severed end high enough above the water so that the water would not slosh into the case.

This operation requires special equipment, which I think I should describe. Above the deck a special pole is rigged, with a line attached at the upper end. The pole is suspended from a position above the deck, with the line going over a pulley so that the pole can be pulled up. A second line is attached to the top of the pole so that it can be pulled down with force. This line is called the downhaul. On the lower end of the pole hangs a special, heavy, narrow, two-foot-long, round-bottomed bucket. The function of the pole is to force the bucket down into the bottom of the case. On the upward haul the bucket fills with the thick, greasy oil—the spermaceti, and is hoisted to the deck.

A bucket brigade is formed and the try pots are filled. Any surplus is poured into the mincing tubs, and if there is still more, into other containers.

While this operation is going on, the smoke stacks are put in place on the try works, the caboose is checked for water, and the fires are started. The oil trying begins, first with the case oil, then the horse pieces, or blubber strips, cut from the blanket pieces. When all of the oil is out of the case, the head is slacked down all the way into the water and cut adrift to follow the fate of the rest of the carcass.

The deck is a scene of bustling activity. Blanket pieces of blubber, laid flat on top of each other, cover large areas of the deck. The boat steerers, with long-handled cutting spades, start cutting smaller strips (called horse pieces) crosswise off the blanket pieces.

The horse piece goes to the mincing tub where one man with a hook slaps it onto the mincing board or table located across the mincing tub, holding it there while the other man cross-cuts the horse piece into leaves or sections about one inch wide, leaving them fastened together at the bottom. If he happens to cut clear through, the cut portion simply falls into the tub. He goes right on cutting until the strip, or remainder of it, is finished and is lifted over into one of the try pots.

Another man, with the long-handled bailer balanced over the raised edge in front of the try pots, empties the boiled oil out of the finished pot into the cooling tank. As soon as the oil is bailed out, he takes a long-handled fork and, using it in the same way as the bailer, he stacks the tried-out blubber scraps in a pile on the deck, from where they are fed into the fire. The mate on watch supervises the operation, and tends to the cooling tanks and the disposal of the oil into casks.

The blocks remain in place on the mast until the end of the three- or four-year voyage, except for inspection and repairs.

The moment that the cutting was completed we set masthead watches and regular ship's watches so that if any whales were sighted we could go after them and have more cutting on hand. You see, the try works operate day and night until the job is completed, which, ordinarily, would take no more than four days, at most. All sails were set except the foresail and mainsail. We were now stowing away oil and looking for more. The try works were soon going full blast. Our try works would handle about one hundred and fifty gallons per hour. The case oil took only a few hours and, because of its premium value, was stored in special casks.

After we built the fire under the try pots with wood, they were kept going with blubber strips. Black smoke poured from the funnels, and light from the flames shooting out with the smoke made a weird, flickering light on the sails and rigging at night, and lighted up the whole deck.

One night we were approached by a steamer which came very close. The captain hailed us, apparently through his megaphone, and shouted, "Do you want to be taken off?" They had come upon us close enough to see the shadows of the men in the red, flickering light. There were shadows dancing on the sails, and more blurs and flashes of light reflected from the try works when the sliding doors were opened to throw in more blubber scraps. It was a weird-looking, ghost ship, lighted up with the fires of hell and tended by half-naked, devilish-looking figures hurrying to and fro.

Our captain answered, "I'm trying my w-e-e-l!" in a long, drawn-out reply.

"Do you want to be taken off?"

"I'm trying my w-e-e-l!" the captain repeated.

"You want to do what?"

"I'm trying my w-e-e-l!" the captain repeated with a still more strenuous effort.

"I don't understand you."

"Oh, I killed a w-e-e-l. I'm making oil!"

"Good luck and good-by. I thought you were on fire." He gave us three short blasts on the whistle, which awakened the watch below. They scrambled up, all goggle-eyed, and rubbing their eyes and crying out, "What's the matter? What's the matter?" Then they saw the steamer fading into the distance and darkness.

CHAPTER XV

A GAM AND A STOP AT FLORES

After a couple more days we finished with the oil, swabbed down the decks and got everything clean and shipshape. We were just getting well into the Western Grounds and cruising along nicely when early one morning, just after daylight, we saw another whaling ship.

Mr. Frates came up on deck a few minutes later and we told him about it. He looked at the bark through the glasses and said, "That's the *Wanderer*. The *Wanderer* with Captain Edwards."

He went down immediately to inform Captain Corvello that Captain Edwards was off to starboard. The captain came up and looked her over.

"I thought we'd start running into some of the ships that were coming from Dominica," he remarked. So we pulled toward each other and had a gam. Now the rule is that on a gam, if neither of the captains' wives is aboard, the captain of the vessel to windward comes to visit the captain on the vessel to leeward. In this case, the captains had been friends for many years. Captain Edwards had been captain of one of the whaling ships since he was seventeen or eighteen. His uncle owned the ship and taught him how to handle it, and made him captain while he was still just a boy.

Anyway, as soon as Captain Edwards hoisted the gamming flag, Captain Corvello ordered a boat ready and said that he was going over. They were such good friends that he didn't worry about the courtesy of position to windward. Anyway, Captain Edwards was the older Captain. The second mate left with his crew and the captain and went over to the *Wanderer.*

From the *Wanderer,* it was now proper for the first mate and his crew to come over to our ship. However, nobody is ever taken from masthead. The masthead watch remains unbroken all day.

The day was spent in visiting and exchanging stories, information and gossip. The visiting members were treated royally, with coffee, the best food available, and the best liquor. The captains, mates, and their crews were a little red-eyed for a few hours afterward.

The mate from the *Wanderer* was a great whaleman—one of the best. He had a lot of good stories and experiences, and I immensely enjoyed listening to him.

Toward evening—just about dark—the *Wanderer*'s flag went up again, calling the mate's boat back. Our captain and our own crew returned and the gam was over, but it broke the monotony of days, yes, often months, at sea, even though one forgot all about it the next day.

By morning we were far apart, with only the tops of the sails visible above the horizon. The rest of the season was the usual thing. We began getting whales—cow whales—and occasionally a bull. Toward the middle of August we were pretty well filled up. Not quite full, but the captain was satisfied.

Of course, he was going to Flores at the end of the season to pick up his new wife. And it looked to me as if the end of the season was going to come a little earlier. After all, he had been married to my sister only a few months and he'd had a fairly short honeymoon several months back.

"Well," he remarked, "we could carry another hundred and fifty barrels or so, but we'd better begin to pull toward the Azores because there's a lot of whales off the Azores."

Of course, Mr. Frates agreed with him. I heard the conversation because I was talking to Mr. Frates when the captain came over. Mr. Frates was a crackerjack whaleman. He was as good as the best—better, in my estimation. And the captain naturally wanted Mr. Frates to agree with his decision. When Mr. Frates indicated that he agreed, with a sly wink in my direction, the captain said, "We might as well start over toward Flores. We will have full sails during the day and short sails at night."

It was now about the middle of August. The weather was beautiful. In about ten days or so we sighted Flores. Of course, both the captain and I were hot and bothered to get ashore on that beautiful little island.

The breeze was light, and since the *Greyhound* was naturally a little loggy, we couldn't make landfall early enough to go ashore. We had to cruise around that night. My sister saw the ship through a good pair of binoculars that my mother had. She told my mother, "It's a bark, just about like father's. It must be the *Greyhound!*"

The next day we pulled toward Fajangrand, quite early, and lowered a boat and went ashore.

Both the captain and I had bought a lot of presents. I had bought quite a lot of nice clothes for my mother and sisters and my girl friend and her sisters. I had two suitcases full, altogether.

The captain had become acquainted with quite a few people from Fajangrand on his last two visits and I had made quite a few friends there on my last trip, too. Quite a lot of them were there to meet us, even though the people from Fajazinha, our own village, hadn't yet arrived.

You see, it was the custom there for the captain's wife to wait at his house for him. Coming in early, as we did, other people in Fajazinha hadn't seen us yet.

Right there among the first of them to meet us, though, was my little sweetheart with her sisters. What a greeting that was! The way that sweet, pure, cuddly little thing threw her arms around my neck and clung to me made homecoming worth many months at sea. Then, of course, a few of the villagers began to meet us, and we greeted them like the old friends they were. As we approached the Center in Fajangrand, we came right in front of the church, the Church of Señora de Saude—Our Lady of Good Health. I had promised to stop in there on my way, so I excused myself and went into the church. My girl friend came with me. We knelt down and I said a little prayer, bade Our Lady good-by, and we went out into the street again. More of the people from Fajazinha had arrived. After greeting them, we went on up the road toward home.

In about an hour we arrived in Fajazinha. My girl friend's house was the first that we came to. There were her mother, the two boys and a girl. We hugged and kissed. We had always been just like brothers and sisters. A lot of the neighbors were there waiting, and more people kept coming. As we came to the little girls' school, the teacher and all the children came out, just as they had done two years before. We stayed a little while and then went on to the boys' school, where the same performance was enacted all over again.

We greeted the old schoolmaster and all the boys, and the older people who were now appearing. From the school we could see my father's house. I could see my mother and Mary on the front porch, where Mary was waiting to greet her husband, as was the custom. My mother could have come out but she remained in the house with my grandmother who was now in her eighties and couldn't get around very well.

The new priest was there, too. He was a local boy whom I hadn't seen before. He was now ordained. I had heard mention that he had gone away to school, but I was just a child at the time. Of course, we greeted him and the rest of the family, and the old folks who had gathered around. My little girl friend never left my side for one minute. When we went into the house to sit down, she very quickly found a chest to sit on so we could be close together.

Mary had a big meal ready. It was really a banquet, with bread, meat, vegetables—enough for everybody.

As you will remember, my father's house was large and there was room for a lot of people. My sister really put on a good show of hospitality for the captain who, at the moment, was naturally quite the center of interest.

We were to stay in Flores only three days. There was room on the ship for a couple hundred more barrels of oil and the captain wanted to cruise around as much as possible to see if we couldn't get a full ship. His wife was going to cruise with him, so what reason was there to stay ashore any **longer**?

The next day we went up to the hills on a picnic—my sisters, Lucy's sisters, and Lucy. We didn't mind having the rest of them along. Anyway we found a good chance to sneak away and do a little loving. After all, I was going to be there only two more days and, believe me, we weren't wasting any opportunities.

The time flew by. Sunday we went to church together. Monday we spent around home. Tuesday morning came and it was time to go. We bade everyone good-by.

When we got to the deck the boat was coming in, about a quarter-mile out, under sail. Final good-bys were pretty hard for Mary. It was the first time she had ever been away from home. We got aboard and under sail. The first thing Mary did was to get seasick. This isn't a pleasant experience, and nobody knows it better than I. I did what I could for her but it wasn't much. Someone had told me that bananas were the best thing to eat, and she had a few with her. The only reason for recommending bananas was that they tasted the same coming up as going down.

CHAPTER XVI

BEDBUGS AND COCKROACHES

We didn't sail direct for Fayal. We sailed south instead of east —out toward the open, on a chance of getting into a school of cows.

We were out only two or three days when we sighted a ship, the bark *Bertha,* under Captain Churchill. When we got close, the captain put up the gam flags. That meant that Captain Churchill would visit us since Captain Corvello's wife was aboard the *Greyhound,* and the first mate and his boat crew would go over to the *Bertha.* That meant I would be going over to the *Bertha,* too.

I haven't explained before, but the *Greyhound,* at least in the fo'c's'le and the steerage, was practically alive with bedbugs. The biggest, fattest, juiciest, most wicked bedbugs I've ever seen anywhere. Anyway, I hadn't been on the *Bertha* long until I was telling the boat steerers and the mates about the bedbugs. One of the mates—the third mate—suggested that we take some cockroaches back to the *Greyhound*. "Why?" I wanted to know.

"Well, don't you know that cockroaches are deadly enemies of bedbugs?" the mate answered. I thought he was pulling my leg, but he said, "No, it's the truth. I was never more serious nor more honest in my life."

I didn't like cockroaches, and I said so. "But they're better than bedbugs," the mate countered, "they don't bite."

That clinched it, even though I hated cockroaches. You remember how they crawled all over me when I stowed away on the *Pedro Varella*. I went to see Mr. Frates about it. "Joe, do the bedbugs really bother you so much?' he asked me.

"Why, Lord yes! The steerage is full of them. Every crack is loaded. I've put oil on them, everything, but they drop down on me. They crawl and they bite. I slap them in my sleep or when I wake up, and they squash all over. Even when I'm dog-tired they still wake me up."

"Is it that bad?"

"It's even worse than that."

"I never heard the other boat steerers complain."

"I guess their hides are tougher than mine, or they sleep harder, or maybe my skin is just sweeter, or something. Anyway, they wake me up."

"Well, okay. Go ahead."

The crew of the *Bertha* pitched in. We really had a time, catching cockroaches. And their cockroaches were as healthy as our bedbugs. We caught five quart bottles of them. Then we got a five-gallon can that had had kerosene in it, rinsed it out and put a lot of them in that.

The captain's flag went up after a while and we went back to the *Greyhound* with our catch. Since the mate already knew about the cockroaches, I didn't bother to tell anyone else. I didn't want to get stopped. The cockroaches in the bottles were okay. I opened the kerosene can only to find that the poor passengers were all dead. I say "poor" because it made me feel bad. To me they were pretty valuable just then. I guess we hadn't washed the can well enough. The kerosene fumes must have killed them.

I dumped one quart jar in the fo'c's'le, one in the steerage, one in the cargo hold, and another in the steerage where I slept—just to make sure that there were enough. There was one jar left. I went to the mate and asked him where I should put it. "You better go ask your sister. Ha, ha, ha."

After he laughed some more he said, "Well, go put it in the main cargo-hold. Open a crack in the main cargo-hatch and put them in the main cargo hold."

That was all of them. Now to wait and see what would happen.

Now, you can believe this or not. I'm not superstitious. I never was. But while we were in Fayal for four or five weeks unloading, the bedbugs began to diminish. After we left Fayal there were no more bedbugs, but believe me, we had the biggest cockroaches I've ever seen. They were everywhere and into everything. They didn't hurt the hardtack. They could be sifted out of the flour. But they got into the drinking water bucket by the dozens. Of course, they were always being fished out, but legs and wings would remain. The other sailors sort of grinned as they drank. They would keep their lips apart and their teeth together and then spit out the cockroaches when they finished. I tried to do the same thing. My teeth were very good but I had a space between my two front teeth just large enough to let a few pieces through. They'd catch in my tonsils and stay there. I would cough until I cried, and I began to hate the idea of drinking.

The third mate came by one day and asked if I had a clean handkerchief. I pulled one out of my pocket. "Get another cup," he ordered, and I did so. "Put it over your cup and pour the water into it." This I did. "Now try it."

This simple device solved the problem. I enjoyed drinking water again and I've carried a clean handkerchief ever since.

CHAPTER XVII

SPLICE THE MAIN BRACE

Two days later, when it was getting close to the time when we should be in Fayal, someone at the masthead raised a spout.
"There she bloooows!"
Then the captain's, "Where away?"
"Off the starboard beam!"
That meant it was to windward, and though the weather was good, still the *Greyhound* was so loggy that we didn't make much headway in that direction. Consequently, the captain gave the order to stand by and lower away. We were in the water in two or three minutes and began rowing toward the spout. We hadn't gone far when we could see that there was a school of whales. As we came in closer, the mate said to me in a low voice, "Joe, there is a bull in the school. They're mating, and there's a bull in there."
I was sitting with my back to the whales because I was rowing. But I glanced around. There was a hell of white, boiling water, like a regular free-for-all fight with lots of kicking and lashing about. Of course, a whaleman knew what it was. The whales were not running at all. It was just an exhibition of sea monsters at play—mating.
The mate told me to stand by. I shed my oar and went up to my little platform on the bow to get ready to strike the whale.
"Now, wait a minute, Joe. You let the bull spout so you can

locate it. Just a minute. I'm going to stop the boat." He stopped the men from rowing. The boat was already dancing about on the turbulent water. We were very close when the bull spouted. I could see it was a good-sized one. I signaled the mate with my hand to come on and get close to him. The mate signaled the oarsmen to pull ahead, and in a couple of dips and jumps we were on him. When I hit the whale with the first harpoon, the boat was going ahead so fast that I was nearly knocked off my feet by the impact. By a stroke of luck, I got the second harpoon in, and the mating season stopped right then and there. He ran and he sounded. He went down to the bottom of the ocean taking all of the line from the big tub and three quarters from the smaller tub. We figured we might have a real fighter on our hands. He slacked up a bit and the mate and I exchanged ends. I picked up my steering oar. We were pretty busy, pulling in the line and coiling it and steering the boat.

Soon, the other boats were ahead of us. The whale was up again and running, and we were pulling in line and coiling it as fast as we could. I had my hands full. I couldn't see what was going on.

The mate shouted to me, "Joe, the other boats are all fast. One is on our bull, and the other two have cows."

You see, two boats always try to get fast to a bull even if there are plenty of cows around. One bull can be equal to a dozen cows. The bull stopped running. We pulled on top of him in no time and in a half-hour we had him killed. He proved to be one of the tamest ones I've ever seen. I didn't even have to strain to hold the line in the loggerhead. The man on the bow had the line clinched under the bow platform and was holding the boat right there on top of the whale while the mate kept on lancing it.

The third mate's boat was on the other side. With two lances going in and out continuously, the whale died very quickly—even before the two cows that the other boats had caught.

The *Greyhound* was hull-down. All we could see of her was the sails. It was so calm that there was no hope for her to come up to us. We had to tow, and it was getting late. We got the three whales lined up and the boats lined up single file, towing them, and we began to tow. We rowed and rowed and rowed. It was after midnight when we reached the ship and we still had to hoist the boats and tie the whales alongside. Everybody was dog-tired. As soon as we had finished, however, the captain shouted, "Splice the main brace!"

On a ship, that means a round of Scotch, or whatever the ship carries. The captain liked Scotch, and he used to consume quite a lot of it when ashore. Everybody went aft. The captain had a gallon jug there. One gallon wouldn't go around. He gave everyone a good shot, pouring out about three ounces for each one, maybe a little bit more. At least it was "double." He was pretty good that way.

We had a fine catch of whales alongside and, too, it was the first catch with his wife aboard. The captain knew I didn't drink and that I would just give mine to one of the other boat steerers, and he didn't want that to happen. "You would only give it to someone and I'm giving them double anyway. Go away, Joe. Go away."

He didn't want any favoritism and he wanted them all to feel they were being fairly treated. After all, it takes the co-operation of everyone to make a whaling voyage successful.

My sister had never seen a whale. Naturally, she was all eyes. I took her up forward with a lantern. In those days there were no flashlights. At least I had never seen one, and certainly we didn't have any. I lowered the lantern down, so she could see. She was thrilled, "Oh, it's beautiful, but I can see it better in the morning." So I took her back to the captain, on the quarter-deck.

We were up at daylight. All hands were called on deck and we immediately began to cut the bull. While the whale is over the side it does not belong to the ship. If a heavy storm were to come up, the whale or whales might have to be cut away. Then they would belong to whoever might find them. Naturally, then, we started on the bull.

Mary was thrilled and delighted. She had a camera and she took pictures of everything, all day long. Pictures of the whale and the blanket pieces; of the blubber going up the masthead; of the boat steerers handling blanket pieces and pulling blubber; of the officers cutting over the side. It was a joy to see the pleasure she was getting out of it.

We worked at top speed. We didn't let up for lunch except for **fifteen minutes. That was all.**

"We want to get those whales in before dark so we can set sails for Fayal," the captain told everyone. "It's a slight breeze but it's a fair wind, and by the time we get the whales tried out we will be close to Fayal, if the breeze holds."

We had all the blubber on board by sundown.

The third mate began to get the try works ready. We set all sails except foresail, mainsail and main staysail. Just enough to give her good steering way. In fact, it was working kind of hard on the wheel, so we slacked away the spanker gaff to make it easier. We could do that because the weather was calm and beautiful.

We tried blubber all night, the next day and night, and were just about through on the second day toward noon when we sighted Pico Island quite plainly from the deck. We had quite a job of cleaning up to do. I was still on the hook on navigation. The captain wouldn't let up on me for one minute, and I knew exactly where we were and about how long it would take to make Fayal.

There was a lot of commotion on deck. All hands were called out with buckets, brooms and what not, to clean up the ship. The windlass had to be cleared and the anchor chains reengaged. We would need the anchors at Fayal.

Everything on deck was full of oil—the try pots, the tank, a cask (partly full of hot oil), and the cooling tanks below. It was all still too hot to stow away in the hold. We were just getting things shipshape as we came in between the two islands and shortened sail to slow down.

A mile from the breakwater, we began maneuvering by hoisting some sails and lowering others, to get up to the anchorage, or at least as close as possible. Coming around the breakwater, we lost the wind. We immediately lowered two boats and used them as tugs to get in the rest of the way. We lost no time. Everyone was dog-tired. The sooner we got it done, the sooner we could rest. We dropped anchor, and the crew had hardly finished putting up the boats when the captain called, "All hands aft to splice the main brace!"

It was unusual to splice the main brace at such a time, but no doubt the captain felt more than usually grateful as well as fortunate. He had filled his ship at the last minute with a catch that could only have been thought of as a gift from heaven. Everyone had worked far beyond the call of duty without complaint. The weather and the wind had been perfect, and the captain's wife was aboard. He poured out half a glass for every man except, of course, me. As usual, when it came my turn, "You'd only give it away. I've given every man enough already. Go away, Joe. Go away."

For a new crew, mostly greenhorns, it was really a successful voyage. Every man had done well except the young lawyer who was so sick. As soon as the doctor, the customs and immigration officers had cleared us, the captain sent him to the hospital.

CHAPTER XVIII

SAILOR ASHORE

The supply ship and several of the whalers were already in ahead of us. All the captains soon came aboard. They knew Captain Corvello's wife was aboard and they all wanted to meet her. The ship's best was brought out and we had a regular feast. Captain Corey, of the mother ship, had not been aboard very long before he sent for me. He had a letter for me from the girl at my aunt's boarding house in New Bedford.

She had gone to the dock and given him the letter and asked him to be sure that I got it. I opened it and read, "Dear Joe. I am very sorry if this will make you unhappy in any way, but I am getting married. I want you to know that you will always be my friend, and my husband will also be your friend. When you come back to New Bedford, I want you to feel that you are welcome."

Because it had been a fine friendship and we had had some very, very good times together, I didn't want even a little letter with her name signed to it left undestroyed. It might at some future time hurt her. So I tore the letter into little pieces and held them on my hand, letting them drift away with the wind and fall gently onto the water. When I got back to New Bedford I would have to look for someone to take her place.

I was on the starboard watch. I had always been. It was like a lucky number. Nothing could have kept me from making that first watch ashore, even if I'd had to buy my way out. I had a little money and I was sure I wouldn't need any more. I wouldn't spend it on liquor or women, as the other sailors would do. I was going to see a very beautiful girl who liked me as well as I liked her. I didn't even have to wait for our own boat. One from the bark *Bertha* was going by and I waved to them to come and pick me up. I jumped in and went ashore ahead of all the rest.

I went straight to my girl-friend's father's store, and they all greeted me as though I were one of the family. And oh, the girl was more beautiful than ever! She had a clear complexion, beautiful coloring, and a lovely figure. She was serving a customer but she grabbed my hand, took me back in the shop, threw her arms around my neck and, oh——! So, her mother came in.

She greeted me as if I were her own son. Then she said, "I'm not going to get much help out of this big girl while you're around here so you kids go ahead. Go and take a walk." That's all we hoped to hear her say.

Leading from the store there was a wide boulevard along the waterfront. It ran past the old fort, and down to the center. We were looking at the whalers out in the bay, but as we approached the hotel I could see a lady waving to me from the veranda. I knew it must be my sister, and when we got near enough she called, "Joe. Where are you kids going?"

"Oh, I don't know. Down aways, and I think I'll stop over at that little church and say a little prayer."

"All right. On the way back stop in. I want to talk to you."

So we walked on down the road to the church. We knelt down there and I said a little prayer before the Blessed Virgin, then we went back to the hotel. My sister was down on the main floor waiting for us.

The first thing she said to the girl was, "Oh, but you are getting beautiful. More beautiful than when we were here two years ago!"

Just then Captain Corvello came in and asked us to have dinner with them. Josephine didn't think we should stay that long because of her father. I reminded her that her mother had told us to go out walking and wouldn't worry, so she thought it would be all right. We had dinner with them and several whaling captains who were at the hotel. Two had their families with them. All of them thought my girl friend was just a bit of all right. After a while I said, "Come on. We'd better go. If we stay too long your father may think we're taking advantage and won't let you come again."

There was still quite a crowd around the store, but Josephine's father said, "Oh, come on in. Let's have a family reunion." So he locked the door and we went into the back of the store, where part of the family living-quarters. They wanted to know all about what had happened since I was there two years before. I told them of my adventures, and how I had liked New Bedford; that I had been to Boston a couple of times, and over to Providence, Rhode Island, once.

About ten o'clock, I thought I had better be getting back to the ship, but her father said, "Wait a minute. Why don't you stay here and go over in the morning? We have a couch and you can sleep on it. It's comfortable, and nice and warm. You won't get cold."

I saw the girl sort of frown. So I said, "No. I don't have permission to stay ashore, so I'd better go back. Thank you just the same. Anyway, this is the first night ashore and the work has to be reorganized. Since I'm a petty officer, boat steerer, I had better be there. My boat has some damage and I have to get it ashore."

I didn't know why the girl had given me the high-sign, but I figured she had a good reason. So I excused myself and went back to the ship.

The captain came aboard the next day. Some captains would never bother to go aboard except on special business, but Captain Corvello was very conscientious. He seldom missed a day. He was always on the job. He told Mr. Frates to have the gear taken off my boat and to send it ashore for repairs. There were three damaged boards, and Mr. Frates wanted them taken completely out. There were good boat-builders on Fayal, with good material, so this was an excellent opportunity to have it done.

All the equipment previously described, except the five rowing oars, had to be removed and lashed on to the spare boat which is carried across the stern of the ship. After I had put all the equipment on the stern boat, I decided I needed a "Keep Off" sign. None being available, I decided to make one. I was pretty proud of my English by now. I really thought I was getting great, so I put up the sign in five-inch letters painted white.

The sign disappeared almost immediately. When I got ashore I heard fellows laughing about it wherever I went. I heard it was on one whaler, and then on another. Finally, I saw it. There it was, big as life, nailed up over the customs house door, my remarkable spelling unchanged, "Kipp ovv dis boat."

My brother-in-law used it occasionally as a nickname for years afterward. In fact, the last time I saw him he greeted me with, "Well, if it isn't old Kipp Ovv Dis Boat himself!" That was in Boston in 1919. I was chief mate on a steamer then, and he and my sister and their daughter had come to Boston to see me off to Europe. It was still a big joke with him. I remember that last greeting so well, for he died of the flu only a short while afterward.

The boat carpenters were waiting for my boat when we got it ashore. I took the oars and locked them up inside the shop. Those oars were expensive. Besides, when you get used to an oar you don't like to change it and use a different one. The mate gave me permission to stay with the boat, so I said I wouldn't be coming back to the ship until the boat was finished. I didn't stay with the carpenters very long—just half an hour. Then I went to have lunch with my Josephine. Her mother had told me never to eat in a restaurant while I was ashore but to come over and eat with them. I never felt that I owed them anything, as I had bought clothes and things in the United States for the whole family. They weren't rich. And now that I was a petty officer, I thought I was a big shot, anyway.

After lunch I went back to the shop. I wanted to see how the carpenters went about repairing the boat. They really were doing a beautiful job on it. I left again, long before they were through, and went back to my girl's house. She was waiting for me, and told me her mother had taken the horse to the center for groceries. They had a horse and wagon. A relative there had a store, so she would be gone for a while, taking the younger girls with her.

I asked her father if he needed us around. "No," he replied, "it's pretty slow around here at this hour. You kids go ahead and enjoy yourselves." That was what we wanted to hear.

We went out the front door, around the corner, through an alley back of two buildings, and back into the house to do a little love making. We had a wonderful time trying to make up for the two years I'd been away. After a while we heard the horse outside, but we made a little blunder. We went out the front door. If her father noticed it, he didn't say anything. I felt pretty silly. But it was too late. We had already given away our little secret.

We helped to unload the bundles and carry them upstairs. The kitchen and front room were above the store on the second floor, much like my father's house. It was a nice house, built of stone, as were all the other buildings there. We came down to help in the store while her mother prepared the dinner.

"This is Saturday, so we will have to stay open late," her father said. "You kids go up and eat and then come down and take care of the store while I have dinner." So Josephine, her sister, and I, went up and ate. Then we came back down, as her father had suggested. The girl and I couldn't keep away from each other. There was nobody in the store for a few minutes, and then suddenly my sister and the captain came in, just in time to catch us in a terrific embrace. Boy, was my face red. They had come in to buy a few things that my sister wanted for her room at the hotel, and some lace for a dress.

They came behind the counter and sat down, and after talking for a few minutes they went upstairs to the living room. They stayed all evening. The captain was feeling good. He gave me a handful of escudos, Portuguese dollars, and told me to get a bottle of Scotch for them and some soft drinks for us.

The girl and I went to the liquor store. Being dressed in American clothes, I was an American so far as anyone was concerned, and buying liquor was no problem. We came back with the liquor and they locked up the store and we all had a nice evening. Josephine, her sister, and I walked back to the hotel with the captain and Mary, and on the way back we made plans to go up into the country the next day. I was going to rent a horse and buggy and we planned to drive to Josephine's uncle's ranch.

Then I returned to the dock to go back to the ship. The girl told me that the reason she would not let me stay at her house, as her father suggested, was that she wouldn't be able to stay away. "Joe, we would get to fooling around, and my father and mother might wake up and suspect something. We can find other places." She was absolutely right.

Bright and early next morning, I got a couple of fellows to row me ashore so I could go to early Mass. Josephine and her family were all there. I knelt down with them.

After Mass we went to their house for breakfast. Then I went to a stable not far away and rented a horse and buggy. The girl did all the driving. I didn't know how to talk to the horse. The only horses I had ever handled were those two on the plow at New Bedford, and they went by themselves. She had done quite a lot of riding and knew how to handle horses pretty well. I didn't trust this horse any more than I had trusted those other two, and I was perfectly willing to let her do the driving.

We drove back to the store. The sister was supposed to go with us, but her mother had taken her off somewhere—so we could go alone. It took us a couple of hours to reach the ranch, and the girl introduced me to her relatives. Her uncle was a big man, but her aunt was very small. I doubt that she weighed a hundred pounds. She was a pleasant and happy person. They had three boys and two girls. The boys wanted to unhitch the horse.

"No, you don't," I said. "Don't unhitch that horse. You'll never get him hitched up again."

"Sure I would."

"Nothing doing. You leave that thing right where it is. Feed him and water him, but that's all. That's all right, but leave him tied just where he is."

Next, the boy wanted me to ride a horse that they had, but I answered, "No. You'll never get me aboard one of those things."

We had a good time around that ranch. The kids were fun, too. I enjoyed it, and I also enjoyed the fried rabbit we had for lunch. They had the table set when we arrived, so they just moved over and made room for us. Then they asked us to stay for supper, and even said they would eat early so that we could drive back to the city. We were not afraid to drive back in the dark, because the stable was near the store.

They had cassiolla for dinner. Here, I think it would be called rabbit stew. It was delicious, highly spiced. I don't care for spiced food but that was good.

We drove back to the city, and made three more trips back to the ranch—for three Sundays. The folks were so much fun. We praised them so much to my girl's family that each time we went, some member of her family went along, and no one was disappointed.

We had been in Fayal quite awhile and we were getting toward the end of our stay. We had been alongside the mother ship. The oil was discharged, provisions and water taken aboard, and in one more day we would be ready to leave for the South Seas.

The last night ashore, the captain invited Josephine and her family to dinner at the hotel. The younger sister had a cold, and her mother didn't feel well. The father didn't want to leave the store so early, so they asked the girl to go and excuse them. Of course, we did as they wished. We hung around the hotel foyer for a while afterward, visiting with the people and especially with my sister. She had some trinkets she had bought for both girls, which pleased Josephine immensely. We bade them goodnight and headed for the house.

On the way, we had to pass in front of the old fort which was situated right next to the bay, and was still in use. A guard with a rifle and bayonet was constantly on guard, walking back and forth in front of the door. We were walking along on the opposite side of the street next to the stores and buildings which, at this time of evening, were closed. Only a couple of barrooms were open.

As we approached the old fort, on the opposite side of the street, we saw a man in a soldier's uniform in front of us near the electric street-lamp—Fayal had electricity at that time. Of course, he was off duty, and he apparently noticed I was dressed in American clothes. Consequently, he took me for an American. He began passing remarks at Josephine. I didn't like it and I told Josephine to keep on walking; that I would take care of him. He was considerably bigger than I and she didn't like the idea. She grabbed my arm and whispered, "Come on, Joe. Don't bother with him. He's twice as big as you."

"Yes, but I can fight, and these Portuguese don't know how to fight." I hadn't mentioned it, but there was a mulatto in the ship's crew who had been teaching me both boxing and judo. He was very good at it, particularly the judo, and I had really worked hard at it and had learned the fundamentals pretty well.

She said, "Don't be silly," and tried to drag me away. I was pretty hot and bothered because he was still throwing slurs, dirty names and curses. I shoved her away a little and told her to stay up ahead a bit. Then I walked up to the guy and plastered him right across the teeth. He threw a few punches that didn't land and I started boxing with him. I began hitting him with everything I had, on the face, the jaw, anywhere I could reach him. But I couldn't get him down. My punches just weren't heavy enough. He was cussing and calling me names faster and harder than ever. Well, after a few minutes of fruitless boxing, I figured I'd better try a little judo. In seconds, I had him flat on the sidewalk. I was tempted to use my feet on him, but that would be dirty. On shipboard it would be considered a crime, so I didn't. I let him get about half-way up, and I plastered him with rights and lefts to the face and eyes. He made a swing at me that left him wide open for a good right to the jaw. It stunned him a little, but not enough. I grabbed him in another judo hold and threw him down. His head bumped the lamp post and he was out—cold.

By this time the guard from across the street had charged up, aiming his bayonet right at me. "Don't you know this is a soldier?" he yelled.

"Of course I know he is a soldier, but no soldier is going to call my girl foul names and talk the way he did."

"How is it you talk Portuguese?" he wanted to know.

"I can talk Portuguese as well as you."

By this time the soldier had started to get up.

"I'm going to hit him again!"

"No. Don't hit him again. I'll take care of him." And the guard went away with the guy's arm over his shoulder. The fellow was still pretty groggy. Apparently the lamp post was a lot more effective than my fist.

As soon as we got away from the light, she threw her arms around my neck and kissed me. "My goodness," she exclaimed, "I didn't know you could fight like that. Why, you were just like a tiger. You hit him a dozen times. He wouldn't go down and then, all at once, there he was flat on the ground. How did you do it?"

"Judo. I used judo."

"What's that? What's judo?"

"Well, that's a Japanese way of conquering the other fellow."

"It's wonderful. You were wonderful."

So we walked on, with her close to me, her head against my shoulder, the rest of the way home.

Her father still had the store open. He was sitting and waiting for us. Right away she told him about the fight. By now, the guy was even bigger than I'd thought he was, to hear her tell it. Anyway, her father was very pleased.

"Now I'll never be afraid to let my girl go out with a fellow like you." I had figured even before this that I was quite a big shot. Now I had no doubt about it.

We went upstairs. I wanted to say good-by to the little girl and their mother. This was the last night ashore and we were due to leave the next morning about ten o'clock, weather permitting. Unbeknown to me, they had made plans with my sister for going out on the breakwater to see me off.

At ten the next morning the captain came aboard with the clearance papers and immediately gave orders to shorten chain—heave up the anchor—and let go the chains from the buoys.

In Fayal, which is a small closed harbor, there was no room for a ship to swing around with the other whalers close by. There were always several small boats daily from Pico, too—forty- or fifty-foot boats loaded with produce and passengers—as well as a steamer out near the end of the breakwater. Often there was the interisland steamer, and a good-sized boat from St. George. At any rate, the ship's stern had to be fastened to a buoy while in the harbor, so that it couldn't swing around and damage another ship. Likewise, when we went out, we had to tow the ship with two of our whaleboats because there were no tugs in the harbor.

The captain ordered three boats down—one to steer the other two between the other ships and out past the breakwater. I was to be in the steering boat. Mr. Frates, the mate, was to maneuver the ship, thus leaving the captain and his wife free to wave to the other ships' captains, and to friends, as they went out.

Then, what a surprise! As we came close to the end of the breakwater, I heard Josephine calling my name as clearly as could be. My boat must have zig-zagged quite a bit, because I couldn't look at her and wave and steer my boat straight at the same time. My sister, Mr. Frates, and the captain had planned this, to give me a build-up with the girl. My sister told me, a long time afterward, that she had told Josephine's mother it made her very happy to know that I would always spend my time with them when the ship was in Fayal, instead of down at the bars and houses frequented by the rest of the sailors.

As we passed the breakwater, I had visions of coming back before long. To a young fellow like me, the rough, hard life at sea with all its adventure was just right, but the romance of a shore leave with that lovely girl on Fayal was the nearest thing to Paradise.

CHAPTER XIX

DANGEROUS HARBOR

The sailors were already setting the headsails and the upper and lower topsails as we cleared around the breakwater. We came alongside with the boats, hoisted them and set the mainsail and foresail, and soon the ship was going full sail for the great blue yonder of the South Atlantic Seas and another season down below the Equator. Only one stop on the way and, at the moment, it didn't interest me a bit.

The single stop ahead of us was St. Nicholas Island in the Cape Verdes. As I said before, the captain stopped here every year for a couple of days so that his Cape Verdian crewmen could visit their families who might be there. As a result of this policy he could always fill out his crew if he happened to be short, or get some good men if he needed them. Also, some of the men living in

New Bedford had relatives in the Cape Verde Islands and they knew they would always have a chance to visit during the stopover. Most of the population of the Cape Verdes is mulatto, similar to the population of Morocco, which is not far away.

When we came around the island to the little harbor, we were very surprised to see two whalers anchored there. We had never dropped anchor there nor had I ever seen any other whaler anchored in the little harbor. One vessel was the brig *Viola*. The other was the schooner *Margaret,* under Captain Mandley. He was a very likely sort of young fellow and I had made friends with him previously, in Fayal. He was always making fun of my English and correcting me. I was always eager to have my English corrected, so he was my man.

When the captain saw that the other two ships were anchored, he said, "Well, we might as well anchor, too. Stand by the starboard anchor." Two anchors are always ready so that if one chain should get tangled up below the hawse pipe, the other one can be let go.

We dropped anchor about a thousand feet outside the two ships which were about a thousand feet apart. The *Viola* was a beautiful little ship with new masts and riggings, new sails, and fresh, bright paint. She was trim, sharp and light, more like a yacht than a whaler. The captain's wife was aboard and I thought it would be nice to meet her. She proved to be a very dignified, elderly lady. She and her husband were almost the sole owners, to the best of my knowledge. I think the *Viola* could sail about twice as fast as the *Greyhound*. To me, she was really a beautiful ship.

By-and-by, we dropped back on the anchor chain. As I recall it now, we gave the ship six shots, shackles, or ninety fathoms on the anchor chain. I think the depth was fifteen fathoms. The captain had said, "Might as well give her plenty of chain." When we slacked back, that put us about four or five hundred feet from the *Margaret*.

As soon as we were settled, Captain Mandley came aboard. I was glad to see him. So were Captain Corvello and my sister. The two captains were good friends and my sister thought Captain Mandley was a lot of fun. He used to tease her a lot, particularly about her English, which was just as bad as mine was. He couldn't speak any Portuguese, either, but he would flirt with her just to tease my brother-in-law.

The captain of the *Viola* came aboard a little later, but his wife didn't accompany him. The two women couldn't have talked together at all, and being of different nationalities probably had nothing in common. I'm pretty sure the wife of the visiting captain must have felt that way about it.

The two captains, Mandley and Corvello, made an appointment to go ashore the next day. I asked if I might be permitted to stay ashore a little while because, I said, "I am going to take you ashore in the boat." I knew that to be the case since the captain and all the mates except the fourth, who would be serving as head ship's keeper, would be ashore.

"Well, I'll think about it." He was always very stern when he was on the ship, and very seldom gave me a direct answer, but that was okay. It was part of his discipline.

Next day, while we were going ashore I asked him again, adding that I'd like to walk around the little town. From the ship, one could see all of it. Some of the houses were unpainted, some painted white. The town rose a little from the water's edge and, although there was no breakwater, a little point of rocks made it smooth enough for landing a boat. The town actually made me think it looked much like an altar, as I saw it from the ship.

I asked him again if I might stay ashore awhile. "Well, all right. You can walk around for a couple of hours, but don't stay too long. The fourth mate may need you. After all, we are anchored in an open harbor. Come back to pick us up about four o'clock."

Right after we beached we could see a boat with the captain of the *Viola,* and his wife, and Captain Mandley coming ashore. Of course we greeted them, but the captain of the *Viola* wouldn't recognize me. He knew me, but I thought he felt it beneath his dignity to talk to me.

Captain Mandley was already kidding me. He was sure I was coming ashore just to see what the girls were like. I could understand that much anyway.

I walked around for a while. First to a house where a relative of Mr. Frates lived, but he and the mate had taken a horse and gone several miles up the coast to the town where Mr. Frates was born. There were two sailors with me. One was a young fellow from Gloucester. He was always grinning at my English pronunciation, but he helped me a lot and I really liked him a great deal. I always favored him because he was the most promising thing I had, in the form of a teacher. He would read to me in English, and then make me read to him and it helped immensely. He was a pretty stubborn guy, which stubbornness caused quite an incident later on.

We came back to the ship at about lunch time. There wasn't any work to do and we were all loafing around the decks, reading and so on. When I wasn't reading I was learning to do something —splicing, making knots, or fighting. The captain had one strict order: no fighting while he was ashore. Around 2:30 P.M. the fourth mate called me, "Joe, come out of there." I went back to the quarter-deck. I had been sitting on the carpenter's bench back by the try works reading to Harry, the fellow from Gloucester.

The fourth mate looked a little worried. "Look, Joe, the barometer's dropping. We're going to have a storm. The captain had it marked 30.10 this morning and now it's 29.10. It's going down fast. Look," and he pointed to the eastern sky. "We're going to get a blow from there and it's bad because it blows right onto the beach. I think you'd better take a couple of the boys and go ashore. The captain may want to get back aboard earlier than the appointed time."

We got the boat off quickly. It was hanging just clear of the water, and we were on the beach before three o'clock. The captain saw us coming, for he always took binoculars with him when he left the ship. He and Mary were already part way down and Captain Mandley was with them.

"I'm glad you came ashore," he greeted us. "It doesn't look good. I'm afraid we're going to have a storm."

"Well, that's the reason the fourth mate sent me ashore. The barometer was down to 29.10."

"Good God, that's dropping fast! I think it was over 30 this morning."

"That's right. You had it marked down 30.10."

"I remember now. I always mark it down three or four times a day." He always had a pad of paper right under the barometer.

"That's a doggone good idea." Captain Mandley remarked. "Let's go back to the ship. I wonder if the captain of the *Viola* is around here."

"Nuts to him!" exclaimed Captain Corvello. "I can't see him, so let's go." He was a little nervous. He was pretty concerned about the ship. We couldn't get up anchor because a majority of the crew was ashore. We had enough men to man the ship for a couple of days although no one knew what was coming, and the eastern clouds were getting very thick.

In that part of the world, the barometer drops pretty fast when a storm is coming from the south and east. The wind was starting to rise by the time we got to the ship, having set Captain Mandley off on the way.

"I'll tell you what we'll do," the captain explained. "We will pull ahead and heave the chain up short. We'll set a jib which will throw the bow away; slack the starboard chain—the one in the water—until we have thirty fathoms more than the depth of the water, drop the port anchor and then slack both chains back until the port chain has five shackles out also, and the ship will follow on the two chains." This, of course, was a very sensible way of doing things, for it gave us two anchors holding at an angle to each other. I didn't realize then what good seamanship it really was. Captain Mandley told us that when we were heaving up the chain short and setting the jib he thought we were pulling out. Later, of course, he saw us lower the jib and settle back on the anchors, but I doubt whether he was familiar with the maneuver at the time.

Well, it began to blow. Before dark the *Margaret* was astern of us and jumping so ungodly high on her one chain that she would come down and sink her jib boom right under the waves, with the waves breaking right over her decks, and she was in a very dangerous position. Apparently she was dragging anchor, and I don't believe she was more than a thousand feet from the rocks.

It wasn't dark yet. Captain Corvello yelled through a megaphone to the captain of the *Margaret:* "Lower a boat and bring me a line. I've got two anchors down. I'm all right. You seem to be drifting!"

Regardless of what Captain Mandley might have answered, we

couldn't hear him. He was off to our leeward. We waited a little while but there was no response, neither an answer nor a light, and it was getting dark fast. We didn't see him try to lower a boat.

I was on the quarter deck with my sister, the captain, and the fourth mate. They were the only officers and I was the only petty officer on board. We also had the steward, the cook, and a few crew members.

"Joe," the captain said, raising his voice above the wind, "your voice seems to carry pretty well. Do you think you can talk to Mandley? Repeat to Mandley what I am going to tell you?"

"I can try."

He started to tell me, word for word, what I should yell through the megaphone and I repeated it after him. A minute later we saw a lantern waved by hand, from side to side, on Captain Mandley's ship. That meant, "I understand you."

On sailing ships in those days, we had no means of signaling except by lantern. There was no electricity of any sort. The night was not yet dark and we could still see the ship leaping and plunging on the anchor. To us, it looked as though the waves were sweeping over the ship. It must have been more spray than waves, but it certainly looked bad from the *Greyhound*.

The captain had his binoculars and I had a pair that belonged to one of the other boat-steerers. My sister had a pair of her own. We were watching intently, for it looked as though the *Margaret* was dragging anchor. Nothing could get ashore alive, through the reefs in those breakers. The captain saw that the *Margaret* was preparing to lower a boat. He got a little excited and I heard him saying, "Oh, no, no. Not now. Count the big waves. Count the big waves. Count three big waves and then let her go."

But, of course, Captain Mandley couldn't hear and he hadn't had the experience that Captain Corvello had, having come up the hard way. Captain Mandley was, I think, on his first trip as captain. His father was a retired whaling captain who had turned the ship over to him. He was a likely sort, smart, and a pretty good skipper. He had a good mate; English, I think, from the West Indies.

He lowered the boat. Lo, and behold, it got clear of the ship without mishap. That boat, the second mate's, had a heck of a time getting up to us against the wind, trying to bring us a line. We kept our eyes on both the boat and the *Margaret*. We feared the boat would be swamped and it looked as though the *Margaret* would be washed onto the rocks before they got a line to us. It took a good quarter-hour for them to get alongside. Ordinarily it would have taken no more than three minutes. We got the line aboard but Captain Corvello didn't like the looks of it.

"This line is no doggone good. It isn't strong enough—Joe!" I was already on the way to the forward hatch.

"That's what I mean," he said. I yelled to some of the guys who were sitting on the fo'c's'le and also back of the try works where there was some shelter. We cracked the hatch open. We had to be rather careful, what with a wave or spray breaking over us every few seconds. I went down and passed up the end of the line. They passed it along the deck and tied it to the line from the *Margaret*. This left the boat free. The crew on the *Margaret* began pulling in the line. They put it on the windlass to get it good and taut, they told us afterward. Anyway, the line held and our anchors held. That three-inch line slapped up and down on the water like a child's jump-rope. Only this rope was well over a thousand feet long, and it snapped like a gigantic whip as easily as a rodeo performer would crack a whip in the show ring. It was terrific, and it kept up all night.

The round, tub-like bow of the old *Greyhound* would rise high in the air and slap down with a reverberating sound, while the waves poured along the sides with the roar of a raging flood. When the stern of the *Greyhound* rose up, it would come down so far that a passing wave would hit the spare boat which was two or three feet above the stern.

None of us left the quarter-deck for more than a few minutes all night. We expected anything to happen, but the line, the anchors, and luck all held throughout the length of that horrible night. The wind howled and shrieked through the riggings. The spray drifted over us constantly. We were worried, wet, uncomfortable, even though we had boots and oilskins.

The *Margaret* couldn't get the boat back on board. They put a line on her. The men jumped overboard and swam to a Jacob's ladder on the side of the ship. They let the boat drift to the stern, held at a distance by the line, until the next day.

At midnight the barometer hit bottom at 28.15. The captain would go down every ten or fifteen minutes to look at it, or send me down. Around two or three o'clock he remarked, "This thing will blow itself out, and we've got the *Margaret* safe."

The wind started to drop at daylight, and we knew the worst was over. We would make it. We hadn't drifted one bit. We'd held the *Margaret* off the rocks successfully, and we began to haul her in. We could see that the *Viola* was all right, too. Her captain had done the same thing with the chains as had Captain Corvello, but he had done it after it had gotten too dark for us to be able to tell what he was doing.

The waves were still running terribly high. With the light we could see what was happening on the *Margaret*. The waves would enter over the bow and sweep over the decks. It was so bad that their potato bin, which was on the raised quarter-deck, about two and a half feet higher than the main deck, was completely gone except for the very bottom.

The storm abated in the afternoon, with only the ground swells to indicate that we'd had a storm. We picked up our three-inch line from the *Margaret* and waited for our officers and crew who were due on board the next morning. Captain Mandley came over to thank us for the help the *Greyhound* had given him. I've never seen anyone more grateful. When we came back to Dominica at the end of the season, he told everyone how Captain Corvello had saved his ship and the lives of all the crew aboard. It was a feather in Captain Corvello's cap, for he showed excellent seamanship in making the maneuver that made the whole thing possible, and Captain Mandley's generous praise added much to his reputation.

CHAPTER XX

THE WHISTLER AND THE BARBEECH

When the crew came aboard we heaved up the port anchor, followed up with the starboard anchor, and set sails again for the winter whaling grounds off the South Atlantic.

Things proceeded quietly, except for one incident that I didn't like but which, because of certain amusing aspects, I shall relate.

One of the inviolate rules on the old sailing ships—whalers that is—is that there shall be no whistling. A whale's eyesight is very poor, but his hearing is exceptionally keen. It was a belief on whaling ships that whistling was the worst form of noise insofar as a whale was concerned.

Anyway, there was this fellow from Gloucester. I have mentioned Harry before, as the sailor who was so good about teaching me English. I had favored him in every possible way in return for his help, and I felt pretty close to him. This incident happened the first forenoon after we left St. Nicholas.

Harry was on the other watch, the port watch, and I don't recall whether I was awake or sleeping, at the moment. It seems that Harry was sitting on the forward deck somewhere around the fore hatch, and he was whistling. The captain heard it and sent the third mate, who was on watch, to investigate. The mate was unable to stop him, so he reported back to the captain. The captain himself went forward and ordered Harry to stop whistling. When the captain raised his voice and started a little cussing I was suddenly conscious of trouble. I didn't know who was involved but, knowing that Harry was a rather independent and pretty stubborn sort of fellow, I had a sudden sinking feeling. I got up on deck, walked forward and saw that it was Harry. Why he was doing it, I didn't know. He was one of the nine who had been shanghaied from New Bedford and just possibly had been on shipboard long enough to want to show defiance of the whole situation. He was the only one of the nine left. The rest had all run away, with the exception of the man the captain had taken to the hospital.

I went to him and said, "Harry, what's the matter with you? Are you off your noodle? You know you can't do this."

"Oh I can't, can't I? You'll see. They can't stop me from whistling."

"The heck they can't. You better cut that out, man. The captain can shove you in irons."

"That can't stop me from whistling."

"There's means to stop you from whistling, Harry. You'd better cut it out."

But, no sir—he wouldn't stop. He wouldn't pay any attention to me and he just laughed at the captain. When he did that, Captain Corvello took out a pair of handcuffs and started after him. Harry turned around and went for the rigging. The captain called for the second mate, Mr. Cruz.

Now Mr. Cruz was that big, powerful mate I described some time earlier. He weighed well over two hundred pounds, all muscle. He was long-bodied with thick, heavy legs and very long, powerful arms.

Harry was by now well up toward the top of the forward lower rigging. When Mr. Cruz came up to us the captain, with a wave of his arm, gave him one short, simple order. "Bring him down, Mr. Cruz."

I had butterflies in my stomach. I was beginning to feel kind of sick. I knew how stubborn Harry was, and to defy the captain so completely and openly, well, I didn't know how that would go, but I knew it wouldn't be good. Not for Harry, anyway.

Mr. Cruz went up that rigging more like a huge monkey than anything I've ever seen. Harry was as high as he could go on the lower fore rigging and, for a few seconds, when Mr. Cruz caught up with him, I was afraid he was going to jump. Then I saw one of the most amazing things I ever witnessed. Mr. Cruz picked Harry off that rigging as neatly and easily as one would handle a kitten. He put him under one of his powerful arms and brought him down to the deck as easily as though Harry were nothing more than a rag doll.

During this time all eyes, masthead watches' included, were on Harry and Mr. Cruz. This made the situation even worse because it interfered with the ship's business, and the captain would naturally be pretty rough on Harry. No masthead watch would see any whales spouting while they were watching the show down below. The captain's face was almost as red as his big handkerchief, and he was madder than a wet peacock.

"Give me a spun yarn. Somebody give me a spun yarn," he ordered. One of the sailors brought him a strand from a piece of tarred rope. I don't remember who it was. I wouldn't do it. The captain ordered him to open his mouth. He was sullen and kept his teeth tightly closed. The captain drew the yarn across between his lips, pulled it tight across his teeth, around over and under his ears, and tied it behind his head. Harry couldn't whistle any more. The captain left him standing, handcuffed, there by the bulwarks at the starboard fore-rigging.

I had been kneeling at the carpenter's bench, back of the try works. Of course, no one can go contrary to the captain, but after things had quieted down, I went over to Harry. I was sick at heart. Harry's gums were bleeding. The blood was running down on his shirt and chest. He was a pitiful sight. As I said, I was tremendously fond of the guy and here he was in irons just because he was stubborn.

"Harry," I said, "if you promise me, nod with your head, I'll go to the captain and see if I can get him to let me cut you loose." He nodded his head and so I went to the captain. All I got in response to my plea was a furious, "Get the hell out of here. Don't bother me. He got what he deserved."

I could see that the captain was really mad because that was one of the very few times he ever cussed me, even though I have to admit that I took advantage of him on numerous occasions because of the fact that he was my brother-in-law, and I knew I could get away with it.

The captain was sitting in a deck chair on the quarter-deck alongside the wheel, working on a whale-tooth scrimshaw. Mary had been below in the cabin, but she heard me ask the captain to cut Harry loose.

I felt sicker than ever. I went and sat down. I couldn't bear to see Harry again right away. I reminded myself that I'd done the best I knew how. I had gone to the captain. He had refused me. There was nothing else I could do.

After another hour I couldn't stand it any longer. I went back to Harry. He was terribly pale and just about ready to collapse. He couldn't close his mouth. His lips were dry, cracked and swollen. He had opened his mouth and his tongue was caught under the yarn. He was gagged and about the same as if he were paralyzed. I was desperate.

I went to the captain again and begged him. "Please, Captain, give me permission to cut the barbeech off that guy. He's looking bad. He's sick."

Barbeech is what the captain called that thing. I don't know where the name came from, and that was the first time I'd heard it.

"I told you to get the hell out of here and leave me alone," he roared.

I did, fast. I went back to the bench and sat down. I couldn't read. I couldn't study. I couldn't concentrate on anything. I felt so sick now that I didn't care what the captain did to me. "Anyway," I reasoned to myself, "the captain can do any goddam thing he wants to with me. He can put me in irons. He can put me up on masthead for twenty-four hours. That won't hurt, and Mary won't let him do anything more than that." I took my knife out of my pocket, went over to Harry and cut the yarn off. Whatever the captain was going to do I would rather have done than see Harry suffering any more. Poor Harry. He tried to grin a little and he raised his handcuffed arms a little, like he wanted to hug me.

"That's all right, Harry. At least you can use your tongue in a minute. I'll get you some water." I got him a drink and after a minute he could work his tongue around a little and begin to move his lips a bit. He was looking a little better.

Well, now I was wondering where I could get the key to remove the handcuffs. I figured I might as well finish the job now that I'd gone this far. I went back to the quarter-deck, making out that I was going to my boat over on the port side. The boat steerer always goes to his boat whenever he feels like it, to inspect his equipment and make sure that everything is exactly right. While I sat on the gunwale of the boat I ran my eyes around the binnacle, the potato bin, and the skylights. The *Greyhound* had a nice, big skylight over the dining room and lo, and behold, there at the after end of the skylight on the starboard side, I saw the key to the handcuffs.

"Well now," I said to myself, "how in the name of God am I going to get that goddam key?" The captain was sitting there on the starboard side of the skylight, just a little way from it, working on his scrimshaw. I couldn't go around the front because I would have to go the full length of the skylight before I could get the key. I couldn't go around the back because as soon as I'd turn the after port-corner the skipper would see me.

I was now crawling around the deck on my hands and knees trying to find how I could keep out of sight. The helmsman, of course, could see me and was practically in stitches because he knew what I was up to. The captain heard him snickering and looked at him. That was enough to make the man burst out laughing.

"What in hell is so funny?" the captain wanted to know.

"Oh nothing, sir. Nothing. I just thought of something funny."

I didn't know what to do, but the guy at the masthead saw me. This was the same guy who taught me boxing and judo. We called him Malhado, a word that meant spotted. He was a mulatto, or looked like it. He had spots all over his body. Even his hair was spotted like a leopard. He was a very handy guy and he was always teaching me tricks and things. Well, he was up at masthead and he, too, had figured out what I was up to. At least, he and the third mate together had.

Malhado had noticed me first, crawling around on my hands and knees. "Look at Joe," he said to the third mate. "What do you suppose he's up to?" The third mate was a pretty wise owl. "I'll bet he's seen the key to the handcuffs and is trying to figure out how to get it."

"He wouldn't dare do that."

"Well, the captain's wife is Joe's sister you know, and the captain wouldn't hurt him too much. Anyway, the kid has helped Joe a lot. You know how Joe's English has improved. Joe owes him a favor or two and the boys are pretty good friends. Let's put our glasses on. Let's give Joe a chance."

So they put their glasses over to the starboard beam and yelled, "There she blows!" Of course the captain jumped up and got up on the second mate's boat to look over the ocean. "Whereaways?" he called out as usual. By this time I had the key and was back behind the try works, on my way to set Harry free. The captain repeated, "Whereaways?"

"Well, I guess we made a mistake. Must have been a fish jumping or something. There aren't any more."

"Well, O. K. It has happened before, and it will happen again."

I had Harry free and down in the fo'c's'le. The captain went back and forgot all about the illusory spouts. I went on masthead at twelve o'clock. I saw the captain walking forward. I'll have to admit I was watching the deck a lot more than I was watching for whales. I wasn't interested in whales. I was thinking only about what was going to happen to me when the captain found out. Right or wrong, I figured I'd pay sooner or later for what I'd done.

"Oh, oh, here it comes," I thought. The captain looked around. He crossed over to the port side and in front of the entrance to the fo'c's'le, between it and the foremast, and back again to the quarter-deck on the port side. I didn't know, of course, but I thought he was looking for Harry. I did know that Harry was asleep down in the fo'c's'le. I had taken him down and told him to go to his bunk and stay out of sight. His watch was going off anyway, so there was no reason he should still be on deck.

At any rate, the captain didn't ask anybody about Harry. I found that out as soon as I came off masthead. Each boat steerer, you see, takes two hours at masthead and then spends the other two hours on deck. So I came down at two o'clock and the captain was below. I had a good chance to replace the key and did so. I still had the handcuffs in my pocket, for I didn't know what else to do with them. About an hour later, three o'clock, it was coffee time. The captain came up with two cups of coffee. He could have had the mess boy or anyone else bring up the coffee but he never did. He never bothered anyone to do things for him unless he had to.

By the time he was on the quarter-deck, Mary was coming out of the cabin. They both sat down in their deck chairs and it looked to me like a golden opportunity to get permission to free Harry, and cover my tracks. I was sure the captain thought Harry was still in irons and had the barbeech in his mouth.

I had my coffee over on the carpenter's bench and when I saw the captain and my sister sipping theirs I went over and said, "Captain, will you give me permission to free Harry now? Don't you think he's been punished long enough? He told me when I first came to you that he wouldn't whistle any more."

"Oh, all right. There's the key on the starboard corner of the skylight."

"Thank you, sir." I picked up the key and went forward to the fo'c's'le to carry off my bluff. Harry was already on deck because it was getting close to four o'clock, which starts the dogwatch. Dogwatch is from four to seven, with both watches on deck. Everybody swabs decks. The boat steerers throw water on the deck and the sailors swab the decks and rails with brooms. I cautioned Harry about keeping out of sight of the captain for a few more minutes, and asked him how he felt.

"Oh, I feel good now," he answered.

"All right, but goddam, Harry, if you whistle again I'm going to beat you up," I said. "I'll beat you up to keep you from getting another barbeech in your mouth." He knew I could do it.

"Okay, Joe. I've had my lesson." And outside of a few chuckles around the deck that was the last of it.

Harry was a nice kid. He was a little older than I, but he didn't drink to amount to anything and he didn't play around the bars and bawdy houses like the rest of the sailors. In other words, he didn't make a fool of himself. I never could figure out why he pulled that whistling stunt. I got the key and the handcuffs back where they belonged and never heard anything from the captain. To this day I don't know whether the captain knew what I had done and just ignored it, or not.

CHAPTER XXI

FLYING BOAT STEERER

Captain Corvello had an ulterior motive in stopping at St. Nicholas Island on this trip. As I have explained, it was a convenient place to pick up crew members when we were short. On this trip we were eight men short when we left Fayal. Eight of the nine shanghaied crew members left us there. One, of course, was the sick lawyer. The other seven followed the usual procedure. They waited until the day before we were to sail and then took to the hills. From then on the procedure was to stay in the hills for a few days then go back to the American Consulate where the Consul would get them passage back to the United States as workaways. In later years when I was captain on steamers, I brought a good many workaways back from Europe and Mexico.

Among the eight new crew-members from St. Nicholas was a little guy about my own age, named Joe. I never heard his last name. He had developed a trick that to the best of my knowledge had never been used before. The first time I saw him pull this stunt I didn't know what was up but apparently he had talked it over with the second mate and the mate had talked it over with the captain, for it went off as smooth as silk.

It had been our practice every time we sighted a sea turtle to lower a boat, harpoon it and bring it aboard. Fresh turtle-meat and turtle-soup were mighty welcome changes in our routine diet; so much so that turtle was practically a delicacy. While Joe was with us our method of taking turtles underwent a sudden and spectacular change.

We were down close to the Equator, running with full sails set, when the masthead sighted a sea turtle. Joe was on watch below. The second mate called him up. The captain directed the ship toward the turtle, and Joe went up on the jib boom. I had been down in the hold but I heard the voices and thought the masthead had sighted whales. I came up, and there was Joe, up on the dolphin strike right under the jib boom. At the precise moment, Joe leaped off the dolphin strike into the water, feet first. The captain ordered, "Wheel down! Slack the fore port-braces. Haul on starboard fore-braces and haul her back. Stop ship."

The ship stopped. There was Joe on the port side, holding a big sea-turtle flipped over on its back, with his hands, and treading water with his feet. We lowered a boat, put a noose around the turtle's head with a hatchet handle between its jaws, and pulled Joe and the turtle aboard. Joe was right at home. I asked him how in the name of heaven he ever learned to do such a thing. "Oh, my father and I have caught turtles that way ever since I can remember. He did it when I was a kid and then he taught me how to do it. I've never caught sea turtles any other way. It's really quite easy. You just jump down on them so that they flip over and you grab them as you go into the water and hold them bottom side up. You know, a turtle can't do a thing when it's upside down, except bite. You do have to keep out of the way of their heads. They can really bite."

It sounded so easy and looked so clever that I secretly resolved I was going to do it too.

We had a fine meal out of that turtle. It was a big one and there was enough for the whole crew. Everyone enjoyed the show, too, for it provided an interesting break in the routine of everyday life on shipboard. Mary, especially, got a big bang out of it. The Captain said he'd heard of the trick but had never seen it done. Joe repeated the performance a great many times, always to the enjoyment of everybody.

After four or five weeks I decided it was time for me to do it. After all, I was sure I could do anything Joe could do, so the mate promised to let me try. It wasn't many days until someone from the masthead yelled, "Turtle ahead on the port bow." I quickly got up onto the jib boom. We were going at a pretty good clip and as I poised out there on the dolphin strike I had my first misgivings. The thought flashed across my mind that I wasn't as good a swimmer as Joe. It looked like quite a way down to the water, and the turtle looked pretty big, too. I leaped. I struck the turtle with my feet at the proper place, near the edge of the shell. He flipped. I caught hold. But there the successful part of the venture ended. I was looking almost straight into those snaky, beady eyes. I was inches from those powerful snapping jaws. For a second or two, I thought my nose was a goner. I tried to shift my hold. It was quite a struggle for a minute, and there was a real commotion in the water. And then I found myself swimming as I had never done before. I was sure the turtle was after me, although I guess it wasn't. Apparently, everyone on deck enjoyed the show even more than they enjoyed Joe's. But, of course, there wasn't any praise. The captain greeted me with, "So you think you can do anything anybody else can do!"

"Well, I tried."

"You've got to give Joe credit. He tried it. He didn't succeed, but he can try again," the mate chimed in. He was a good guy, always taking my side.

"He'd better not. Joe, if you ever go overboard after another turtle you'll hear from me. Don't do it again. That's orders."

From the captain—well, that was that. And Joe kept on catching the turtles. If we were in a calm and the ship couldn't get to the turtle, we'd lower a boat and Joe would leap from the bow platform just as successfully as from the dolphin strike on the ship. He always knew just how to come up on them, and I can't remember that he ever lost one. If he had, I'm sure I would have remembered it.

We had arrived at the winter season's whaling grounds in the South Atlantic and we were in a dead calm. We had been so for a couple of days. We'd had all the sails out except the flying staysails. The sails were just flapping with the roll of the ship. Suddenly there was a spout right near us. In fact, it was so close that we could hear the air and vapor coming out of the whale's spout hole, almost like steam from a locomotive. By the spout we knew it was a sperm whale—a big bull, all alone. It was swimming and we could see it going down for the next spout. It went down, and when it came up it breached. It came out of the water like a torpedo, but there the likeness of motion ended. That huge mass came clear of the water and then fell flat with a terrific reverberating boom, and a wallowing splash that sent great waves circling out from the center. When they reached the ship, we rolled with each succeeding wave until the water was smooth again. Then the whale sank below the surface, rose and breached again.

This time the bull rose even higher from the water, turning over sidewise in the air, and coming down flat on his back with an even greater boom and splash than before. It was a magnificent spectacle. A little frightening, too. To see that huge mass in action, completely clear of the water, made one think of the tiny whaleboat going out to throw a tiny dart against a monstrous Goliath of the deep; one that could crush the boat like an eggshell, between that huge head and that long, flat underjaw; or could, with one swipe of its gigantic flukes, destroy the boat and every member of the crew.

No one yelled the usual, "There she blows!" We were too close. Captain Corvello signaled Mr. Frates with his hand, raising one finger—one boat. He was afraid more boats would make too much noise in getting into the water. I already had my shoes off and was ready to relieve the forward gripes. Mr. Frates was ready at the after gripes. We lowered the boat nice and easy, allowing it to slip quietly into the water. As we shoved off, the mate said softly, "Use paddles." With paddles we could make seven or eight knots, while making practically no sound. I could see the second mate lowering his boat as we pulled away. About five hundred feet from the ship, the mate signaled to me to get ready with the harpoons. The whale came up for the next spout, rubbing the port bow of the boat. The position was almost perfect. I drove the harpoon with all my might right into the middle of his back. I grabbed the second harpoon, and let him have it again. He took off as though he had wings, and the tail was going under the bow. I'm sure he didn't kick purposely, or I'd have met my patron saint right then and there. But he must have flipped his tail a little bit, for he struck the bow right under my feet with a sharp upward blow that sent me flying into the air.

Mary was only five or six hundred feet away, watching through the glasses. She claimed I went a hundred feet into the air. The mate said, "No, but it was twenty-five or thirty." Anyway, it was high enough. I came down headfirst, right beside the boat. One of the oarsmen stuck out his paddle. I grabbed it and climbed aboard. The mate left the line slack to give me time to get back aboard. It was running out with a sizzling sound around the loggerhead, and over the bow it sounded more like an express train. The instant I was aboard, he tightened the line, and we were off like a speedboat. Mr. Frates went to the bow, and I took the stern. The second mate's boat got into position and struck the whale just about when I got on board. Shortly after the whale slowed down, the third mate also got fast. We then made short work of the whale, which was a good one. It was between eighty and ninety barrels.

Back at the ship they thought I had probably broken my legs. Mary was sure I was hurt, but the captain saw me go headfirst into the water, and he assured her that, at the worst, I'd only have one or both legs broken. "And at that age," he assured her, "they are easily mended. I can take care of that, very nicely."

We had the whale in tow and, as our boat came alongside, the captain called to Mr. Frates, "Leave the whale to Mr. Cruz, and come on in." Mary was standing with him, anxiously waiting. When the captain saw me get up to go up the forward block, I could hear him say, "Thank the Lord, Joe isn't hurt. Look, he's standing on his feet."

When I came aboard, my sister was crying with happiness. She wanted to kiss me, but I wouldn't stand for that. I didn't want anybody to think I was a sissy. She made me roll up my pants legs and she felt my toes to make sure I was okay. She had always been like a mother to me and I can't tell you how good it made me feel to see how happy she was. The captain seemed to be pretty happy, too. I guess maybe he liked me more than he was willing to let on. He was probably relieved, too, because I had no broken legs to set.

CHAPTER XXII

STRANGE MEDICINE

It was about the first week or so in November that we got the whale. I had noticed that the captain's face had been looking a little drawn for a few days, and I asked Mary, "What in heck is wrong with the old man?"

"His stomach is out of whack and he isn't well."

He kept getting worse and, along in December, he was pretty sick. He could come up on deck for two or three hours and sit around, all doubled up, then go back to bed. I was doing all the navigating. As I mentioned before, I had started learning when I was on the *Pedro Varella* and I had become interested in celestial navigation while I was in New Bedford. A fellow named Arthur LaFrance had started me on it; then he gave me his book, saying that he knew everything that was in it, anyway. I had kept right on studying on shipboard, four or five hours a day, mostly navigation and English. I showed the captain several times how to navigate by stars, but he wouldn't believe it was accurate, and consequently he didn't trust it. Of course, you can't use the Polaris in the South Atlantic, but there you cross the two stars, one with the other, with two longitudes, and two lines of position, with a resulting position more accurate than by using the sun with only one line of position (which must be taken between nine and twelve or between twelve and three o'clock). By using stars, you lay your lines down and get a cross or fix, right there. I was confident by now that I was a better navigator than the "old man."

The captain wouldn't give orders where to go, but he would tell the mate, "Try this direction. Try that direction." We had been catching whales right along and had a very good catch by the middle of January. The mate suggested that we should take him and his wife to Barbados and leave them ashore.

"Joe seems to be a very good navigator. After we drop you off, we can come back to the West Indies whaling grounds, which isn't too far from Barbados, and finish up the season there."

The captain wouldn't hear of it. "No," he said, "I am not that sick. We will finish the season here." He was losing quite a bit of weight, but, in my opinion, he was too fat anyway. I didn't like to see him feeling so bad, however, because it made Mary so unhappy. We followed the captain's wishes and kept on until we had a full ship, at which time we headed for Barbados. By this time I was doing all the navigating. Mr. Frates told me he could do it a little, but not enough to bring the ship straight into port.

Several hours before we were due to sight the lighthouse at Barbados, I took our position by the sun. We had good weather, a light breeze, and we were making an easy eight or ten knots. We had the log out to mark the miles. I had my noon position, my three o'clock position, and at twilight I had a position by the stars. They all agreed. I was making my first landfall and, of course, I was a little nervous. So was the captain. He was down in the cabin so, of course, I showed him the map. And he agreed with the two sun positions. He sort of sneered at the star position. He didn't understand it, and naturally it rubbed him the wrong way.

At a little before ten o'clock, just as I was about due to pick up the light, I climbed up the foremast. When I came up, with my head just over the foresail, I caught the flash of that southeast lighthouse. At that moment, making my first landfall, it was a very beautiful white light, and in the biggest, loudest voice I could muster, I yelled out, "Light-o-de-e-e-ad ahead!" I couldn't have hit it any more directly. We didn't have to shift course, except that as we approached we had to steer a little to port to pass it. Also, since we were coasting off the coast at night, the captain insisted on staying pretty well out in order to steer clear of fishing boats and to allow for unfamiliar currents. Even in the West Indies, where the winds are pretty steady, he was cautious.

We shortened sails to slow down, as we didn't want to get into the harbor before eight or nine o'clock, allowing plenty of time for going around the south side of the island to get into the bay. After daylight we sighted the pilot boat. The captain was so doubled up with stomach cramps that we had to bring him up on deck. The pilot, a native colored man, was a very clever fellow. He had piloted us in the *Pedro Varella*. He knew the captain, and the moment he greeted him, he said, "Captain, what's the matter with you? You look sick."

So the captain told him about the horrible stomach trouble he had experienced, beginning way back in November.

The pilot wanted to know exactly what it was like.

"Well, everything I eat turns sour and I have terrible cramps all the time," the captain told him.

"Do you have a coal stove? Do you carry coal on board?"

"Yes. Of course. We have some coal."

"Have someone bring me a lump of it."

The pilot took his knife and scraped the coal until he had a teaspoonful of black powder; then he called for a cupful of warm water, put the powder in and stirred it up. Then he told the captain to drink it.

"What the hell will that do to me? That's no medicine," the captain retorted.

"You won't be sorry. You just wait and see what it does to you, Captain." Mary saw all this and she told me about it.

So the captain drank it. Mr. Frates was there and he, also, told me about it. In half an hour the captain was on his feet. I saw him walking the deck, so I came up to him and remarked, "Captain, you seem to be a lot better. What did you have, land fever?"

"No. The pilot mixed up some coal medicine and it seems to have straightened me out. My stomach isn't hurting and I can stand up and walk around."

He took charge and began maneuvering the ship, tacking back and forth three or four times to come into the anchorage.

"Before I go ashore," the pilot told the captain, "I am going to give you another dose of medicine." This time it was I who went to the galley for the cupful of warm water. I watched the pilot scrape the coal into powder and stir it into the water. It didn't look good, but the captain drank it. About an hour later he went ashore with his wife, looking as though he had never been ill.

Next morning, I checked at the hotel to see how he was. He told me he felt fine, and that whenever his stomach began to feel bad he took his medicine and was all right. So far as I know, he was never bothered by stomach ailments again.

The next day, Mr. Frates called me and said, "Joe, I want you to go ashore again today and see if the captain is all right. You'd better dress up a little, because he told me yesterday they would be spending the day with an English captain and his family. You'd better get there early because they are going out into the country."

We had just had breakfast. I dressed and called a bumboat. The bumboats will take passengers ashore for a couple of shillings. I went to the hotel to look for the captain and Mary. I found their room locked, so I went into the dining room, where I found them having breakfast with the English captain, his wife and daughter. They invited me to sit down and I had coffee and crumpets with them. Barbados is an English island and for that reason the traditional English crumpets were served.

Soon I bade them good-by and said I would have to get back to the ship. Mary said, "Oh, Mr. Frates will understand."

But Captain Corvello said: "Did you have permission to stay ashore? If not, you'd better go back."

I knew the captain was himself again. I walked back to the dock and got a bumboat to take me out to the *Greyhound*. I told Mr. Frates the captain would not be aboard today, and that he was feeling fine. The word spread around the ship and everyone was glad to hear the skipper was all right again.

CHAPTER XXIII

NOT MY TYPE

It was a pleasure to stay at Barbados for a few days. There wasn't much to do there but splice some line and mend some sails. There were no watches to keep.

The bumboats came alongside all day, selling wares and bringing girls who were eager to get onto the ship and go to the fo'c's'le with the sailors. Of course, the mates would try to stop that, as far as possible, but the regular fellows would look the other way when some of the girls came aboard. On one occasion, I went down into the fo'c's'le and there were five girls in there with the sailors. I turned right around with my eyes closed. It was my duty to report it to the mate but I didn't say anything. "After all," I thought, "we are all human."

I walked back and got my book and began to study. In the afternoon, just before dinner time, Mr. Frates asked if I was going ashore. "You can go ashore if you want to. I'll talk to the third mate."

"No. I don't care to go," I said.

"Well, tomorrow I want you to go ashore again and see the captain. Make sure he's all right. You won't have to return to the ship. If your sister wants you to stay, it will be all right. Stay the rest of the day if you want to."

Mr. Frates was a sensible guy and he was a good friend. He

always thought of nice things that I'd like to do. He knew I was studying hard and he went out of his way to help me. I stayed on board. I could have gone ashore and made up to the daughter of the English captain, but she didn't appeal to me much. She was a little on the skinny side and her features were rather sharp, and her English sounded rather peculiar. She was English, and I had not quite accepted the English people as yet.

The next morning I had only coffee on board. I hoped to get to the hotel in time for breakfast with the captain. They were still in their hotel room when I arrived, so I sat down and waited. The captain began teasing me. "What's the idea, trying to get away from that girl? That's the first time I ever saw you try to get away from a skirt."

"Oh, I don't know. I just didn't care for her. She isn't my type."

"We have an appointment with them. We'll have breakfast at the same table at eight o'clock. Have you had breakfast?"

"Of course not. I knew I was coming ashore. Mr. Frates told me yesterday, and I didn't see any reason for eating that stuff on board when I could eat in a restaurant and have someone wait on me."

When we reached the dining room, the English family was already there. We sat down and, being willing to give her another once-over, I sat next to the girl. She was about my age. Her name was Marie. I soon discovered she was nice enough, and admitted to myself that the trouble might have been with me.

We stayed at the breakfast table for a while, just talking. They talked and I listened. When everyone got up to leave, Marie took my hand and said, "Come on, Joe. Let's walk around. Let's leave the folks together."

"Well, that's all right," I replied. So we walked around the hotel grounds, and a little later on I suggested that we go and see some of the island.

"We saw it yesterday," she said. "We rented a horse and wagon. Your sister and her husband and my father and mother and me. You should have stayed."

"Well, we will go now. Would you like it?"

We decided to go, so I rented a horse and a sort of cab. I expected to drive it, having learned how in Fayal, but in Barbados the driver goes along. He's part of the deal. That was just fine. In fact it suited me a lot better. There was a compartment in the carriage. The driver couldn't see us and we couldn't see him.

I saw a little of Barbados—a few cultivated fields. Marie wasn't the cold English girl I had expected her to be. She was warm and she was loving, and she didn't care about the scenery, either. We closed the cab and let the driver go where he pleased. From about nine-thirty, we were very busy making love. About four o'clock, we returned to the hotel for dinner. The trip had cost me only a handful of shillings. This was about five dollars. Neither of us had even thought of food, and the driver had driven all day without any. I thanked him and gave him a dollar bill as a tip.

When we reached the hotel, the others were sitting on a bench under the trees. "You kids sure took your time," Mary remarked.

"We've been all over the island."

"How did you do it? Did you get a carriage?"

"Yes. We rented a buggy and went all over hell."

Marie's mother thought that was pretty rough language but I didn't know too many expressive words in English. Naturally I used the ones I heard most.

After dinner, Marie and I went for a walk along the pier. Several of the crew from the *Greyhound* met and passed us. As we walked along the bulkhead where small boats are handled, we met another fellow. He was a tall man with a gray scarf around his neck, as the English dress. Behind him were a couple of others. Marie whispered to me, "That fellow is from my ship." We heard the fellow remark, "Look at Marie with a bloody Yank." I went up to him and he said, "Get off. You bloody Yankee."

I had never heard that expression before, but I was sure it didn't mean anything good. He was too big for me to box with so I used a judo hold on him and had him on his back in a flash. He hit his head pretty hard and was a little dazed. As he got up, he sort of apologized. "Hey, I didn't mean anything by it. You are a Yankee, aren't you?"

"No!" I assured him. "I'm from an American ship."

He apologized to Marie, and then we walked on down to the end of the bulwarks, and then back to the hotel. The rest of the party was sitting up, waiting for us.

It was getting late, so I said good-by to everyone. To my surprise, Marie kissed me in front of everybody.

The captain and his wife were remaining in the hotel over night, but the ship was to sail the next day. I returned to the *Greyhound,* reminiscing over the day. When I got aboard, I told Mr. Frates and he smiled and said, "Well, I figured you'd have a pretty nice time with a girl your own age. That's why I told you to come back when you pleased." I thanked him, with a warm feeling inside of me, and I said to myself, "What a wonderful guy!"

Next morning, knowing the captain and Mary would be on board fairly early, we set about making ready to sail.

CHAPTER XXIV

CAPTAINS' RENDEZVOUS

Usually it took about twenty hours to sail from Brighton Bay, Barbados, to Dominica. We passed around the northwest corner of the island and ran into the strongest trade winds I'd ever seen up to that time. Fearing that the pressure would be too great for the foremast, the captain ordered the sailors to take in the flying jib and the fore degans'l (so called during my whaling days, but referred to as topgallant sail or topgans'l in strict whaling terminology). A little later, he had the main-topgallant sail taken in also. We were making such fast time even then, that along about midnight the captain ordered the foresail and mainsail clewed up and the jib topsail taken in, otherwise we'd have been coming into the harbor before daylight, 'way ahead of schedule. At daylight, however, we were just coming around the point where we could see into the bay. Ten or twelve whalers were already in ahead of us. As soon as we turned the point we were in the lee of the island and in smooth water. We set sails again—foresail, mainsail, topgallant sail—to head her as close into the wind as possible. The breeze was so good and we made such a good run that we headed right in toward the river where we always took on water; made only one tack to the south whereas it usually took five or six, tacked back toward the ships and sailed right up to the anchorage. We dropped anchor at around eight or nine in the morning, after having completed the most beautiful run into the anchorage that, in all likelihood, had ever been made by the old tub-nosed *Greyhound*.

The *Greyhound* was almost immediately surrounded by whaleboats. Each and every whaling captain came aboard to meet the captain's wife—some for the first time, others for the second. All of them wanted to greet her and shake hands. When Captain Mandley came to see her, he did more than shake hands—he threw his arms around me, picked me up and waved me like a feather. He really appreciated the fact that my voice had carried to him through the megaphone, in the storm at St. Nicholas. He must have described the whole episode very vividly to all the captains, with plenty of praise for all of us, for the captains all congratulated Captain Corvello on the maneuver, and the captain of the *Viola*, to my utter astonishment, came over and shook hands with me.

There was really a gang on board. Each of the whaleboats came with the captain and a crew of five, leaving one of the crew below in the whaleboat to keep it from bumping against the ship. The steward, of course, put the big coffee pot on immediately, serving some other stuff with the coffee, including crumpets (those things I'd had for the first time in Barbados), and we really had a swell time.

Captain Corey, from the mother ship, came over in a motor boat; the first time I'd ever seen the *Clark* with such a craft. He had a letter from my father with two twenty-dollar bills in it. My father was such a good guy. He was always doing things like that. As Captain Corey handed me the letter, he said, "And your father wants to know if you are studying hard."

"Look," I said, "I'd rather you asked the captain or Mr. Frates about that. They can give you the answer."

He laughed, "I'm 'way ahead of you. I've already talked to them. The mate says you study all the time, and the captain says you are even navigating by the stars."

"That's right," I replied, "but I didn't think the captain thought much of it."

"Keep it up," he said, "I've done it for years. I went to navigation school to learn how. But tell me, how did you come to learn it?" Then I told him about the big, fat French guy, Arthur LaFrance, and the book he had given me.

"Good boy," he said. "I could see that you were studying even if they didn't tell me. Your English is better every time I see you. It shows in a lot of ways. When I see your father, I'll tell him and I know he will be very pleased."

It was a nice compliment and I left Captain Corey with that nice warm feeling that all was right with the world. I didn't know it then, but Captain Corey had talked with my father several months before and my father had told him that instead of going home to the Azores for the winter he was going whaling down into the South Atlantic. I discovered also, a little later, that Captain Mandley had gammed with the bark *Fairhaven* some time during the past few months. Then Captain Corey and Captain Mandley had conspired with Captain Corvello the moment they came aboard, to keep Mary and me from finding out that my father was due to arrive with the *Fairhaven* within the next couple of days. The letter from my father was genuine, but Captain Corey had slipped the two twenty-dollar bills into it to make it look as though my father had no expectation of seeing us. Captain Corey was really pulling my leg, and doing a thoroughly good job of it. Then, to make a good gag better still, the two skippers figured out a scheme whereby they thought they might be able to work out a clever surprise. Now, no one can tell when a whaler is going to arrive, but the fact that the *Fairhaven* wasn't yet in made it just that much more certain that the next day would be the day that it would show up. Like a couple of schoolboys, they were eager to try.

Plans were carefully laid. Captain Corvello was to see Linda's mother and set it up with her. Meanwhile, Captain Corey was to tell Mr. Frates that my girl friend's mother (remember, we were now in Dominica) had seen him and that I had an invitation to go to a cousin's place for the night, which was four or five miles down the coast, and come back the next day. I was to stop at the hotel late next morning, to see Captain Corvello and report back to the ship.

That afternoon, a couple of hours after things had quieted

down, Mr. Frates called me over. "Joe," he said, "I suppose you're going ashore tonight."

"Well, yes. I'd planned to."

"Look, Joe. While Captain Corvello was ashore a little while ago he saw that girl you run around with, and her mother. They would like to have you walk over to a cousin's place a few miles down the coast; some kind of a little party or something, and you won't need to come back until tomorrow. Just one thing—before you come back tomorrow, stop at the hotel and see if Captain Corvello has any message."

Coming from Mr. Frates, it all sounded just right. You see, Mr. Frates had sailed with my father as third mate, second mate, and first mate. He was aboard when my older brother and sister were born. I guess he knew my family better than I did, and he was almost like a father to me.

Everything went as planned. I found Linda shortly after I got ashore, and I had a nice time with the family. About an hour before sundown, we started to the cousin's place, figuring it would take over an hour to get there. I don't know whether anyone warned them beforehand, but however it was, they carried it off nicely. We sang and danced until pretty late. They showed me where I was to sleep and, after Linda and I had spent an hour or so in the moonlight together, we all went to bed. We had a nice breakfast the next morning, fooled around for a while, and walked back to town. I left Linda at her house.

When I got to the hotel, there were a lot of people on the veranda. Mary saw me coming and waved to me and told me to come on up.

"We have a table down at the end, Joe." I went up, and there were several people seated around a table having soft drinks and so on. My sister was facing me. So was the captain, and two or three other skippers had their backs to me. Others were standing around. I got almost up to the table and I caught a little of the side view of one gentleman's face—just enough to see the end of a black bushy moustache.

My heart simply stood still. My sister couldn't keep quiet any longer, and she laughed and clapped her hands. The man stood up, with his back still toward me, but there was no mistaking who it was, even before he turned around. I threw my arms around him. Believe me, we acted like a couple of schoolboys, and we didn't care who saw us. After all, I hadn't seen him since I started sailing, almost four years before. Mary was actually crying for joy, and it took a little while for us to quiet down and become normal human beings.

Captain Corey was there, of course, and getting as big a bang out of it as anybody. He and Captain Corvello were really tickled to have their scheme work out so perfectly, and they had to explain how they had done it. When they got through, my father took out his wallet and handed Captain Corey two twenty-dollar bills. "Captain," he said, "it was worth every penny of it, and Joe can keep the money."

I went back to the *Greyhound* and reported in full to Mr. Frates. He was very pleased that the scheme had gone off so well.

"Now listen, Joe. It's a long time since you've seen your father and you need to get acquainted while you have a chance. I have already spoken to the third and fourth mates and they will be responsible for any of your work that has to be done while we're in port. You are relieved of all duty as long as your father is here, and you are free to come and go as you please."

That was as good as captain's orders—for the first mate is in command while the ship is in port. "Thank you, thank you, Mr. Frates." I couldn't think of anything else to say.

I did as Mr. Frates said. I spent part of the day occasionally with one or the other of the two girls—I'll tell about the other one in a moment. And a great deal of the time I spent with my father. I slept on the *Fairhaven* in my father's cabin every night but one, until we set sail again.

I spent a good deal of the time on board the *Clark* largely because my father and Captain Corey were very close friends. He was there and so was I, and I loved it, for I was fascinated with the way the chief mate handled the oil casks with the power winch. Naturally I knew how much cargo we had on board, but as I watched the casks come out of the hold and go swinging up to the *Clark* and into the hatch, it seemed incredible that there could be as many as there were. I think it was because the *Greyhound* looked so small beside the *Clark*—about like one of our own whaleboats alongside the *Greyhound*. The *Clark* was almost twice as long as the *Greyhound,* with decks much higher above the water. It was very wide by comparison, and the masts, I thought, were terrific.

I liked the *Clark* and spent a lot of time aboard her, especially this time in Dominica, because my father spent so much time with Captain Corey. Better still, Captain Corey liked to have me. He was a close friend of Captain Corvello, too; in fact it was due to Captain Corey's and my father's influence that Captain Corvello got his first ship, the *Pedro Varella*. Captain Corvello was a very good sailor, but his English was poor and it was hard for him to get ahead. Once he got his ship, however, he became very successful. He had the experience that was necessary, and the ability. All the education in the world could not have helped to make him into a successful whaling captain without those other two qualifications. He tried very hard. Hours meant nothing to him, neither did his own comfort. He had one objective—to keep everything in top shape, the better to get whales. He was a good skipper, but I really didn't like him. He was just too doggone rough on me, at least to my way of thinking. As I look back, however, I realize that it was probably pretty much my own fault. I took advantage at times and I think he wanted to show that he wasn't showing any favoritism just because of the fact that I was his young brother-in-law. I defied him several times, too, which of course didn't improve my situation.

Among the whaling ships at Dominica when we arrived was the *Morning Star*. The skipper, Captain Rose, was a Cape Verdian. He had picked up his daughter in the Cape Verde Islands and had brought her with him on the ship. He called her Rosina. If she had another name, I never heard it. She was not nearly so dark-complexioned as her father; she was nice-looking and had a nice figure. Her father, the captain, was a dignified-looking gentleman who looked more like an athlete than a sailor. He was quite friendly with Captain Corvello, too.

Captain Rose had met my sister in Fayal and knew that she spoke very little English. His daughter spoke only the Portuguese dialect of the Cape Verdes, but it is understandable to anyone who knows Portuguese. Consequently, he brought Rosina over to the hotel and introduced her to Mary. The four of them were at the hotel the next afternoon when my father and I arrived. I didn't know the girl was there, and I had expected to spend a little of the afternoon with Linda. Mary introduced me to Rosina and the three of us walked around the town for a little while. We walked down the main street and stopped at the little place where Linda worked, and I introduced the three girls to each other. I was careful not to mention dinner because I was sure that Mary would insist on paying for it and I didn't want her to do that. We had a few soft drinks, and went back to the hotel. My father was visiting with some of the other captains and having dinner with them, so I left the girls at the hotel and went back to see Linda.

I had purposely taken Mary and Rosina down there so there wouldn't be any misunderstanding. Dominica could be a very lonesome place if one didn't have any friends there. Linda had to work for another hour, so I had dinner and waited for her. Then we walked down to the beach where we'd been other times, and talked about the party the night before. I told her about my father and what a wonderful surprise it was; also that I would be spending a lot of time with my father. She began kidding me about Rosina. I thought she was serious, but finally she said, "It's all right. She's not on your ship. Anyway I'm better-looking than she is and I have a better figure." With all of that I had to agree. We had a nice time together—a little loving, of course—and got back to the house a little late.

I was afraid her father wouldn't like it, so we sat on the steps and laughed loudly two or three times to make it appear as though we'd been there quite awhile. Soon she went in and I went back to the hotel to meet my father. Together we went back to the *Fairhaven* to sleep. We sat and talked quite awhile. He wanted to know a lot about what had happened to me, so I told him how it all had started—how I'd blacked my face and hands and so on, and later how I'd begged the captain to kill me and throw me overboard. He laughed a lot and gave me a big man's hug and we finally said good night.

The excitement occasioned by my father's arrival soon settled down to a daily routine that didn't vary too much, but just enough to make the four weeks a nice holiday and vacation for me. Most mornings and often early afternoons we spent on the *Clark* with a group which usually included, besides Captain Corey and my father, Captains Mandley, Corvello, and Rose. Others were often present, and Captain Rose always brought Rosina with him. Oftentimes I took her over to one of the other whalers to meet some of the friends I'd made there, and I also took her over to the *Greyhound*. In the afternoon, or sometime just before lunch or dinner, we would go ashore and have lunch or dinner with Mary. Occasionally, when the two girls were together, I'd take them down to the little eating-place where Linda worked. At other times, the three of us would go for walks around the town, along the streets, through the crooked little alleys, and up into the hills.

One day I sent all my work clothes by the boat steerer, to be laundered. It was always the duty of the oldest of the boat steerers to supervise the water-making job at the mouth of the river. This was right next to the place where the women of Dominica went to wash their laundry. Consequently, the sailors all sent their laundry down there to be washed in fresh water. On shipboard we had to do our own laundry, and the rinsing always had to be done with salt water. Naturally the salt left in the clothes attracted moisture, and it was always a relief to get clothes that were free of salt so they didn't have that damp, muggy feeling. I sent everything, both clean and soiled. There was much activity around the place, with probably a third of the village women washing clothes, plus lots of sailors coming and going from the eighteen or twenty ships in the harbor. It was an interesting and picturesque place. I walked with the girls—Mary and Rosina. It was a warm day but they both had parasols, so when we got there we sat down and talked. I found the woman who was doing my laundry and she told me that for an extra shilling she would take it home and iron it, too. I was delighted, and I told her I would pick it up the following afternoon.

The girls enjoyed the scene of bustling activity so much that they asked to come down with me again next day. Well, I picked them up the next afternoon and we went down to get the laundry. I took them over to greet the crew from the *Greyhound*. We talked and laughed for a while and then started back. At a little distance from the *Greyhound*'s water-making crew there was a crew from the *Alice Knowles,* a group unfamiliar to us. As we were passing, I overheard the boat steerer say, "Who does he think he is, sporting those two classy-looking janes around—but then there are a lot of cheap girls around who will go with any guy who has a little dough." The girls heard the remark, and my sister's face flushed. I turned around and demanded, "What did you say?" Well, the guy was quite a bit bigger than I, and Mary grabbed my arm. "Joe, Joe. He's too big for you. Come on. Let's get away from here."

"You heard me, sailor. Want to do something about it?"

I shook Mary's hand off my arm and started toward the guy. He rushed at me with teeth clenched and his fist ready. I didn't wait to try any boxing. I gave him a judo hold right away, and over he went, flat on his back in the sand. He got up mad as a hornet and called me a couple of vile names as he rushed me again. My back was sort of toward the river. There was a woman behind me on the bank, although I didn't realize it at the moment. Well, I was in just the right position, and the way the guy was rushing me was a perfect setup for another judo maneuver. That guy went over me and over the stooping washerwoman into the river. As he came out of the water, I caught him with a couple of rights and lefts in the face and then I backed up just enough to let him get up on the bank as he came out of the water a second time. Quite a crowd gathered very quickly—a lot of sailors besides the ones from the *Alice Knowles* and the *Greyhound.*

"Look, you. If you haven't had enough I'll drown you. That was my sister, Captain Corvello's wife, you insulted. You better apologize, quick."

Everything was set for a free-for-all, but when he realized he had insulted a captain's wife, the fight was all over. He knew what would happen when he got back to where his captain could deal with him.

He said, "Oh, I didn't mean—I didn't realize—"

"Tell her you're sorry," I yelled at him. He did, and we turned to go and pick up my laundry. Mary had a tight hold on my arm. "Joe," she said in a slightly hushed voice, "I didn't think you could handle a fellow so much bigger than you."

"Look, sister, you don't know your little brother very well. I've learned lots of things since I started being a sailor." We walked back to the hotel, and I felt nine feet tall.

CHAPTER XXV

GOING UP

During our stay in Dominica, I had been sleeping in my father's cabin on the bark *Fairhaven*. We almost always had breakfast together in the morning and, of course, we had a few hours to spend afterward, which gave us a good chance to get together in a father-and-son relationship. It was one of the few times in my life when I had such an opportunity. I enjoyed my father's companionship very much, and I look back on that experience as one of the really fine things in my life. I learned to appreciate my father for the fine man that he was, and all of my life I have been grateful for those few weeks together.

About three days before we were due to leave Dominica, my father and I were having breakfast together. There was a difference in my father's manner—an extra satisfaction in the way he smiled, and in the way he spoke, and several times I found him looking at me with a sort of gleam in his eye. I had a feeling there was something in the wind, and then I decided he was just happy because we had had such a nice time together and, although we were about to go our separate ways, he was feeling pleased, as I was, that we'd had a close companionship for a few weeks.

We had just finished breakfast when a boat from the *Greyhound* pulled alongside. The man at the steering oar yelled up to us, calling to my father, "Captain Gomes! Captain Gomes! We have orders to take you and Joe over to Captain Corey's ship—over to the *Clark*."

"All right," my father answered, "we'll be right down."

We went down to the cabin and got caps and coats, climbed

down and got into the boat. In a few minutes we were aboard the *Clark,* and the first thing I noticed was that the quarter-deck was covered with people, mostly captains and their wives. There were Captains Corey of the *Clark,* Mandley of the *Margaret,* Tony Edwards of the *Wanderer,* John Edwards of the *Carleton Belle,* Hagerty of the *Alice Knowles,* with his wife and three children, the captain of the *Viola* and his wife, and several others whom I didn't know or didn't specifically remember. And, of course, there was Captain Corvello with Mary. I think all the skippers from the whaling fleet were there. They all greeted us, and Mary gave me a little hug and a kiss as she always did. I think she would do that if we met fifty times a day. She whispered in my ear, "Joe, I have some good news for you." Only, she didn't tell me what it was; just sort of hung onto my arm and steered me over to where a group of men were talking—all captains whom I knew, including my father.

What had happened previously was that Mr. Jones, who was first mate on the *Alice Knowles,* had been quite sick during the last season, and was getting no better. To replace him, Captain Hagerty had to have a man of experience who was both a good whaler and a man who was capable of handling a bark. Our second mate on the *Greyhound,* Mr. Cruz, was just such a man, and since the only source of getting such a man there in Dominica was from the whaling fleet itself, Mr. Cruz was a natural for the position. Captain Hagerty had talked it over with Captain Corvello who, though he was a rugged man to work with, would never stand in the way of any man's promotion—not even in the way of a man as valuable as Mr. Cruz.

Captain Corvello had talked it over with our first mate, Mr. Frates, and apparently they had had quite a discussion. For the next problem was to replace Mr. Cruz with someone whom Mr. Frates could depend upon. It could mean a shift all the way down to the fourth mate and the boat steerers.

Mr. Cruz actually didn't want to go. He liked the *Greyhound* and he was a close friend of Mr. Frates. He liked everybody and everybody liked him—one of the reasons, no doubt, that Captain Hagerty selected him.

Captain Corvello and Mr. Frates finally convinced him it was the thing to do; that he was wholly capable of going first mate, and that for his own good and for the sake of his family it was the only thing to do. In the first place, it was a definite promotion, and in the second place, the pay was better and the job provided a much better lay. The lay, in whaling terminology, is the portion of the ship's profit that goes to the individual members of the crew at the end of the voyage. A first mate's lay was about one-seventeenth or one-eighteenth, as compared to a second mate's of about one twenty-eighth. The lay would vary according to the size of the ship, the number of the crew, and the number of boats. The *Alice Knowles* was a larger ship, but she was at that time only a four-boater. At one time she had been a five-boater. Now, though only a four-boater, she could carry more oil than the *Greyhound* if she was lucky enough to get it. However, any ship, regardless of capacity, would have no grounds for complaint if she filled equal to the *Greyhound*.

Mary steered me into the middle of the group of captains. Captain Tony Edwards, who was sort of a far-away cousin of mine, gave me a pat on the back. Captain Mandley, who was always fooling with me anyway, slapped me on my seat and ruffled my hair. The captains spread out and I was left standing a little in front, inside the circle. Mary was just back of me with my father, and Captain Corvello was in front. There was a moment of almost awkward silence, and then Captain Corvello cleared his throat as if he were going to make one of those short speeches.

"Joe," he said, "you know Mr. Cruz is going first mate on the *Alice Knowles*. We talked it all over yesterday and last night. It's made several problems. He's a good mate and we hate to lose him, but it has all been decided, and you are to go second mate on the *Greyhound* in Mr. Cruz's place."

I was dumbfounded. Everybody was looking at me. I looked back at my father. He had that same gleam in his eye that I had noticed at breakfast, only more so, and he was grinning so that he had to shift his plug of tobacco. Mary was actually crying with joy.

"Oh, no," I finally blurted out. "I'm boat steerer and I like my job. I know how to do it. I'm happy where I am. I'm not going any second mate. Anyway, there's a third mate and a fourth mate, and you don't need me for second mate."

"Joe," he repeated. "It has all been decided. Mr. Frates convinced me you are ready for it. I am master of this ship and as long as Mr. Frates says you are ready, it is okay with me. Captain Corey is part-owner and he says you are ready. Your father is part-owner, and he does not object. It has been decided. You are now second mate. That's orders and there's nothing you can do about it." He sort of waved his hands. The whole affair was over and dismissed. Mary grabbed me and gave me a big hug and kiss. Captain Mandley raised me clear off the deck and set me down again. Captain Corey shook my hand and gave me a hard squeeze with his other arm around my shoulders. My father took hold of both my arms and said, "Joe, you'll make a good second mate. I know I can depend on you, and you're going to be a captain before too long. I'm sure of that. Captain Corvello told me he'd make a captain out of you, and I know he's going to do it."

Everybody congratulated me. I walked around for awhile. I felt kind of funny. After all, it was quite a shock. When Mary told me she had good news for me I never expected anything like being made a second mate. If it had been at the end of the voyage, I might have expected it—or when a new crew was being shipped. But this was different, and I didn't understand it until I heard more about what had actually happened.

At the conference the night before, Mr. Frates, as usual, took my part right away. When Captain Corvello brought up the question of replacing the second mate, Mr. Frates spoke right up. "I want Joe. Joe is ready for it. He isn't afraid of whales. He isn't afraid of anybody. I've let him stay in the bow a couple of times and kill a couple of cow whales." Captain Corvello didn't feel it was quite right to go over the third and fourth mates. When shipping a new crew, on a new voyage, it would have been perfectly all right.

Captain Corey had agreed that as long as Mr. Frates wanted me it was all right with him. As part-owner, he would throw in his vote for me. He relied completely on Mr. Frates' judgment and opinion. Then Captain Corey asked my father, who was also part-owner, how he felt about it. My father simply said that it was entirely up to the captain. He would not vote for me just because I was his son, nor would he stand in my way. It was up to the master of the ship. Captain Tony Edwards made the remark that such things had been done before and that three of the ship's four owners were present, one of whom was my father. He said that anyway everyone knew I was going to be captain before many years went by. And then Captain Tony Edwards had said to Captain Corvello, "Tony, sure Joe is your brother-in-law, and he has given you some trouble, but probably you would do the same thing if your brother-in-law were captain on the same ship you were on. What do you say, Tony?" So that was the way they left it. Everyone who had said anything was in favor, and no one had spoken a word against me.

Captain Corvello accepted it as the wish of the majority, and in spite of the fact that I felt he was very rough on me, I believe he was really glad to have the opportunity to give me such a big boost toward the goal of my becoming captain.

Before I left the *Clark* to go back to the *Greyhound,* Captain Corvello called me and said, "Joe, you'd better go and talk to Mr. Frates right away, about your boat steerer. He has to have a new boat steerer for his boat, and you be sure you don't pick the same man for your boat."

I walked forward and went down into the hold where the second mate on the *Clark* was stowing away oil from the bark *Bertha*. I talked to him for a little while, and then Captain Corey called me. "Joe, how do you like it?"

"I don't like it," I answered. "I'm too young. I know what the second mate's job is. I'm not any good for the stage. I'm not strong enough to swing a spade."

"Oh, the heck you aren't. You're as strong as the fourth mate, and he does it. You're all right. You won't be sorry, Joe." We walked around together for a while, and Mary and Rosina came over to us. Rosina came at me with her arms wide open.

"Joe, you sweet thing, you. I'm so glad you are going second mate." And she kissed me right then and there. I was a little embarrassed because her father saw us, but he was a good scout—he didn't let on he'd even seen us.

I went ashore in the first boat and went directly to the restaurant where Linda worked and told her the good news. Most of the fellows from the *Greyhound* were there. Mr. Frates had told someone, and word spreads rapidly aboard a ship. They knew where to find me after four o'clock when they came ashore, and they were all there to congratulate me. I don't think one of them missed. It made me feel good to know that they were glad for me, but I didn't yet feel quite happy about it. I guess it was because of the third mate—it didn't seem quite fair somehow. Anyway, when the third mate came ashore that evening he also congratulated me, and I told him, "Gee, I'm sorry, but that was none of my doings."

"Of course, Joe. We all know that. We have all known about it. From here you will go captain. We've seen that before. We know you are a good navigator and that if anything happens to our captain—if he gets sick or anything—you'll be our captain. There isn't anything to be sorry about. We are all happy for you and we are all your friends. We will all be back of you."

Well, his little speech made me feel very good. I knew then that I had really been worried about how he would take it. In fact he put me so much at ease that all at once I realized that I was beginning to feel important, and I reminded myself that I'd have to watch out or I'd be acting like I had the big head.

Of course, being at the restaurant as all this went on, Linda took it all in. I think she was extra nice that evening, and when we got away by ourselves later I think she was closer to me than ever before. I had always given her a little money before we left port—twenty dollars or so, which was a good deal in Dominica. Perhaps, now that I was promoted, she might feel that I should add a little to it. Anyway she seemed to be sincerely happy for me and it made me feel good indeed, after all the congratulations from the crew.

We had only another day to stay in port. We had just about finished with the casks. In fact there were only two left to settle down in the main hatch, and we did that the next forenoon. The mate ordered the hatch closed and the deck washed, but he told me not to stay on board—that I'd better go over to see my father. "Joe," he said. "You'd better spend as much time with your father as possible, and you know this is our last day in port." My father came by just then and we all went to see Captain Corey on our way to the dock. I stayed with my father for quite a while, and I think he gave me all the advice he thought I would listen to. I'm afraid I was just cocky enough that it showed a little bit. After all, I was still just a kid, and going from boat steerer to second mate was a pretty big jump. I did know that it would never have happened if I had not worked hard and (more important still) studied hard and learned to become a good navigator. As I look back, I realize that any kid in my place would have felt pretty darned important at that particular moment.

I spent the whole day ashore. Linda's mother told the owner of the restaurant that we were busy and that Linda wouldn't be in that evening. We spent the evening walking around and doing a little love-making. I thought a lot of her and we were very good friends. She was a nice little sweetheart to have in an otherwise lonely port. She was probably a mulatto, but very light, and she had the appearance and the ways of a white girl. No serious thoughts, such as marriage, ever entered my mind. I was too young, anyway, to be serious about any girl. After all, I had no money nor means to give cause for such ideas. I was young, and life was full of interest and adventure. We were good friends, lighthearted sweethearts, and that was that.

When I left her that night, I emptied my pockets of money and gave it all to her—about seventy dollars. To her it was a small fortune. To me it was just stuff that I had no use for during the next six months at sea. I wasn't going ashore at Santastatia, and I could draw some money when we got to Fayal. Why carry the stuff around when it could make someone very happy? My one ambition was to become a sea captain, and money had little to do with it.

I went to pick up my father at the hotel as soon as I left Linda, and I went on the run. I hadn't realized how late it was—almost twelve o'clock, but father was waiting. There were three or four other skippers with him, sipping liquor of course, but everyone else, including Captain Corvello and Mary, had gone to bed. I bade good-by to the other skippers, as I didn't expect to see them again for a long time. Some of them, including my father, were on the short two-season voyage, and would be returning to the United States. Father didn't like to go on those long voyages any more, so he spent most of the summer on the North Atlantic and then went to Flores in the winter, or stayed in New Bedford. Why, I don't know, but this year he had done differently, starting in the North Atlantic in the fall for a short while, then going down across the Equator where he'd made a good winter season with a catch of over eleven hundred barrels. All he had to do now was to finish the season on the North Atlantic and go on home to spend the winter with my mother in Flores.

CHAPTER XXVI

TIDAL WAVE

The next morning was time for departure. One of the boat steerers from the bark *Fairhaven* took us over to the *Greyhound*. As I had a lot of new duties to perform, I left my father with Captain Corvello and Mary. First I had to get my clothing and belongings moved to my second mate's cabin. Moving into a room all my own was a new experience. The third and fourth mates shared a two-bunk room, so the process of moving into my own room helped greatly to strengthen the feeling that I had really moved up in the world. I did a few other things, and then asked Mr. Frates if there was anything in particular he wanted me to do. "No," he said. "I don't think the captain intends to sail until after lunch, so there's no hurry, and I want you to spend the time with your father."

"Would you mind if I went first to the *Morning Star* and said good-by to the captain's daughter? She has been very nice to me."

"I know what you mean, Joe. Go ahead, boy."

The second mate's boat, stripped of whaling gear, is always the work boat, and was on the water ready for use. I called four fellows for the oars. On whaling ships, if an officer wants one man, he calls, "One!" If he wants two, he calls, "Two!" and so on. I called "Four!" and told them what I wanted. Very shortly, I was aboard the *Morning Star*. The captain had seen me coming and was waiting on deck. He said they were getting ready to say good-by to Mary, so I asked, "Do you want me to take you over in my boat?"

"Oh, no," he answered. "You folks are going out to sea, so I'll go in my own boat and you won't have to bring me back."

"Well, there's no need of my going down to say good-by to Rosina then."

"Oh, sure. Go on down. She is expecting you, anyway," so I went down and we kissed a couple of times, but that was all, for we didn't know when the captain might come down. Rosina knew she was going over to say good-by to Mary, anyway. I went back to my boat and over to the *Greyhound,* and spent the rest of the forenoon with my father. Several captains had come aboard and Mr. Cruz was with them. He had come over to say good-by. He acted like someone who was leaving home. I know that I was really sorry to see him go.

Soon it was time to depart. Mr. Frates said, "I'm going to heave up anchor, so get the captain's orders on what sails he wants out and have them unfurled."

I called all hands up. Mr. Frates took a few to heave up the anchor—the chain had already been shortened—and we set sails and left Dominica. I was out on the wide blue sea on my first trip as second mate. I was trying hard not to show how important I felt, as I didn't want to be criticized for being a swell-head, and I guess I must have succeeded fairly well because everything went smoothly and I soon felt that I fitted into my new position. The men accepted me as though I belonged. In fact, as though I had never been anything other than second mate.

On the passage from Dominica to Santastatia the wind is off the starboard quarter, so we set everything except the outer sails. We didn't want to get to Santastatia too early next morning. It was something new to me not to have to stand watch. I spent most of the time around the quarter-deck with Mary and Mr. Frates and the captain, who was sometimes on deck and sometimes below, until it was time to say good night and go to bed.

When I got into my own bunk in my own room and stretched out, I began thinking to myself, "Joe, you're getting to be somebody. Here you are on a passage, without standing watch. Isn't that wonderful!" With these happy thoughts I dropped off to sleep, while we kept on sailing down in the lee of the islands on the smooth sea, almost as a steamer moves, with just a perceptible roll.

I slept so soundly that when I awoke it took me a moment to realize that we were under way. The ship was rolling a little and I could hear the squealing of the tackles and the main and fore braces. I didn't know what time it was but I got up and went out of the cabin. It was too early to get up, so I went back to bed, but I couldn't sleep. I came up on deck. The fourth mate was on watch so I stayed with him for a while and then went over to the carpenter's bench where the two boat steerers were on watch. After that, I went to the fo'c's'le head and talked to Harry. He had been very happy that I'd made second mate and he congratulated me heartily and sincerely. Up to now, I hadn't picked a boat steerer. In a way, because of all the help he had given me in studying English, I wanted him. Though I didn't feel that he was quite the man for the job, the sense of personal obligation was strong. I didn't say anything about it, one way or the other. I decided not to, until I had talked with the mate. He, Mr. Frates, came up about six o'clock. I went to the galley and got two cups of coffee—one for Mr. Frates and one for myself. As soon as we sat down, I said, "Mr. Frates, will you please give me some advice on picking a boat steerer?"

"No, Joe. You do your own picking."

"But, Mr. Frates, I have so much confidence in you that I wish you'd advise me. You know, Harry has been very good to me and he has done me a lot of favors."

"Yes, Joe, but this is different. In picking a boat steerer you are not picking a man for yourself. You are picking a man for the ship, for the captain, and for the ship's owners, and for the rest of us. You must have a man who can harpoon whales; one who can steer so that you can kill them; someone who can use good judgment and not be reckless with the boat and the crew."

"Yes, Mr. Frates, but I owe Harry so many favors that I didn't have the guts to put him out of my mind."

"That's true, Joe, but that is personal and this is not a personal matter. I don't think Harry is the proper man. I don't think he'd be good for killing whales."

"That's just why I came to you, Mr. Frates. I didn't want to go to the captain because, regardless of what I would say to him, he would bawl me out. So I would rather take it up with you."

"All right, Joe. You know that little guy that catches the turtles?"

"Yes, I do. His name is Joe, same as mine."

"Well, I think he would make a good boat steerer. He is short, stocky, and very much like you. He is very lively and not afraid of anything. I don't think he'd be afraid of the devil. He is quick and he's very smart. I think he would make you a good boat-steerer. I had him in mind myself, but I took Mr. Cruz's boat steerer instead."

I went up in the fo'c's'le head. Joe was drinking coffee. I sat down with him and said, "Joe, would you like to be my boat steerer?"

"Would I! Yes, sir."

"Look, Joe, when we're alone you don't have to say 'yes, sir.' Of course, if the captain is around, you do, but otherwise, no; so start getting the boat ready. It's dirty from being used as the work boat, and all the gear has to be put back. Check everything. I'll help you as soon as we get to Santastatia. I'm not going ashore there, so we'll have most of today and tomorrow to get it shipshape. Good luck."

Joe was just about the happiest guy I ever saw. He shook my hand and even wanted to embrace me, but I objected. He rushed down and told everybody. It wasn't more than five minutes later, when I was back on the quarter-deck with Mr. Frates, that I saw Joe moving to the steerage with both arms full of his belongings. His enthusiasm never lagged. Mr. Frates was pleased with the choice, as was everyone else, for Joe proved to be one of the best. He was attentive and responsible, and everything in his boat was always shipshape. I was always glad that I had picked him.

Santastatia was showing up dead ahead. As we were finishing breakfast, the captain said, "Well, it's no use to try to make any record trip, so you might as well clew up the foresail and mainsail." You see, in coming in to anchor, you never furl the sails until the anchor hits bottom, because you never know when you might have to use the sails to stop the ship. I relayed the order to the men. We slowed down some, and soon the captain ordered the headsails taken in, except the forestaysail and the spanker. The spanker topsail hadn't been out at all, neither had the topgallant sails. As we came in to anchor, the first mate stood by, waiting for the captain's order. It came a moment later. "Stand by to drop the starboard anchor.'" Why the captain preferred the starboard anchor to the port anchor, I never knew. They were both the same weight. In order to haul back the ship on the anchor, you slack the lee fore-braces and haul on the weather fore-braces, which turns the yards the opposite way, allowing the wind to hit from forward. This acts as a brake does on a car, or in the same manner as reversing the propeller on a steamer. As soon as we had hauled back on the anchor, the mate ordered me to take in the topsails. Then followed the order to furl all sails. Everything was made fast and put shipshape. The doctor came aboard with the customs officials in due time, and the captain and Mary then prepared to go ashore.

Mary called me and asked if I wanted to go along, but I said, "No, it wouldn't be a good idea. Mr. Frates wouldn't mind, but the rest of the crew might not understand. I don't want anybody to think I have any special privileges, so let's keep it out of the family altogether. Anyway, I don't know any girls, so what's the use of going ashore?"

I stayed aboard, and they returned before dark. Next day, they went ashore again, as they had been invited to dinner with some old friends of the captain's. Again, Mary asked me if I wanted to go. But I declined, saying, "No. Anyway I have a lot of work to do on my boat. Joe is new and I don't trust him too much yet."

Naturally, I wanted everything to be perfect for my first strike at a whale after making second mate. One never knew how soon we might raise whales after leaving Santastatia. By afternoon my boat was in top shape, and I spent the rest of the afternoon with the three mates, playing cards, mostly; no gambling, though. Mr. Frates was too sensible to gamble, and I followed his example.

Early the next morning, right after breakfast, we unfurled sails, picked up anchor, and went around the lee side of Santastatia, out into the blue yonder of the North Atlantic. The captain thought that, instead of sailing straight into the Western Grounds, he would keep to the windward a little and see if we could raise some whales on the grounds off the West Indies.

We were out of Santastatia three or four days, going under full sail, when one of those incidents happened that—for old sailors—usually is the inspiration for all kinds of tales of the unusual: ships mysteriously lost at sea, and such.

It was full moon, or nearly so, and we were sailing through the upper part of the Sargasso Sea. The weather was warm. All four portholes, the two opening into the captain's cabin, the one in the mate's cabin, and the one in the linen closet, were open. The big door in the middle, which opened into the dining room facing forward, was wide open. The sky was clear, the sea smooth, and we had a northwesterly wind at our beam. We were on the starboard tack, sailing by the wind. In other words, close hauled. I was talking to the third mate and had not yet gone to bed.

We saw a white squall coming, but paid no attention to it. We were running away from it, and sailing as we were with all sails set, all that would happen would be that we'd pick up a little more speed.

The squall struck. There wasn't too much wind with it. The ship listed a little more and we picked up a little speed. We were going eight or ten knots.

I was walking toward the carpenter's bench at the waist of the ship and had reached a point between the main hatch and the main rigging when suddenly the bow of the ship lifted, up and up, as though some terrific force were standing the ship on end. Then it came down, and the bow, with the jib boom pointing the way, simply dived right into the ocean. The whole ship shuddered and trembled as though she were making a supreme effort to rise. Her head came up. A surging wall of water rushed back toward the quarter-deck. The sailors on deck instinctively dived for the rigging and clung to it. I made a beeline for the main rigging where the lines are fastened, and started climbing into it. I heard the three pigs squeal in terror and the sheep made about the most piteous cry I've ever heard. The chickens—I always called them egg machines—just squawked. On shipboard, whoever got the eggs first could keep them. I was always watching for them so as to give them to Mary. As soon as I heard the animals cry out in helpless terror, I wound my arms and legs around the lines and clung to them with every ounce of strength I possessed. The water struck. It washed over me. I felt as though I were having a horrible nightmare and couldn't get to the surface. Then I felt air again as the water washed off and spilled across the quarter-deck, down the open door, through the portholes of the quarter-deck's forward wall, and out over the sides and the stern, back into the ocean.

I heard a couple of muffled, gurgling screams as the water spouted through the porthole directly over the captain's bed. Of course, I didn't know what had happened. I only heard Mary's screams and what sounded like a couple of muffled curses from the captain. The ship began to rise again. Again it plunged, but this time it did not scoop up a shipload of water; only a little water washed over the bow and sloshed down the deck. I dropped down onto the deck from the rigging and ran toward the captain's cabin to see what had happened to Mary. I met Mr. Frates coming up from his cabin with a lantern. "Joe, what happened?"

"We hit a tidal wave, I think, but I guess we're still right-side-up. I heard Mary scream." And I ran on to the door of the captain's cabin. The captain was coming out. "What happened?" he gasped, still coughing from the water he had taken in.

"Is Mary all right?"

"She's half-drowned but she's all right. The cabin is knee-deep in water."

We went back to see what damage had been done on deck. The potato bin was gone. There was no trace of the livestock, except one scared sheep that had been washed squarely through the open door and down the steps into the dining room.

CHAPTER XXVII

FREE SHOW AT SEA

We were sailing along on somewhat shortened sails a couple of days later, due to a strong wind and heavy seas. It was really pretty rough going, but we were still standing masthead watches, for it has to be almost impossible to launch a whaleboat before the captain will call them off. In fact, in all my whaling experience, I never saw the masthead watches called off but once.

We were just entering the Western Ground when the watch raised whales up ahead off the port side. We hauled pretty close to port and slacked off the lee braces, at the same time getting the whaleboats ready. The truth is, I was hoping the skipper wouldn't send us out in that weather—not that I was afraid of it (actually I was very anxious to get my first chance at a whale as second mate), but I was afraid we would smash against the ship and wreck the whaleboats while getting away or while getting back on the ship.

Of course, it takes only two or three minutes to get ready, so the captain gave orders to stand by to lower. We could see only one spout, quite a distance away. With that wind, and sails set, we could get to the whale much faster in the whaleboats, literally flying from wave to wave. We got away without incident and went for the whale with only the mainsail set. It was too rough to use the jib.

The whale turned flukes and went down. It stayed down for about thirty or forty minutes, indicating that it was not a very large one, since a larger bull would stay down from fifty to seventy minutes. It came up right ahead of us, just off our starboard. I held in the sheet, put the rudder over, and sailed for it.

When you go alongside a whale like that, in rough weather especially, you go on the lee side if possible. The whale wasn't running directly into the wind. Therefore, I sailed right up on it. As we closed in, I gave Joe the usual, "Let 'im have it!"

It was, of course, Joe's first whale as boat steerer, and he was just as eager to strike it as I was to kill it. He buried that first harpoon to the hitches. There was no time to strike with the second. Almost at the instant the harpoon struck, the whale half breached and ran, which was a good thing to have happen as it gave Joe and me time to change ends, as well as time enough to get the mast down and the sail stowed away. Then Joe took a turn around the loggerhead and snubbed the line.

All this time, the ship was coming closer. It was only about a mile away when the whale ran and took off in the opposite direction. We had only about one-third of the big tub of line out, but the next thing to do was to get close. That whale was taking us on a real Nantucket Sleigh Ride. We were simply jumping from one wave to another, just hitting the crests as we went. I don't know how long it continued—only that the *Greyhound* was hull-down with nothing but the topsails in sight, when we noticed a steamer fairly close by. As we approached, the whale slowed down. I don't know why, unless perhaps it was because of the sound of the propellers. We were probably about a mile away when we first noticed the ship. It must have been a second-class passenger ship, because it had only one and a half decks above the main deck. We could see the passengers lined up along the rail. By the time we got close to the whale, the ship was so close that we could see that the passengers were taking pictures with cameras and watching us with glasses. It must have been quite a sight for them, for they followed right along. The weather was rough, so I don't believe they even slowed down. We were heading right into the wind and so was the steamer. The waves were flying right over the steamer's bow. It must have been quite a show for the passengers, with that little boat looking like a mosquito attacking the whale. The steamer stayed right with us.

In later years, when I had more experience on steamers, I realized that since the waves were flying over her bow, she was driving to keep up with us. Except for the steamer, we were all alone. The third and fourth mates' boats were out of sight. The first mate's boat we glimpsed occasionally, as it came up on a wave in the distance. By the time we pulled on top of the whale, I had the darting gun across the bow, and the shoulder gun ready also in case we didn't get near enough to use the darting gun; both were loaded, ready for instant use.

When the flukes were about at the middle of the boat, I "let 'im have it" with the darting gun. The whale shook as if there had been an earthquake. Its hump and flukes quivered with the shock, and down it went, probably two or three hundred feet. To my great good fortune, it came up spouting blood. The steamer wasn't more than three hundred yards away by this time, and I was calling them all kinds of damn fools—to send them away—

though of course they couldn't hear me. There was no telling what direction a dying whale would take, or what it would do. It might foul up the ship's propeller or rudder and put the ship completely out of use. But, fortunately, the whale was dying fast. It quickly became so tame that it couldn't get out of its own way.

When it was apparent that I had finished it with the lance, the steamer gave us a salute with three short blasts and headed back on its course, with the passengers cheering and waving as it went. It gave me a good warm feeling to have made such a lucky, perfect hit with the darting gun. From a different angle, the shot could have gone right through without doing much damage to the whale, and that crazy steamer might have been crippled when it was right in the middle of the ocean. I felt that it was my lucky day. Certainly, too, not everyone could have such an enthusiastic gallery to witness the killing of a new second mate's first whale.

The other boats soon caught up with us. Mr. Frates was first, and he congratulated both Joe and me as soon as he came alongside. He remarked, "What will the old man say now?" I couldn't help grinning as I replied, "I had an awfully good teacher."

The first mate's boat and mine soon had the dead whale in tow and we had been rowing for some little time when the third and fourth mates' boats caught up with us, followed shortly after by the *Greyhound*. The wind had subsided somewhat, but the sea was still very rough and I knew it was going to be a tricky and difficult job to get the boats back on the davits without damage. With the ship rolling and pitching as it was, a whaleboat could be smashed like an eggshell.

As soon as we were within hailing distance, the captain called to me through the megaphone. "Joe, cut your boat loose and come alongside first." He then proceeded to tack ship so that the starboard side would be the lee side while we got my boat up on deck. The other three boats were always carried on the port side, so I could see that his maneuver was planned to get my boat and crew on deck while the starboard side was leeward, giving us as much protection as possible. Then, with my crew to assist, the whale could also be secured in its proper position on the starboard side, taking advantage of the leeward position.

As I went around the stern of the ship, I realized that I had never been out in a whaleboat in any rougher weather. The stern of the *Greyhound* was pitching and heaving as much as I'd ever seen it do. I didn't anticipate getting my boat back on the davits with anything but a great sense of apprehension.

"Pass up your bow line and keep it slack," ordered the captain. This would keep the boat from dropping back, but wouldn't snub the bow too close in.

"Pass down the tackles," the captain ordered the ship's keepers, half of whom were standing at each of the falls, "and stand by." The last part of the order was to everyone. Each man had a job to do and was standing poised and ready for action.

The captain waited, watching the weather and the sea for the opportune moment. "Hook on and hoist away!" Instantly, my boat steerer hooked on to the forward block and I hooked on to the after block. Two men with long-staffed boat hooks fended the boat off the ship's side, so that it wouldn't crash against the ribbing strip. The two remaining men assisted in the fending operation with the oars. The men on deck heaved just as the boat came up to its highest lift at the crest of the wave, and we were off the water. Quickly, the men with the boat hooks and oars stowed them away and climbed on deck to give a hand with the falls. In another minute, the boat was lowered onto the cranes and secured.

With the men in my crew on board to help, we soon had the whale properly secured on the starboard side. The captain tacked again, giving the port side the leeward position, and put out more sails to give the ship a little headway, as the slightest increase in speed reduced the rolling and pitching considerably. The first mate's boat was soon hoisted up and, with the added crew, the task of hoisting up the third and fourth mates' boats was easy enough. The whole operation was completed without incident. Apparently, I wasn't the only one who felt a sense of relief as the final boat—the fourth mate's—was secured. I distinctly heard the captain say aloud, "Thank the Lord for that," followed by an order that *everyone* heard: "All hands aft to splice the main brace."

The sea was too rough for us to start cutting, so we hove to and settled down for the night.

Mary had been a keenly interested spectator from the moment

the whale had been sighted. For the first few hours, she had been exceedingly worried. Just as things began to quiet down that night, she came to me and said, "Oh, Joe, I'm so happy. I was terribly worried, and now everything is all right. You did so well and Tony is awfully pleased. I know he is going to tell you." Then in her own words she explained how things had gone on board from the moment the captain's order, "Stand by to lower," had been relayed to all the crew from end to end on shipboard.

"Tony," she narrated, "grabbed his glasses when he heard the cry, 'There she blows,' took a quick look, and said, half-aloud, 'She isn't too far away.' Then he gave the order, 'Stand by to lower,' and he was already starting to climb up to masthead before the first mate got down. He stayed up there and watched, all the time you were waiting for the whale to come up again, and didn't come down until you'd got fast and had gone out of sight. When he came down, he looked kind of worried and I asked him, 'Is something wrong, Tony?' and he said, 'Joe got fast to that goddam whale and it took off before Mr. Frates or the other boats could get up to him. He's all alone with it, and in this rough weather they'll never catch him. He'll have to kill it all by himself.' He went down and took his customary swig but he couldn't settle down and went back up to masthead, where he stayed until he sighted you towing the whale. Then he yelled down, 'Mary, they've got it; they've got it okay.' And, oh, Joe," she repeated, "would you believe that Tony said you did a nice job on that whale?"

"Good," I answered, "I think I did, anyway."

"Yes, you did, and Mr. Frates praised you a lot when he got the old man alone—and your boat steerer did, too. Tony is really very pleased with the way things are turning out."

A few minutes later, the captain joined us. The first thing he said was, "Well done, Joe. You did a nice job on your first whale, and it was pretty rough weather, too. I am very glad we chose you for second mate." That was another of the very few times he ever praised me, and as I went down to my cabin it was with the feeling that the killing of my first whale had been a successful and exciting experience, and that I'd had a very busy day.

CHAPTER XXVIII

THE CAPTAIN'S FESTIVAL

The wind kept going down all during the night and by morning conditions were fairly good to start cutting. I soon found that my earlier misgivings about handling the work on the cutting stage were ill-founded. I discovered that I could handle it very nicely, and I liked it much better than handling blanket pieces up on deck. By the middle of the afternoon, we had the blubber and the spermaceti on board. Of course, my next job was to fire up the try works. I knew well enough how to do it and found it to be no chore. The third mate gave me a hand. While the blubber is being hoisted on board, the third mate has about the dirtiest job of all, excepting perhaps the boat steerer, who goes over the side.

The third mate is then constantly under and handling those wet, slimy, greasy, dripping blanket pieces. I was always just a little bit glad that I had skipped being third mate.

We set watches again, and as soon as the fires were going satisfactorily, I turned the try works over to the mate on watch and went back to my cabin to change my clothes before going down to dinner. Having dinner in the cabin was a new experience and I had enjoyed it thoroughly ever since being appointed second mate. As boat steerer, I was used to the little table, actually nothing more than a wide, hinged shelf that swung down from the partition separating the steerage from the cabin. Even that had been a step up from the lot of the sailor. As a sailor on the *Pedro Varella*, I had done exactly as the rest: grabbed my tin plate, tin cup, spoon, knife and fork, got my food and gone to whatever place best suited my fancy—the carpenter's bench, the fo'c's'le head, some place on deck or, in stormy weather, down in the fo'c's'le.

The dining table in the cabin of the *Greyhound* was large enough to serve ten people. I felt that this was really in a class by itself. Sitting down to a table with the captain and his wife and the three other mates made me feel almost as though I had stepped into a new world. The places were set just as at a hotel, with dishes, and the steward brought down the food (the same as that provided for all the crew) on platters or in bowls and set it in the middle of the table where everyone could help himself. Here there was conversation, too, and this evening it turned, naturally, to the incident of the whale just killed. The captain again surprised me with a pretty direct bit of praise. He remarked, "Well, I guess Mr. Frates knew what he was talking about when he insisted on choosing Joe for second mate." I was terribly pleased and a little proud, too, and most of all I enjoyed the expression of happiness on Mary's face. It filled out for me what I thought was another perfect day.

My masthead watch was now on the mainmast, twice daily, to relieve the mate on watch. After two or three days, we raised some more whales and kept on having pretty good luck. We went to a small whaling ground called forty-forty: forty north and forty west. From there we went to the Western Grounds. Captain Corvello always seemed to have better luck there than anywhere. In July, we got one school of seven cows and another of six, but no bulls. By the middle of August, we had almost a full ship. The old man remarked one day that it wouldn't be long before we were back in Flores. "Yes," I said, "we haven't got much more to go. There are only a few casks left and they are full of water. I don't think we should depend on just one cask."

"We are going to pull toward Flores," he said. "I will take in sails at night but in the daytime we will get under way pretty well."

This we did, and during the last week in August we sighted

Flores. The captain told Mr. Frates to pick us up in five days. Shortly after that, Captain Corvello, Mary and I went ashore. I had hoped to have a week, but it was a God's gift to be in Flores for even five days. I hadn't realized before quite how proud Mary was that I was second mate. She told everyone she met, and she must have repeated about a hundred times, "Don't you know that Joe is second mate, and has been doing very well? He's been killing a lot of whales. Only the first mate got one more whale than Joe in the whole season!" Lucy didn't want to believe it. "Is that really correct, Joe?" she asked. "I don't really know, Lucy," I answered. "I really never kept count. I never paid any attention to how many whales I got. If Mary said so, she probably kept count, but I didn't."

Of course this all took place right there on the dock at Fajangrand. The ship had been sighted at Fajazinha first thing in the morning, and by the time we landed, half the village was there to greet us. Of course, too, Lucy was one of the first to get to the dock and was waiting there as we pulled in. I didn't wait on courtesy to the captain or anybody. I just jumped ashore and grabbed that sweet girl and kissed her and headed up the street at the head of the parade. I didn't wait for Mary. After all, she had the captain and a lot of friends to give her a hand, and I was busy hugging and kissing my girl for the first few minutes, anyway. When we got in front of the church at the center of the village, I said to Lucy, "Come on, let's go in. I promised Our Lady I would say a prayer if she helped me killing whales and, my goodness, she certainly did." We went in and knelt down and said a little prayer and when we came out the first part of the parade had gone by. We kept on going toward Fajazinha, and the greetings and huggings and kissing started all over again. Everyone I knew was glad to see me, and I was glad to see them. Lucy's mother, brothers and sisters had all met us before we got to Lucy's house. In fact, as I recall, the boys and girls were right at the dock behind Lucy.

Mary was the real center of attraction. She had grown up there and was loved by everyone. This was her first time home since getting married. One little sister clung to each arm. (They were sweet little girls, anyway.) A flock of friends surrounded her from the moment she landed. Captain Corvello soon gave up trying to walk with her, and he walked along with some of his old friends.

Mary had to keep repeating how well I'd done as second mate, and it wasn't long until I felt like quite a celebrity. The school children came out to greet us, and the usual crowd was at my father's house and in the village square by the time we got there. The greetings continued.

You shake hands only with the men. The girls and women all kiss you. That is, if you are a native son. Our arrival was quite an occasion and gave us a very good time. Mary was as happy as anyone could be.

My mother had made a huge pile of sandwiches and lots of coffee. It was really quite a homecoming celebration. Lucy stayed at home with us to have dinner and afterwards she and I slipped away to the hayloft to make a little love. When we came back an hour or so later, Mary called me and said, "Joe, we have something to tell you."

"Well, let's have it," I replied.

"We're going to have a Holy Ghost Feast next Sunday," she said.

"How come?" I wanted to know.

"Well, remember that first whale you got, out of Santastatia? I was awfully scared and I promised the Holy Ghost that if you caught it and killed it and nobody got hurt, why, Tony would stop here long enough to have a feast for the Holy Ghost. It's all agreed and Tony has already ordered the cattle that are to be killed tomorrow afternoon. We wanted to tell you now because part of the promise was that you would be the crown-bearer. You'll have to carry the crown on Saturday while the bread and meat are being delivered to the houses in the village, and again on Sunday you'll have to be the crown-bearer and carry the crown to the church."

"Well, why didn't you let me in on it before?" I asked, for I would be losing a lot of valuable time with Lucy. This was my first reaction, and then I realized that my remark sounded pretty sharp and that Mary was thinking of what an honor it would be for me to act as crown-bearer in the village. So I followed up quickly with, "Well, thank you. That's quite an honor. So long as the promise is that way, it's quite all right."

So we talked there for a little while. The captain kept looking at her while she was talking and he glanced at me a couple of times, but he didn't say anything or deny anything, so I was sure everything had been settled and that I'd better plan accordingly.

About ten o'clock, I walked Lucy home. My two little sisters wanted to come for the walk with us, so we went into Lucy's house and visited for a little while before going home and to bed. Everybody treated me as sort of a local celebrity and it was quite a pleasant sensation to feel like a big frog in a little puddle.

The next morning, which was Friday, Lucy and two of her sisters came over and asked if they could help. My mother was a good manager and soon had everyone at work getting things ready for the visitors who were expected for Saturday. There would be quite a few from other villages, mostly relatives (some from Fajangrand) including the captain's two sisters, who were his only living relatives on the island. The younger one was a couple of years older than I, and the other one was married. They were very nice girls and I liked them both. Then there would be some of the captain's friends from Santa Cruz. It was going to be quite a gathering next day, Saturday.

The cattle arrived about one o'clock and were taken over to a knoll on the hill—a little grass square that faces the village—where they were to be slaughtered. It was a long time since I had seen such an event, so I went along. I had an enjoyable time, talking with everybody while the cattle were being killed, skinned and quartered.

At about four o'clock, the job was finished. The Holy Ghost musicians came over from the Holy Ghost house. A group of young men came up to carry the meat, each one taking a quarter on his shoulders. The procession accompanied by old-fashioned music and singing, went down to the village square and on to one end of the Holy Ghost house, where the meat was hung up on hooks provided for the occasion. It was quite a procession. Usually four cattle were provided for a feast, but this time the captain had an extra animal killed to allow for the many guests from other villages.

The meat was left to hang there over night. Next morning, a number of people skilled at cutting the meat would come down and get it ready for distribution, and for the Sunday feast. Everybody knows a little about it so everyone helps, and no one works for money. There are always enough people on hand to get the job done in plenty of time.

Meanwhile, the captain had found that there wasn't enough flour in Fajazinha to bake all the bread that would be needed, so he sent five strong young fellows over to Fajangrand to fetch back five hundred pounds.

The flour was brought to my father's house where the women who were to do the baking would come to get as much of it as they could handle. There were at least thirty women to do the baking. They lived close to the village square and had large ovens that were used for such an event. They made two kinds of loaves —round French style, to be eaten at the Sunday feast with sopa, and long loaves to be delivered to the houses. The women were very busy getting everything ready, and my mother was managing everything very capably and smoothly. She had made sure that the men who hadn't gotten their wood ready ahead of time had gone home to get it cut and split so the baking wouldn't be delayed. The men who had their wood ready, or who had nothing else to do, hung around the village square and visited and told tall tales.

Of course, this was still Friday afternoon, rapidly drawing toward dinner time. On such an occasion, no one knew who or how many would be on hand for dinner. There was plenty of salt fish— no meat, of course, on Friday—and lots of fresh vegetables. The women were expert at handling such a situation. The extensions were put on the dining-room table, and I have no idea how many times that table was set. Lucy was helping all this time, so I was not very far away. As soon as the dinner was over, we disappeared. We came back about nine o'clock and Lucy's sisters wanted to know where we had hidden.

"Wait a minute," I said, "that's a secret. Where we hide, nobody will ever be able to find us." Little did they know we were right below them in the basement, on top of the hay, making love. After all, we didn't have much time to spend together so we had to make the most of it.

It was daylight Saturday morning before I realized I'd even been asleep. I tried to sleep a little extra but I wasn't used to sleeping after daylight and I found it impossible to do so now. I got up and went to the Holy Ghost's house and found the men already cutting up the meat.

At about ten o'clock they had finished, and the loaves of long French bread had begun to arrive. The men went to get the priest, and shortly after he came in, the rest of the bread arrived. He blessed the bread and meat, and at about eleven o'clock the distributing began, with its colorful ceremonial procession. It took longer than usual because many of the people in whose homes I appeared with the crown wanted to ask questions. My answers were very brief, but even so we were delayed considerably. By the time I got back to replace the crown on the altar, a good many people from other villages had arrived. I had to talk to everybody because I knew almost everyone. Some of the youngsters I didn't recognize. In a few years they had grown just too fast. Two beautiful girls, grown young women now, looked familiar, but I couldn't place them. I was really surprised when I learned they were my cousins. I hadn't seen them since they were twelve, and I never expected to meet any relatives as good-looking as they had grown to be.

There were a number of officials from Santa Cruz, friends of the captain's, to whom he introduced me. They had come to Fajangrand in a motor launch and had then walked over to Fajazinha. There were the customs officials, a doctor, and two priests from Santa Cruz.

It was quite a problem to find places for all to sleep. The ladies gave my mother and sisters a lot of help and divided the visiting women among them in houses around the village square. Spare beds appeared from everywhere and were set up in the Holy Ghost house for the men. Everyone was finally accommodated.

As soon as we could do so, Lucy and I slipped away. I didn't have to check in at home, and I forgot all about the time. It was almost twelve o'clock when I took Lucy home. I was afraid she would catch the devil from her parents, but she sneaked in without awakening anyone, and she told me the next day that everything was all right.

I got up early Sunday morning and went home for breakfast. My mother and the captain were in the kitchen, talking. The women and girls weren't up yet. The captain saw me through the window and motioned for me to come in and have coffee with them. I remember that my mother said she had told all the girls to come early and clear the beds out of the Holy Ghost house before Mass. They responded nicely, and by nine o'clock everything was cleared out. People began arriving from both directions —from Fajangrand and from Caldeida and Quada. Everybody is welcome at one of those feasts, and the captain expected a very large crowd and had prepared for it. There was going to be plenty of bread, meat, and sopa for everybody.

Mass had been set for ten o'clock. I was the crown-carrier and, with the musicians (I was singing, too) and the girls in their lovely dresses, we formed a procession that must have been quite appealing. I thought the eager, smiling faces of those happy girls made quite a touching sight. I noticed how quiet and attentive the people were as we marched down the aisle and up to the priest with the crown. The great church was filled with people, so I realized there must have been a good many there from neighboring villages. I wondered how tables could be set for so many people for the festival dinner. We continued on down the aisle, and the priest received the crown.

When the Mass was over, he came down to the Holy Ghost house accompanied by the sexton, and replaced the crown on the altar. The village square was full of tables. A lot of benches had been taken from the Holy Ghost house and from the church. Planks had been laid across them, making tables, which were covered with cloths.

Where so much silver and so many plates came from I couldn't imagine. It seemed that they came from the whole village, because there were lots of women and girls who hadn't gone to church.

Mary acted as hostess and directed the families from other villages so that they could sit together. The men were served at the first tables. There were too many people for serving the women and girls too, but the women had it all worked out. As soon as the men finished, each woman or girl who had been serving grabbed a man and put her apron on him. It was good fun and we all enjoyed it. It was really quite all right, and it went off smoothly and beautifully.

Everybody ate. When all had finished, the dishes were picked up by their owners, the tables were taken apart, the benches were set around the square, and everybody began to dance. There were plenty of musicians with guitars and accordions, and they kept four square dances going simultaneously.

At about five o'clock the people began departing. Finally, everyone had gone except our close relatives, who hadn't seen much of us. They stayed until the next day. Between my cousins and Lucy's, I couldn't get one minute alone with her. Every time either one of us got up to move, someone pulled us down. They liked us, and we liked them, so we all spent the evening together and finally everyone went off to bed and that was the end of the festival.

Monday morning, Lucy and her sisters came over for breakfast. We visited some more with our relatives, who intended to leave at about ten o'clock. We all went to Mass, came home and had sandwiches and coffee, and the visitors departed.

The ship was scheduled to leave on Tuesday, so Lucy and I walked around the village and talked to those we knew best. We returned home for dinner, then went to Lucy's house so that I might say good-by to anyone I might not see next morning. And then we disappeared into our haypile for a little rendezvous.

There were quite a few people at the house when we went in later. We visited, and conjectured on the happenings and changes that would occur before we all were together again.

My mother invited Lucy and her sisters and the captain's sisters to have breakfast with us next morning. By nine o'clock we were taking leave. Many people walked to Fajangrand with us, and others waited in front of the church. Others wanted to see the ship and went to the water front with us. The ship was not far out, and the men were rowing in.

We said good-by, boarded the boat to go to the ship. Soon we had the sails set to go around the south end of the island on a northerly breeze, with the course set for Fayal.

Parting in a boat is rather a definite sort of thing—the boat leaves and goes to the ship, and the ship fades away. You expect to be back again, but one never knows when. Friends stand waving, and they get smaller and smaller and less distinct, and time seems to have been left behind with them. You carry away a dream and a memory, and move on into another world.

CHAPTER XXIX

SAILOR'S HOLIDAY

The breeze was too light to make it in one day. Even with all sails set, we never picked up the crown of Pico Island until afternoon. Pico is pretty high, about seven thousand feet, so we still had a good distance to go. We would get in between the two islands at about midnight, and since it was impossible to go in at night, we shortened sails—the topgallant sails, spanker and topsails—and approached the breakwater after daylight. We went around it and dropped anchor at about eight. By ten, the stern chains were fast to the buoys. Everything was shipshape and we were all ready to go ashore.

However, it was too early for anyone to get permission to go ashore. I wanted to go but didn't dare mention it. The captain and his wife went, of course, for that was the usual procedure as soon as the ship was tied up. The bay was pretty well filled up. There were nine other whalers and the *Clark* in ahead of us, and we were fairly close to the inside breakwater. After we finished tying up, I heard someone call my name. I looked over the side and saw Josephine, her father and her sister. I yelled back, and we waved. Mr. Frates saw us, and said, "Joe, tell them to go around where we disembark, and wait. I'll send a boat to take you ashore."

I was surprised and very pleased. I changed clothes in a hurry, and by the time I got back on deck, Mr. Frates had the boat ready. Josephine met me and threw her arms around my neck and kissed me, in front of everybody. She was so attractive, and I was so proud and happy. I was becoming more dignified and, of course, I felt the importance of my position as second mate, although Josephine didn't know about that yet. I thought I'd tell her on the way to the store; then I decided to surprise her and not say anything until we got there. I wanted particularly to surprise her mother. There were several customers in the store, but Josephine's mother dropped everything and hugged and kissed me, so I said, "Just for that, I've got a surprise for you. I am not Joe any more. I'm Mr. Gomes, second mate."

She looked at me and said, "Oh, my goodness! For that you deserve another kiss." She smacked me again. Her father gave me a big bear-hug and asked, "How could you get there when you are so young?"

By now I felt like giving myself a pat on the back, so I said, "Oh, yes, I am young, but I'm able to handle it okay."

The mother remarked, "This deserves something different. How would you like a good chicken-dinner?" The father and mother had wine with dinner, but the rest of us didn't take any. We had a wonderful time and danced and sang after we finished eating. Then Josephine wanted to see Mary, and we were just about to leave when the captain and Mary walked in. We went into the house and visited. Soon, Josephine and I decided to go for a walk. We hadn't been alone together and she was as eager as I was.

We said good night to Mary and the captain because we knew they would be gone by the time we returned. We knew where to go to get out of sight, and we stayed away for a couple of hours. Josephine's mother served us coffee and cake. Her father wanted me to stay, but I had orders and had to get back to the ship and, of course, there was work to do on board ship, or there might be, next morning. I didn't know what day Mr. Frates would want to break oil casks out of the hold, and I knew it was the second mate's job, so I wanted to be on deck. It was about twelve o'clock when I got to the dock and in a few minutes I was on the ship, and asleep.

Next day was Friday. Mr. Frates called me aside after breakfast with, "Joe, I want to talk to you." We sat on the rail with our backs against the stern boats and he went on. "Joe, I've decided to have the third mate work the holds. You are too young for that dirty job, and he is used to it. Anyway, he has been second mate before, and he knows all about it. I don't want you to do that dirty job; and why should you, when your next raise will be to captain? I've been thinking about it for some time, and that's what I've decided."

"Well, Mr. Frates," I replied, "as far as I'm concerned your word is law. I won't insist on anything. You are the boss." I went to my cabin and sat there for a while, drinking a cup of coffee. I hadn't thought about it before, but I began to question myself.

"Well, Joe, is Mr. Frates keeping you out of the hold because you are not capable of doing the work? Doesn't he trust you to take out the casks, or store cargo in the hold? Or is Mr. Frates just being a good guy?" I wasn't sure, so I went back up on deck and said to him, "Mr. Frates, are you sure my sister and the captain didn't put you up to this?"

"Oh, no, Joe. This is my own decision. You know Captain Corvello would not interfere with my handling of the ship's work. That's the way I feel about it, so it should be satisfactory to you."

"But of course I'm satisfied," I answered, and that settled it.

I didn't know whether or not he had told the third mate yet, and I didn't dare find out, so I let things stand just as they were. In the middle of the afternoon, Captain Mandley came by on his way to port, so I called him over and asked if I might go with him. "Are you going to the hotel?" he inquired, with a twinkle in his eye.

"Oh, I think I'll go over to the store."

"Oh yes, the one that cute little girl's father owns, I'll bet. I think I might need something at the store. I'll go over with you." So he went up to the store with me, and I introduced him. They all fell in love with him right away. He was such a pleasant guy. He couldn't talk Portuguese and they didn't speak much English, but they got on very well, regardless. He smoked a couple of cigarettes and Mr. Souza gave him a drink. Then he said he had better get on over to the hotel. It was almost dinner time. Mrs. Souza wanted him to stay, but he declined.

I wanted to see Captain Corey, so I asked Josephine if she would like to come with me and walk Captain Mandley over to the hotel. "Fine," she said. Both girls went along.

I met a lot of skippers I knew. Tony Edwards of the *Wanderer* was there with his brother, Joe, who had come from New Bedford. Joe was learning navigation. "I don't know if I'm going to like it or not. I was a little seasick," he told me. "Nobody was ever more seasick than I was," I assured him. "I know all about it, but you'll get over it." He was a good bit older than I, about thirty, I guess.

He had been a storekeeper in New Bedford and had decided to go to sea. I introduced him to the girls, and we stayed awhile before going back to Josephine's for dinner.

We made plans to go see the folks on the ranch on Sunday. Mrs. Souza was very agreeable—said she'd like to go.

We ended up the next day with everyone going to the ranch except Mr. Souza, who stayed to take care of the store.

It took about three weeks until our turn came to go alongside the *Clark*. Until then there was little to do on board. The mate found little jobs to keep part of the crew busy but as for me, I felt more like a gentleman and a scholar than anything else.

Mr. Frates told me I could go ashore any time, so long as I came aboard once a day or so. I told him I would always sleep on board and gave him my reason.

I explained that Josephine's father and mother wanted me to stay at their home but it was just too convenient, and Josephine and I were too much in love to trust ourselves. So I would always come back to the ship at night.

About the middle of the third week, I asked Mr. Frates if he would mind if I took a boat out for a sail on Sunday. "Those people have been so nice to me and I haven't done anything in return except rent a horse and buggy now and then, which is little enough. So I'd like to take them for a boat ride."

He replied, "Joe, you can do anything you like." So I had my boat steerer take the gear out of my boat and get it ready. I asked Harry and Joe and a couple of other fellows if they would like to go sailing on Sunday. Joe asked, "Who's going?" I told him there would be Josephine's family and maybe one or two cousins from the ranch. I said they would be here on Saturday, so it was all arranged.

The relatives arrived. We told them we'd planned to go sailing. The uncle remarked that he didn't care much about sailing but that if John Souza wanted the store kept open on Sunday, he would stay so that John might sail with us. "That's not necessary.

I've already spoken to a man down the street. He'll take care of the store and we can all go."

We were ready quite early, and left the dock in high spirits at about seven o'clock. We didn't go to Mass; we said a little prayer by ourselves instead. There were three boys from the ship, the four Souzas, the uncle, his daughter and two boys.

I had plenty of soft drinks and lots of food, and Mrs. Souza had brought a hamper of fried chicken and a big cake. Somebody was having drinks or eating, most of the time.

It was a beautiful day, and the boat just skimmed along the water. Part of the time I would sail, and part of the time I turned the job over to Joe or Harry, who were both very good at handling the boat. I was afraid to go clear around the island because of running into contrary winds and getting someone seasick, so when I thought we had gone far enough, we turned around and went back the way we had come. I had a lot of fun giving Josephine instructions on sailing, and she enjoyed it.

We got back to the dock and I sent the boat over to the ship with the boat steerer. Then I took everyone over to the hotel for a nice dinner. In spite of all the food we had consumed, the sailing had given everyone an appetite. Mary and the captain joined us, and we had a jolly time. Afterward, we walked back to the store, which was still open. Josephine and I went for our usual walk, and then the big day was all over.

We began discharging oil the next day. We transferred the oil casks to the *Clark* as usual. The only difference here at Fayal, compared with Dominica, was in making water. Here we stowed the empty casks in the hold. Then the water boats came alongside with a hose and filled them. It was a lot easier and faster. We were soon ready to leave Fayal, and I still remember that last night ashore. I was, without a doubt, a most confused and unhappy person.

I was still just a kid, of course, but I was nevertheless a second mate, doing a man's job and carrying a man's responsibility. Probably I convinced myself that I was older than I was, and I'd begun to think and plan, in an offhand way, for the future. At Flores when I left, I was sure that Lucy was the sweetest, most loving, most wonderful and beautiful girl in the world. Now at Fayal, I was leaving again. And Josephine was just as sweet and loving.

I knew that I would have done anything for either of them. I loved them both deeply and, I am sure, one just as much as the other. No matter what I wanted to do or where I wanted to go, each was Johnny on the spot. Neither one was ever ill-tempered or disagreeable. In fact, it was just the opposite, to a degree that I've never seen in any other persons. I was deeply confused, but then, as I said before, a parting at sea seems to be like going off into another world and leaving everything else behind, not knowing when one will return. Little did I know how long it would be before I was to see either of those two lovely girls again.

CHAPTER XXX

KILLING THE SCHOOLMASTER

From Fayal we sailed directly for St. Nicholas, to give the usual liberty to the officers and crew who had homes or relatives there. On the way to the Cape Verde Islands, we got four cow whales—seventy or eighty barrels of oil—which delayed us four or five days. But as we had no specified date or schedule, it made no difference. We were always glad to get whales wherever we found them.

Just as we were coming into the bay, we noticed a boat with oars and sail trying to hail us. The captain pulled over, and when we got to the boat, we held the foreyard back and hove to, to let the boat come alongside. It was Mr. Frates' youngest brother, who had come from New Bedford to get married. He had been Captain Corvello's boat steerer when the captain had been second mate with my father.

He invited the captain, Mary and me to come to the wedding. "Captain," he insisted, "we have waited to set the date until the *Greyhound* got here, so you and your wife and Joe and my brother, Frank, could attend, so will you please honor me with your presence, Captain Corvello?"

"I can't say. I don't know yet," the captain answered. "We may drop anchor, but I doubt it. The last time we dropped anchor here, we took an awful licking, but you go ahead and set the date for day after tomorrow. I'll get ashore somehow, either from anchorage or cruising."

Mr. Frates got off right then and there, on the little fishing boat his brother had come out in. When we got up toward the village, we stopped by, using the sails, of course, and about twenty men went ashore in the boat. It was a real boatload that I took ashore.

I returned to the ship, knowing that the captain wouldn't care to hold that position very long. We hoisted the boat and prepared to sail around on the lee side of the island where we could shorten sails and stay in smoother water.

"Brace the foreyard," the captain ordered, and we cruised the rest of the day on that tack. It was after dinner when the captain sang out, "Wear around," so we wore around, which means the same as tack ship, except that the wind is at the stern instead of the bow.

We headed back close to the bay but stayed six or seven miles out and headed in that direction until morning. I was standing watch because the fourth mate and I were the only mates on board. The captain could very well leave the ship and go ashore for a day or two. He called to me and said, "I think I'll go ashore this afternoon. Tack ship. We'll make a tack over toward the northeast end of the island, go by the wind over there, head back and be in just the right position to let me go ashore."

When we got in position, the captain ordered the fourth mate to take him ashore. I wanted to do it but the captain said, "No, you are the second mate. You stay on board."

In a little while, the fourth mate came back with the boat and we set sails. It was a great feeling. It was really swell. I was in charge of the ship. I was in command, I, the second mate. And I was having a hell of a time trying not to show how important I felt.

I don't think I slept much that night. The fourth mate was standing his own watch and I was standing the third mate's watch. We were very short-handed with so many of the crew ashore, but we had only one greenhorn—Josephine's cousin, the older of the two boys who had been on the sailboat with us. He said he wanted to come to the United States. I smuggled him aboard at night, and after three or four days of being seasick he was able to get around and start learning the ropes. There are lots of them on a square-rigger, with many different names, and a sailor has to know them all, and which to haul and which to slack when the order is given.

We tacked back and forth until the third day, when we were to pick up the captain. I sent the fourth mate ashore, and the captain and Mary came aboard, bringing all kinds of wedding cake and cookies. Mr. Frates sent me a special cake since I had to miss the wedding, and some native drink that tasted good. I divided it with the crew and told myself that I would miss a wedding any time to be master of a ship.

The captain was very pleased with the wedding, and Mary had enjoyed herself immensely. She said, "Joe, you know, these people are ever so much like the people in Flores. They are good, and straightforward. They don't talk about each other, and everyone seems to be happy."

The officers and crew were to stay ashore two more days, so we went on a cruise until time to pick them up.

We got into more than the usual calms down in the tropics and the rain was very heavy. It was no use to send anyone up masthead for it was impossible to see more than a half-mile. For about ten days it rained, night and day. It was nearly unbearable; no sun, no stars, and sails flapping back and forth. We couldn't take sights, and with no headway the ship did nothing but go around and around. Finally we got a little squall, a little breeze, and some clear weather, and we began to move.

As we left the tropics we passed within sight of the Ascension Islands, an English possession. I don't believe there is any population there except a garrison of soldiers. We passed about ten miles out, and two or three days later when I was up on masthead, I raised a school of whales. Every morning I would get up about daylight, get some coffee, hang a pair of glasses around my neck, go masthead and look for whales. When I yelled, "There she blows," the captain ran up on deck and shouted up at me, "How far away?"

"Oh, not far. Six or seven miles, maybe."

"Okay, come on down. All hands on deck," he yelled.

The weather was fine and the whales were to windward. We could sail right on top of them. When we got within lowering distance and lowered away, we discovered it was a school of cows. Somehow the fourth mate beat me to it. I was third to get fast to a cow, but peculiarly enough, Joe got the harpoon sunk in such a way that the whale was down only three or four minutes and came up spouting blood. Only a little line had gone out—I hadn't had time even to stow the sails or get the darting gun ready. We pulled right onto the whale. I threw the lance ten or fifteen times and there the whale was—dying.

A little distance away I noticed a big spout as I glanced back toward the stern of the boat. "Joe," I yelled, "isn't that a school over there, with a bull—a schoolmaster?"

"My gosh, yes. It looks like it," he said.

As soon as the cow whale was dead, I stuck a red flag on it, cut the line, and picked up a harpoon. Then I thought, "Why use a harpoon? Why not rig up the darting gun in case I get a chance at the bull?" So I pulled out the darting gun, set the harpoon in the gun and fastened the line to it. Then I saw that I had put the line through the head chock but had forgotten to pull it through the jack. I had to let go again, but we didn't lose any time because we were making sure that it was a bull—a schoolmaster.

It seemed that he was coming right toward us, and we were right in the middle of the school. It was mating season, and they were playing, really raising Cain. I had the line properly fastened by now, and asked Joe again, "Is it a bull? Are you sure?"

"Yes, I am positive. Look at it right ahead—look at that big head!" he answered.

I did, and I felt like blessing myself—the only time I can remember feeling that way when going on top of a whale. That head was so high and so wide that it looked like some huge monster—and it *was*—coming down almost on top of us. My worry was that I might mistake part of the head for the body and not make a proper strike. You see, I was still at the bow. We hadn't changed ends after the first whale. "Joe," I directed, "put me close to her on the lee side, and be careful."

On an occasion like this we could talk. There was so much noise on the water from the frolicking whales that they would pay no attention to us. The water was so rough that the boat was dancing and bouncing like a cork.

The whale spouted just as the bow went by, and I got wet from the spray. The whale was moving slowly at the moment and hadn't seen us. They can see only straight out from the sides of the head, and in seconds I was in position to let go with the darting gun. I threw that thing and the whale rolled. Fortunately, it went away from the boat instead of toward it, or it would have smashed us. It was badly hurt. The bomb must have exploded right in its vitals. It shook and shook, and rolled again. It was crazy. I was going to pull on top of it, and then I saw Mr. Frates coming in, so I waited for him to get fast. He did, and the bull turned toward the third mate's boat. They had a hell of a scramble to get out of the way, and barely made it. They didn't have a chance to get fast.

We were off on a Nantucket Sleigh Ride for a while, then the whale turned again and headed back toward the ship. It veered again and went toward the dead whales, coming fairly close to the third mate. He got fast, and shortly afterward we pulled on top and started lancing it—Mr. Frates on one side and I on the other. It wasn't long before it was spouting blood. By the time the whale was dying, we were so close to the ship that Mr. Frates told us to stay away from the whale. I looked over toward the ship and I could see Mary standing up on the stern boat with a pair of glasses, watching us. Just before he got fast to the bull, Mr. Frates had ordered the fourth mate to pick up the dead cows. By the time we got back to the ship with the bull, the fourth mate was busy putting chains on the cows. Mr. Frates told the third mate and me both to go to the ship and give the captain a hand. None of the boats was hoisted. One or two men were left in each boat to fend them away from the ship's side while the rest of us climbed up to help with the four heavy, clumsy chains for the four cows.

After the whales were tied up, I had time to think about what had happened. I could still see that huge head as it loomed up over us, looking, at the moment, to be as big as a house and as high as a steeple, and I could see the open jaw under water. It was one of the biggest whales we ever took. We couldn't tell how many barrels we got from it alone, but we had a hundred and sixty from the five whales, and both Mr. Frates and the captain figured that the old schoolmaster must have yielded over a hundred barrels.

I wondered why the whale didn't spout blood when it was so badly hurt by the darting gun, but Mr. Frates told me he had seen a lot of them killed that way—by the bomb exploding in the belly. "They only spout blood," he said, "when they are hit in the heart or lungs."

CHAPTER XXXI

NANTUCKET SLEIGH RIDE

We kept on catching whales, heading south and going from one ground to another. One day we raised a school and the captain ordered to lower away. We did, but there was no wind, so we rowed out toward the school. We were probably a mile from the school. Mr. Frates was a little ahead of me and the other two boats were a little behind. Suddenly there was a terrific spout right alongside my boat. All Joe could do was to ship his oar, jump on the bow, and take the first live harpoon. He sank it right into the whale, and got the second one in, too. The whale took off like lightning, passing right by the third mate's boat, about a yard off his bow. His boat steerer got fast and we were off on one of those famous sleigh-rides. In about twenty minutes the ship was hull down and I knew I had to get the compass and make sure of the bearing, for that whale wasn't going to let us get close. I pulled the compass from under the stern, and that whale kept on going and going. I took the bearing and hoped we wouldn't get out of sight of the ship, but the whale had other ideas.

I knew the captain would know the direction we had taken, but the ship was in a calm and would stay right there until a breeze came up. It was early forenoon when we got out of sight of the ship and the whale wasn't showing any signs of slowing down. We were probably twenty miles from the ship when the whale finally began to slow down and we were able to pull up on her. I changed ends with the boat steerer and went up on the bow. I started to get the darting gun ready and then decided I'd better use the shoulder gun instead. I was afraid that when we got close she would take off again and I wouldn't be close enough to throw the darting gun. Well, we got close—just past the flukes—and I let her have it. I shot a bomb into her, but it must have gone clear through her before it exploded. I loaded the gun again, though I didn't like to use it because it kicked like blazes. Joe said to me, "You'd better clean that thing before you use it again or it'll kick your head off."

"Oh, to hell with it," I answered, "let her kick." I shoved another bomb into it.

We were still right on top of the whale because we hadn't slacked off the line at all and we were just behind the flukes. I yelled at the boys, "Come on now, we've got to get closer. I want this one to do the job." But try as they would, they couldn't get any closer. The third mate was right behind me, and he was pulling up on his line, too, but of course it was my whale and he wouldn't come any closer unless I called him. Of course, if the whale slowed down we would both lance it, but until then it was my responsibility.

We fought and fought, but we couldn't get any closer. I took the shoulder gun and let her have it again. This time it appeared to be a good hit. The whale shook and trembled. Both the third mate and my boat steerer yelled, "There's the red flag." Well, it spouted a little blood—a tint, but hardly enough to call it the "red flag." I put the gun aside and got set with the lance. My arm and shoulder were so sore from the gun that I wasn't sure I could use it again unless I used the other shoulder. I was afraid it was too far to throw the lance, but I threw it a half dozen times anyway. I was pretty sure it had some effect, as the whale slowed down a little. I kept reminding the boat steerer every little while to check the compass. We were running in the four points between northeast and east; we couldn't get any closer than that. As the whale slowed down we were able to pull up on her. The third mate and I were then able to make short work of her. When we had finished the killing, I asked the third mate if he had noticed which direction the ship lay from us. He said, "Yes, she's approximately southwest." "That's right," I said, and I knew we couldn't both be wrong.

We got ready to tow. We were probably over fifty miles from the ship, and if a breeze didn't come up it was going to be a long, hard pull back to it. "Let's take it easy," I told the crew. "We know where the ship is and they knew where we are. We'll eat a little and get a drink of water."

It was well after noon when we settled down to towing. The third mate was next to the whale and I was in front, going by my boat compass. The job ahead of us could be a rough one. In a boat such as ours, one would naturally be rowing a good deal of the time, but there wasn't much choice of position for resting. One could kneel, and at times, stand up, but there was no room to lie down, and towing a dead whale is hard work. It was a twenty-four-hour-day ordeal that lay ahead.

I told the boys there was a possibility that it would breeze up a little at night and we could put the sails out, but I warned them, "Don't kill yourselves. This may last for a day or two, or even five or six. It all depends on whether the ship can make any progress toward us."

This was in December—the middle of summer in the South Atlantic—and the weather was good, but quite hot. Around six or seven o'clock, I signaled the third mate that we were going to stop and have a bite to eat. Ever since I had been boat steerer on Mr. Frates' boat, I had carried three or four cans of beef in my stern box. We dropped back alongside the third mate's boat and I opened a can of the beef. The hardtack and corned beef made a lot better meal than hardtack alone, with water. Sailors always called the corned beef "salt horse," although there is no reason to emphasize it here. We had only one cup to drink from, but we were soon satisfied with both food and water.

"What chance do you think we have for a breeze?" I asked the third mate. "Not too good," he replied. "I was brought up on St. Helena, not far from here, and I know about what to expect."

We rested for an hour or so. The boys smoked their pipes, or cigarettes, and then we went back to rowing.

At about midnight, I dropped back again and told the third

mate that we'd better let the boys have some sleep. "One of us will have to stay awake," I said. "All right, Joe," he said, "you go ahead and take a nap and in a couple of hours I'll wake you up." So I sat down in the bottom of the boat and slept for a couple of hours, and then I told the third mate to get some sleep while I stayed on watch.

Some of the boys were awake. Some were sleeping, but it was too uncomfortable to rest well. About daylight, the third mate called out, "Well, shall we get moving?" I said, "Yes, but we may as well have a bite to eat first." The boys all agreed to that, and after some food and water we started rowing again. We kept at it, off and on, all day. When night set in, there was a little breeze, but not enough to keep a course with the sails set. By ten o'clock it was a little stronger, so I asked the third mate if he thought it was strong enough, and he agreed that we could keep on course. We set the sails and shipped the rudder. With oars, you use the steering oar. With sails set we made less headway than with oars, but it provided a chance to give the boys some rest and at the same time still enabled us to make forward progress. We kept on sails the rest of the night.

In the morning the third mate signaled to me, so I yelled back to him, "As long as we can keep on course with the sails, I'm not going to kill the boys off at the oars. Let the ship come to us. They know where we are."

About one o'clock in the afternoon, the breeze died down altogether. We took the sails down but we left the mast up. The third mate did likewise and we all went back to rowing. The boys were pretty well rested, for while we were sailing they could eat a little or drink a little as they felt the need for it.

At dark, I dropped back again and told the third mate we might as well give the boys a little rest. He disagreed. "No," he said. "They might as well eat a little, but we may get a breeze again and then it will be time enough to rest." "That's a good argument," I agreed. So we did that. At ten or eleven o'clock there was still no breeze, so we took another rest. There was still no sign of the ship, so I knew we still had a long way to go. We would be able to see the light at masthead long before they could see our lantern. The breeze came again and we sailed until morning. Later in the morning we sighted the ship's topgallants—in other words, we could see the tops of the masts. One of the boys suggested it could be another ship. "Oh, no. That's the direction in which the *Greyhound* went out of sight. It's the *Greyhound* all right," I said. We were making a little headway. So was the ship. By afternoon we could see a lot more sails, but it was still hull down.

"Do you think we'll make it aboard tonight?" one of the boys asked.

"I doubt it," I answered. "I think it will be close to another twenty-four hours, the way the weather is." By late afternoon we could see that the ship wasn't steering a good course. The breeze was too light. We got the oars out again. About ten o'clock, I lighted the lantern and sent Joe up to the top of the mast with it. He was the lightest one of the crew. I knew the captain would keep a man at masthead and that they would soon see our light. At morning, we knew we were not over ten miles from the ship, for we could now see the ship's hull. We had our sails out and we knew they could see us. The third mate ordered his men to put the oars out. I could see it was a doggone good idea to get to the ship as soon as possible, now that we were near enough to make the effort, so I ordered the men to put the oars out, too.

When we got close enough to the ship, I let the third mate's warp off and came alongside. They picked up my boat, and shortly afterward the third mate came up and we tied up the whale.

The ship was going so slowly that they never even clewed up the mainsail. They just clewed up the foresail in order to haul the foreyard back.

When the captain saw that the whale was tied up, he said, "Joe, when you saw that you were going out of sight, you should have cut off."

"Cut off?" I asked, surprised.

"Yes. I thought you had a bull."

"Oh, no," I replied.

"Well, too bad. In the future when you go out of sight with a cow, cut your line. I am not blaming you, but I am just reminding you that the customary thing is to cut. When a cow is taking you for a sleigh ride, cut the line before you go out of sight. It isn't worth the punishment you hand out to the men and the worry that your disappearance causes on the ship. Cut the line and come back."

"Aye, aye, sir," and I turned away to get things ready for cutting. I had never thought of cutting the line, but I realized that the captain was one hundred per cent right, and that he had rebuked me nicely for taking a poor risk. I realized it even more fully when I learned that our miserable cow yielded only twenty barrels of oil, but still that wasn't too bad for a cow, either. I felt that every little bit counted. I'd had the whale fast and I'd had just one thought in mind—kill it and get it back to the ship. It had taken three nights and the best part of four days to do it, and we had succeeded. I resolved to follow the captain's directions in the future, but I didn't feel any remorse for what I'd done. Secretly, I felt that it was something of an achievement.

CHAPTER XXXII

THE DOLL OF ST. HELENA

The weather remained pretty calm—so calm, in fact, that I would say that a few days later we were picked up by a school of whales, out of which we got seven. All of us got two, except the third mate, who was called back to the ship after his first kill. We were cutting whales on Christmas Day, and we had the ship more than half-full of oil. After we finished, we headed on south toward the Carol Grounds, which lie between the west coast of Africa and St. Helena. We were on the edge of the whaling ground when we sighted a whale. Mr. Frates lowered away and got fast soon after. Then the fourth mate and I also got fast.

Mr. Frates hit it with a bomb from the shoulder gun and we had started killing it when a whole school of cows came up all around us. Mr. Frates immediately ordered the rest of us to cut our lines. He kept on lancing the bull, and the rest of us each got fast to a cow. Then the school disappeared. We started cutting immediatley, and we had no more than started firing the try pots when someone raised another school, from which we got four more cows. We had no chance for seconds because they immediately disappeared. Apparently they were on a passage. We had plenty of blubber to try out as it was. The try pots were full of spermaceti, at the time they were fired, and the deck tubs were full of it—all from the bull. We had the heads of three cow whales on board, from which the spermaceti had not yet been taken, and the deck was loaded with blanket pieces, stacked level with the top of the bulwarks. Now we had four more cows over the side.

We kept the try works going full blast. The deck and the waist of the ship were so clogged with blubber that the first objective was to get a little space cleared. As soon as we could, we took the spermaceti from the heads of the three cows and ran the case oil right in with the rest of the oil, the sooner to get those three heads overboard and out of the way.

The captain decided to keep the try works going for at least another twenty-four hours before starting to cut on the last four whales. At the end of another day and night, the waist of the ship was pretty well cleared but there was still a lot of blubber on deck. However, as you will remember from an earlier comment, a whale doesn't really belong to a ship until it is on board, so as soon as the captain figured there was room on board for the rest of the blubber, he ordered Mr. Frates: "We might as well get those cows on board. We have enough room now for the blubber."

This was early morning, and by noon we had them all cut. We were even more crowded than before, so the first thing we did was to take the spermaceti from the two heads, throw the cleaned-out heads overboard, and repeat the process with the remaining two. We had room on board for only two at a time. It took us almost a week to get all that oil down below.

We were making very little headway—only two or three miles an hour—having only the upper and lower topsails, two headsails, and the spanker set, and some of the time we had the gaff of the spanker slacked down.

Just as we were ready to wash decks, someone raised spouts again. I didn't like it too well. We were all tired and we had almost a full ship. Furthermore, we were so far from Barbados that we had to hold four or five casks of water. The captain didn't consult anyone, however, and gave orders to stand by to lower. We lowered. But, between you and me and Davy Jones's three-pointed gaff, I said a little prayer for those doggone whales to disappear.

Of course, we all made a try, or at least a bluff, at it. The third and fourth mates' boat steerers each threw a harpoon, but the whales were on passage and actually moved too fast to get a strike. We lost them, and I was glad when we got back to the ship. We scrubbed decks and finished cleaning up. And for the next three days we had a good rest.

We were only about a hundred miles out from St. Helena, which was the home of the fourth mate. Unbeknown to the captain, Mary was telling me the same thing the captain was telling Mr. Frates. "You know, we are so early in getting almost a full ship that we are going to surprise the fourth mate. He hasn't been home for years, so we are going to put him ashore on St. Helena and give him a little liberty. We can get some vegetables and some other fresh food, too."

When Mary told me that, I gave her a hug and a kiss. We'd had very little luck with turtles and porpoises (called sea-pigs by the sailors) and some fresh meat would taste very, very good. I was glad that the captain had decided to visit St. Helena. I had never been there, though all the other mates had, and Captain Corvello had been there a good many times. When he was second mate with my father, they used to stop there frequently.

Mr. Frates told me to say nothing to the fourth mate. Only he, the captain, Mary and I knew our exact position. It was of no interest to the rest of the crew. We were simply out whaling on a wide blue ocean, with considerable time ahead of us before we would be heading for Barbados.

Now, with an almost full ship, the captain was willing to forget business for a short while and take a little time off. It would be the first time since I had started whaling that a ship I was on would put in at St. Helena. Some of the other ships, like the *Wanderer,* who had several crew members from St. Helena, would stop there from time to time.

On the second day, we sighted St. Helena. We pulled in close to the harbor, and I wondered if we were going to cruise or drop anchor. I decided to ask the captain. So I went up to him and asked, "Are we going to drop anchor or stay out cruising?"

"Oh, no. This is a good harbor. We'll drop anchor."

"Is there going to be shore liberty?"

"Of course. This is a nice place. I've been here many times. Your father used to stop here quite often."

"Oh, that's wonderful." I was searching the shore with my glasses, and it looked very appealing.

I asked Mr. Frates, "Have you very much work lined up to do while we're here?"

"Oh, no. Today we aren't going to do anything at all. Tomorrow we'll just break out some shooks from the fore hatch because the captain wants to make some more casks for use for deck cargo if we need them. He's going to get two or three coopers on board tomorrow." I thought to myself that the captain hadn't forgotten about business after all.

"How long are we going to stay?" I asked.

"The captain didn't say. If his wife likes it, we may stay three or four days. If not—well, it won't be long."

The stop was really a surprise for the fourth mate. He was pretty chagrined and upset at first, for he'd had no idea that he'd have a chance to visit home when the trip began. Consequently, he had none of the usual gifts to present to his family, relatives and friends. When a whaleman comes home, particularly after such a long absence, it is really an occasion. He comes from a big, wonderful outside world of many ports and places, and naturally he brings gifts for everyone. The poor fellow didn't know what to do. He'd rather have never gone ashore than go empty-handed.

We all knew how we would feel under the circumstances. Mr. Frates and I got together and took up a collection. I had quite a lot of new things I'd never worn. So did the others. We got underwear, extra pairs of pants, shirts and miscellaneous things, including a few trinkets for the womenfolk. Mr. Frates, the third mate, and the steward also put in all the new stuff they had. It was heartwarming to see how happy it made that fellow feel.

The captain told the doctor it would be all right for the fourth mate to go ashore with him if he didn't mind. The doctor was agreeable to the suggestion, and the mate went ashore with two suitcases filled with gifts.

I was just wondering how soon I would get ashore when Mr. Frates called to me. "Joe, you can go ashore any time. Only one thing, be careful with the girls."

"What do you mean?"

"Remember, half the population here is white and some of the girls are pretty good-looking."

"Oh, oh," I exclaimed, "here we go again. No. I'm going to be true to my girls. I'm not going to go monkeying around with girls here. Anyway, I don't know anybody. I've never been here before. The first place I want to see is Napoleon's Prison. I've read about it and I want to see it, if there is a horse and buggy to rent, and provided I am lucky enough to get a driver."

"You can get anything you want here, Joe, so long as you have something to jingle."

"Oh, heck. I'm okay. I've got that all right."

I dressed up like a duke and went ashore. This was an English island and I knew they would take you by the way you were dressed. First I went to a little restaurant (there were no large ones) and ordered the best steak they had. It was served with some of those "morphodite" potatoes, but it was a good meal and I thoroughly enjoyed it. I asked the waitress if it was much of a walk up to Napoleon's Prison. "Oh, yes," she replied, "it takes an hour or more." Apparently, the owner of the restaurant thought I was flirting with her. It turned out that she was his wife, so she told him what we were talking about.

"Do you want to ride—to go by horse?"

"Oh, hell no. I don't want anything to do with horses. I want a horse and carriage and driver to take me there."

"That's easy." He stepped to the door and waved his arm. A fellow came in and told me what it would cost. "But I want you to wait there and bring me back."

"Well," he said, "that will be a couple of shillings more."

So, good enough. He brought up the carriage and I sat in the driver's seat with him, where I could have everything explained to me as we went along. When we got up to the hill, he stopped, and I asked him if he would come along. He declined but I offered him a couple more shillings, telling him my English was poor and I'd like to have him show me around. I was pretty nearly winded when we got up there and I realized what was meant by "sea legs." Whether the fellow knew what he was talking about I don't know, but he described and explained everything anyway—where Napoleon ate, slept, and so on. After a while we came down and went back to town.

By the time we got back to the center of town I was getting tired. We came to an eating and drinking place where there was music and some dancing going on. I stuck my head in the door and saw the fellows from the starboard watch on the *Greyhound* dancing and having a hell of a time with some white girls. The sailors appeared to be very nearly drunk, but the girls were sober enough. When the music stopped, they sat down at the tables.

My boat steerer, Joe, noticed me and called out, "Mr. Gomes. Come over here." I went over and sat down, and he turned to the girl with him and asked, "Can you get a girl for Mr. Gomes?"

"Oh, no, thank you," I cut in. "I'm going back to the ship. I don't want anything to do with girls."

There were three other fellows, including Harry, their girls with them at the table. They started kidding me about wanting nothing to do with girls. While I was sipping a soft drink, Joe's girl friend excused herself and slipped away. I thought nothing of it.

The dancing started again and Joe and I remained at the table. A few minutes later, in came the girl, arm in arm with a regular doll. One look at that creamy-white complexion, those red lips and rosy cheeks, and my resolutions melted away like a horse piece in the try pots. She had a figure to go with her looks, and a smile that shattered any vestige of a negative resolution. Joe's girl friend lost no time in making us acquainted. The music picked up with a lively tune and she took my hand with a "Come on, let's dance, Joe."

"I wonder if I can do this jig," I remarked.

"If you can't, I'll teach you," and in no time we were off.

She had no more than nestled softly against my shoulder when I said to myself, "Oh, yoi, yoi, what an evening this is going to be!" I felt as though I'd come into a very snug little harbor filled with soft music, sweet perfume, and every delight a man could wish for. What a doll! Snug, cozy, warm, exciting. I was in heaven, drifting on a cloud. The music stopped. I didn't want to stop dancing but, of course, we had to sit down and wait—and then I realized I was hungry. I asked the rest if they'd like to eat. Everybody was hungry, so I ordered fish and chips for the whole table.

It was the only thing they served, in a piece of paper—no plates —just as it was done in England. They handed the paper to you. You took it in your left hand and used the right hand to feed yourself. I ordered more drinks and we kept on eating and drinking until we'd had enough.

We danced some more, and my little doll seemed to like me as much as I liked her. She snuggled closer and closer. After three or four dances, I remarked, "Let's get some fresh air. It's getting awfully smoky and stuffy in here."

"Fine," she agreed, "let's go for a walk."

We found a cozy little nook and I soon discovered that her kisses were as good as her dancing. That was a blissful hour. It made up a little for five months at sea. We had left Fayal in September, and it was now January. Looking at sailors and whales for five months gets rather monotonous.

By the time we got back to the dance floor, most of the fellows and girls had disappeared. Others were coming and going. Everybody was happy because there was a whaler in port and there was fresh money floating around.

Before going ashore, the captain had given Mr. Frates money for an advance for all hands. I hadn't needed any, as I'd left Fayal with fifty or sixty dollars. One thing I learned—American money is good anywhere in God's world. Everybody loves American greenbacks. All you have to do is change them.

About midnight, I decided it was time to return to the ship. My little doll didn't think so. "Oh no, Joe. It's too early yet; two or three o'clock is soon enough."

"It's a working day tomorrow," I argued.

"Joe, you don't have to work tomorrow. I know you don't."

So what could I say? I went back on board at three A.M. I had her name, but next morning I realized I hadn't gotten her address. And I'd made a date for the afternoon. I had my usual six o'clock coffee at seven, and Mr. Frates began to rib me. "You had a pretty good time last night, didn't you, Joe?"

"Yes, I did."

"I could see that by the time you came aboard. It was three or four o'clock, wasn't it?"

"Yes, it was after three I'm sure. In fact it was after three when I left the landing."

"Well, we've got a little work to do today. As soon as we finish breakfast, I'm going to get some cask shooks out of the hold."

"Okay, I'm finished. I'll go down and break them out."

The third mate was sitting there with us and he spoke up quickly. "You won't need to do that Joe. I know right where they are and how they are stowed away. I'll break out the shooks myself."

I thanked him and went to order the fore hatch opened up. I rigged a hand billy to bring up the shooks, and soon we had eight bundles on deck. I didn't expect to get that many casks set up but Mr. Frates suggested that we pull them out so the coopers could get as many done as they would have time for. We'd have that many less to set up out at sea.

Four coopers, each with an assistant, were ready to go to work by the time we got the shooks up on deck. The captain had ordered them to put the casks together first, before flagging them. The flags are leaves from a plant, inserted between the staves, to make the casks watertight. They serve the same purpose as caulking on a ship. Mid-afternoon came and they had each set up a cask. Mr. Frates asked me if I wanted to go ashore.

"Well," I said, "I'm really sick and tired of sitting here watching these coopers and, you know, there's a real, live, beautiful doll ashore. The only trouble is, I forgot to find out last night where she lives."

"That's no problem. All you have to do is show any ten- or twelve-year-old boy a shilling and tell him it's his as soon as he brings you the girl. You won't have to wait fifteen minutes."

"Thanks a million, Mr. Frates," and I was off to my cabin to get dressed. I was ready with the shilling when I got to the landing, but I didn't have to use it. That gorgeous doll was waiting when I got there. She greeted me with, "I knew you'd be coming ashore soon and I told my father you were second mate on the whaling ship—that you were a young fellow about twenty.

" 'Look,' he told me, 'he's an officer. They haven't any work on board. He's young and he'll be ashore most any time this afternoon. Why don't you go and wait for him?' And so I did."

"Have you waited long?"

"Oh, no. Not over an hour, anyway."

"Have you been up to Napoleon's Prison?" I asked.

"Lots of times."

"I went up yesterday but I didn't enjoy the company. Would you like to go up and show me around?"

"Fine. We'll walk. It's not too far."

"Let's get a horse and buggy."

"What are you talking about?" and she took hold of my hand and off we started.

"Look," I said, "by the time we get there, we'll be too tired even to kiss." She kissed me right there in front of everybody, so I said, "Let's walk."

It took us over an hour to get to the foot of the hill, and then we had those ungodly steps to climb. To me they seemed endless. I was used to climbing rigging, but not a mountain of steps. I was exhausted when we got to the top, and she was fresh as a daisy. I apologized for being out of breath. "Oh, Joe, think nothing of it. You've got sea legs and it takes a long time to get used to walking. My father was on a whaler when he was young and I know all about it."

She showed me all around the place—all the various quarters. And everywhere we went we bumped into sailors with their girls—in corners, making love. Most of them were from the *Greyhound*—fellows I'd talked to the day before about my trip up there. We talked, and I asked about her family.

"Is your father home?"

"Oh, I think so. He should be back by now."

"How many in your family?"

"Five. My father, mother and two sisters. One sister is married and has a baby. Her husband is second mate on the *Wanderer*."

"Oh, I know him very well," I said.

"My other sister is engaged to a fellow in New Bedford. He didn't ship out this year."

"What would they say," I asked, "would they come if we went up to your house and asked them to have dinner with us?"

"Do you mean it?"

"Of course I do."

"Why, Joe, they'll be tickled as could be, just knowing you and that you'd like to come up to the house. They're very friendly."

We walked back to her house, which was about a mile from the landing. They were wonderfully friendly people and I liked them instantly. The married sister had a cute little boy about two years old. She was expecting her husband to stop by soon. Captain Edwards would be in with the *Wanderer*. They accepted my invitation for dinner and we went to the same little restaurant where I'd had the steak the day before. We had a nice steak dinner. Her sister told me she had seen me there the night before. But I hadn't seen her. I had eyes for no one but the doll I was with.

By the time we finished dinner, some of the crew from the *Greyhound* had come in. One of them was from my boat crew—a fellow from St. Nicholas. And he was the fellow the sister had been with the night before. We all went dancing and sat out intermissions eating fish and chips or going somewhere for a little lovemaking. I forgot all my resolutions and we had a wonderful time.

CHAPTER XXXIII

FULL SHIP AND LINDA'S SISTER

The coopers came aboard again next day and by the middle of the afternoon they had four more casks set up—eight in all—and had started to flag the first four. The captain came aboard with his clearance papers and said that we would be leaving on the following morning. He had given the fourth mate orders to be aboard by six o'clock.

We set sails bright and early in the morning. We were no sooner out of the harbor than the captain ordered masthead watches. The casks would soon be ready and we could take on more oil.

"We are going to travel night and day until we get on the other side of the line," he remarked. He never mentioned the Equator—it was always "the line." After we got in the West Indies ground, he said that we would shorten sails at night as usual, and see if we could fill the casks.

Next morning, before sunrise, it was still and quiet. A whale blew out a spout so close to the ship and so loud that the cook jumped out of the galley and called out, "There she blows." He didn't dare yell loudly, so he ran all over the deck calling out the familiar phrase. By the time we were all up on deck the whale was behind us. With all sails set and a light breeze, we were moving right along. The whale hadn't been scared, even though it may have brushed the ship or seen its shadow—probably just took it for another whale.

Anyway, I ordered the men on watch to come with me and we hauled back the foreyards to stop the ship. The captain checked our positions and then ran back to his cabin to get more clothes on. By the time everyone was dressed and ready to maneuver the boats and the ship stopped, we were a mile or so past the whale. The captain came back on deck and said, "I think we will tack ship." Then he saw that we were only a mile or so from the whale, so he said, "No, we're okay. Stand by to lower."

We lowered and set sails because it is easier and safer to go up on a whale with sails than with oars, when the breeze is good. The mate got fast. It was a small cow that apparently had become separated from the school. The rest of us were taking our sails down to go on oars and I was making ready to get fast, when the fourth mate yelled, "There she blows," and pointed eastward. We looked, and there was a school coming at us, head-on.

As they came up, I warned Joe. "Beware of the head. Let enough of the whale go by before you strike." He signaled that he understood, and we went in between two of them. The boat touched one and it took off. Joe struck the one on the starboard side. It didn't kick. It didn't swim—it simply rolled. Fortunately, it rolled away from us or we would have been almost instantly swamped and smashed to pieces. How a whale can start from a still or standing position and change instantly into a furiously, madly rolling mass, is something I have never been able to understand.

It rolled—rolled with such amazing speed that one could not

count the revolutions. The line sizzled, rumbled and smoked as it streaked out over the bow from the turn on the loggerhead. The water boiled and churned under us with such vibration that I thought the bottom of the boat would be broken in pieces before it stopped.

We were all utterly helpless and unable to do anything other than get down as low as possible and hang on to thwarts and gunwales, ready instantly also to jump overboard if the line caught or fouled. We were shaking from the vibration and the pounding, so that we could hardly see. Everything was a blur of color, sound and furious motion. A half of the big tub of line was out and the whale was swathed in at least a hundred revolutions of the line. Then it took off in an instantaneous flight that actually began at full speed, as unexplainable as the sudden, full-speed rolling. A few turns of the line pulled off over the flukes as we started on the sleigh ride. Then it pulled tight and we were away. At the instant all this was happening—and it was really only an instant, fifteen or twenty seconds—we were too busy to notice what was happening on board the *Greyhound*. All hands left on board—steward, cook and all—were frantically working to get the ship under way and away from the school. Our whale didn't run far and I soon had it killed. Mr. Frates had killed and flagged his first one and was already killing his second. The third and fourth mates had each got fast and were also lancing theirs. As soon as the whales were dead, the *Greyhound* tacked ship and came up to us.

The next several hours were filled with bustling activity. The killing and securing of the whales had been accomplished with record speed—less than two hours. The captain and Mr. Frates, both excellent coopers, each with a sailor assisting, set to work flagging the remaining four casks. The third and fourth mates and I went to work on the staging, making the cut. Mr. Frates' boat steerer, the oldest and most experienced of the four, took the third mate's place with the board-ho knife, while the other three boat steerers worked at the ship's waist, handling the blanket pieces. The rest of the crew was on the windlass. At mid-afternoon, the cut was finished, and we had the heads on deck, taking out the spermaceti.

FULL SHIP

By dinner time the job was finished. The whale heads had been thrown overboard and the captain and Mr. Frates had each completed the flagging of one cask.

"When you throw the last head overboard, Joe, let me know," the captain had ordered. I did so, and he said, "We were so busy that I forgot something, and the boys all deserve it. I forgot to splice the main brace." He went down and yelled just once. The crew gathered as quickly as if the captain had yelled, "Stand by to lower!"

Officers first, then the boat steerers and the crew. Everybody got a good slug of the captain's Scotch—all but me, that is, for I didn't want it.

That is one resolution I have never broken. I would never even start drinking liquor. I had seen too many sailors—officers too— ruin their lives by getting the habit. A beautiful girl could melt any resolution but that one. To this day I have kept it, and now I'm too old to learn new tricks even if it appealed to me.

I immediately began firing the try works. The captain ordered all the new casks that were finished to be lashed down on deck with the bung up, in order to fill them with salt water and test for leaks. The captain ordered the third mate to light up the big torch and take it to the quarter-deck. I wasn't happy because I knew what it meant. The captain and Mr. Frates would be working on casks most of the night, plugging leaks and tightening hoops, and I would be working right along with them.

I got a hammer and driver and we set to work. The coopers had done a pretty good job and it didn't take as long as I had thought it would. We finished with the lashed-down casks at about ten o'clock and Mr. Frates reminded the captain that it was time to quit. Anyway, the mate who was off watch right under us, as well as the men in the steerage, had to get some sleep. Of course, the crew on watch kept right on at the try works. Two boat steerers were busy through the night cutting horse pieces, with the rest busy at their usual tasks.

I was dreading the next day because we were sailing with everything out except the foresail and the main staysail. They had to be clewed because of the smokestacks on the try works. The mizzen interfered too, so the captain ordered it clewed up. I asked him if

I should go masthead. The response was quick and definite. "Oh, no. You're going to work here on these last two casks."

"I don't know a hell of a lot about it," I countered.

"All the more reason for you to learn." No sympathy from the old man. I didn't want to get my hands blistered, and he knew what I was thinking. "Anyway," the captain added, "I'm pretty sure we'll have all the oil the casks will take, so there's no use sending anybody up on masthead to look for whales."

My initiation into coopering began. Each of us had a set of cooper's tools. "What about these flags?" I asked.

"When one is too thick to go between the staves, use a thinner one."

"What about the hoops?"

"Slide them down. They have to go down as far from the head to the bulge as they will go. They have to be correctly placed, and you have to be careful with that screw that you have there under your arm."

I never learned the name of that particular tool, but it has two prongs that spread the staves, and a lever or sort of handle that you lean against with all your weight and strength to spread the staves apart so you can insert the flag between them. It worked fine for the captain and Mr. Frates because they were both heavy men, but my stern was just a bit too light for the job. They took over the flagging and set me to putting in the heads and pounding hoops. They kept me at it all day. By three or four o'clock, I had five blisters on my right hand and I was getting pretty tired.

Mary would come out every little while and say, "Here, Joe, let me try it," and she would take the tool used for pounding, and the hammer. She didn't pound very heavily, but it was amusing enough to keep everyone laughing. About the time the blisters began to bother me, she brought out coffee and homemade cookies. She had taught the steward, and he had baked enough cookies for the whole crew. She got the credit for the cookies and everyone was pleased.

We kept on heading north and trying out the oil. Our casks were filling up and the captain remarked, "It looks like we're going to have more oil than we can handle. We'll have to do something about that water."

He went below and checked it. There were one full cask of water and part of another. The mate remarked, "Well, the water is far more precious than the oil. We don't have any too much water."

"Yes," the captain agreed. "There's enough for four weeks or a little more, and that is about how long it will take us to get to Barbados."

"If we don't get becalmed at the Equator," Mr. Frates put in, and he added, "When the empty casks are filled and the cooling tanks and try pots are filled, we'll just have to throw the rest overboard." The captain knew this made sense, so he said no more about it. We had a few blanket pieces left when the casks, tanks and pots were filled, so over the side they went.

We lost the wind at the Equator, but were becalmed for only twenty-four hours. Even at that, it worried us, for at other times we had been becalmed for as long as two weeks, and of course we didn't know how long we'd be going in aimless circles with flapping sails. I could fairly visualize what would happen. I knew both the captain and Mr. Frates well enough to realize that if the water became dangerously low they would revive the old custom of making every sailor on board climb up the masthead to get the one lone tin cup allowed for such use, to get one single cup of water, nor would he be allowed to hand the cup to another sailor before replacing it.

My imaginings were short-lived and I was glad of it. We picked up a breeze and at seven or eight degrees north latitude we began to get the trade winds. We crossed the Equator about February 1. I recall that we were in Barbados on my birthday, March 3.

I remember the occasion because Mary got up a nice little dinner party for me, to which the captain invited the other officers. I enjoyed it, and I appreciated it, although I reflected that it would have been a gayer time if that English captain and his daughter had been present. There wasn't much to do but walk around and visit some of the English ships. I went on board five or six English steamers to get acquainted and see what steamers were like—not for any other purpose, of course.

On the third day, we left Barbados for Dominica. When we came around the point, it didn't surprise me to see that neither the *Clark* nor any whalers were there. We were almost a month ahead of time. We could have stayed in Barbados, but the captain was better acquainted in Dominica. Also, Barbados was only a stopover—a place to check new hands with the American consul, pick up some fresh food, and so on. But Dominica was always a long layover while unloading oil and taking on supplies. And the captain was like a little duke there. An American captain in Dominica was almost like visiting royalty in a foreign country.

We tacked back and forth until we came to the anchorage and dropped anchor. The doctor came aboard, and shortly afterward the captain, Mary and I went ashore. I took my customary course down to the restaurant where Linda worked.

To my surprise, I found her younger sister behind the counter. "Hey, what's this? What are you doing here? Where's Linda?" The questions tumbled out of my mouth.

"Oh, Joe. Don't you know?"

"What happened? Is she sick or something?"

"No. She's married."

"What?"

"She's married. Just a minute. I'll send a boy for her. She lives just down the street."

A few minutes later, Linda and a young fellow came in. She threw her arms around my neck and kissed me, and then introduced me to her husband. I was dumbfounded.

"Well," I said lamely, "it's going to be kind of lonesome around here this trip."

"Oh no, Joe. Why should it? Look at my sister. She's bigger than I am and she likes you. It will all be in the family. In a few weeks, Manuel is going to Razore. He has a job there, and we'll still be friends. You won't be lonesome."

For the first time, I noticed something rather peculiar. Anyway, before when we were in port there were very few men around. This was the first time our ship was the first in port, and there were lots of men around. That evening I asked Linda's mother, "How come there are so many men around? Other times when I've been here, there was hardly a native man to be seen."

"Well, Joe, as the whalers arrive the men disappear. There isn't much chance to make any money here, so, as the sailors get acquainted with the women, their boy friends and husbands leave and give the women a chance to make some money. It's part of the tradition—part of the business—and we have to keep the whalemen happy. If you pay attention, you will see. After a while my husband will leave too, until the whalers are gone."

I found it a little disconcerting to give up Linda, but a lot can happen when you see a girl for only a short time once a year.

I went back to the restaurant to get a bite to eat. Linda and Manuel came in and I suggested that we all have some food. As we finished eating, Linda suggested, "Why don't you kids go for a walk? I'll mind the counter." I looked at her sister. She smiled and said, "That's fine," as she grabbed my hand, and away we went.

I wondered where we would walk so early in the evening. It was still broad daylight, but we were hardly out of the door when she said, "You know my mother isn't home, and neither is my father. Why don't we go to the house?"

"Well then," I said, "I don't think we should. It's broad daylight."

"That's a good reason why we should. There's no other place to go." So we went to her house. There are no locks on the doors of those houses, just a sort of wooden latch to keep them from flying open. Linda's sister put a chair against the door and in a matter of minutes convinced me that she could take Linda's place very well.

The long and short of it was that, in the ten days before the *Clark* arrived, we went walking practically every evening. Then the *Clark* arrived and soon after that the *Carleton Belle* hove into port, followed daily by others of the fleet. I went immediately to visit Captain Corey, of course, because to me he was captain of all captains, and I idolized him.

Soon Linda's husband left for Razore, and then I had the company of both girls for the rest of my stay in Dominica. Mary enjoyed teasing me by saying, "Joe, I saw you with one of your dusky beauties today." I would answer, "Yes, they are nice girls and they are very good company."

CHAPTER XXXIV

SUDDEN BLOW

We unloaded our casks and pulled over toward the river, about halfway from the regular anchorage, so as to be in a position to make water. After the usual stay of about four weeks and the completion of the customary routine of taking on supplies, we were ready for sea by way of Santastatia. From Dominica to Santastatia, the wind is at the starboard beam and you make almost the equivalent of steamboat time. We couldn't carry full sails because that would put us into port before daylight, and with only one little light at the dock it was too risky to try to come to anchor with a sailing ship. It was essential to pick up a good anchorage preparatory to taking on the fresh vegetables, potatoes, onions, yams, and so on, for the summer. On the third day, as usual, we were off for the Western Grounds.

One thing happened at Dominica which I didn't care for. We had been given orders to meet the mother ship at Grand Canary Islands instead of Fayal. The authorities at Fayal had been taking an increasingly larger toll on duties, so the New Bedford owners had decided to shift operations to a port that would be more favorable. Also, the price of the whale oil had been dropping, and some of our ships, especially those with heavy mortgages, were being taken out of service.

Naturally, I had a personal interest in stopping at Fayal, and what this change would mean I wasn't sure. But I figured it wouldn't be good—not for me. I could only wonder how long it would be before I saw Josephine again.

We began to catch whales in April and made four or five catches in May. By the middle of June we were half-full. Then one day the barometer started dropping very fast. At first the captain thought the barometer was faulty, for this was summer time and no reason to expect storms.

Naturally, since we were on the whaling grounds, we carried only light sails at night—lower topsails, two headsails and mizzen trysail. There was very seldom anyone at the wheel at night unless a good breeze was blowing. Most nights the wheel was in the jack —two lines, one port and one starboard, to hold it amidships.

At about midnight I was practically thrown out of my bunk. The ship was rolling heavily, so I dressed and came up on deck. The captain and Mr. Frates were already up and were over on the starboard, the weather side, talking about this freak storm.

"How do you like it, Joe?" Mr. Frates greeted me.

"What the heck is this? A freak storm or something?" I asked.

"Yes, it certainly is. The barometer is 28-10."

"28-10! I thought this was summer time. Can this be a hurricane?" But I knew there could be no hurricanes in June, and these weren't the right conditions anyway. We had no sails set except the ones I mentioned, but the wind was still increasing and the ship was listing pretty heavily and beginning to make considerable headway from the force of the wind. Shortly after we took in the main lower topsail, we figured the wind was better than eighty miles per hour. The waves were becoming terrific. We were on the port tack and the captain wanted to go over to the starboard tack.

He was worried about the three boats carried on the port side. The way the ship was listing, they were getting too close to the water, and a big wave breaking against the side of the ship could do a lot of damage to them. We had one hell of a time pulling into the wind and tacking ship. When you pull on the wind, the port and starboard sheets are slackened and they start to jump around furiously. Before the ship fell over on the starboard tack, the jib had gone to pieces. The wind slammed into it and, with the sound of a cannon, it just went to pieces. It simply flew away in ribbons.

Before the ship could come up to an even keel, two or three waves hit the fourth mate's boat from underneath, with such force that it stove in the bottom. The third mate's boat was in almost as bad a position except that as it was a bit farther back, the force of the water was somewhat broken. We were exceedingly fortunate that neither of the other boats was broken or damaged. We finally got on the starboard tack, but then we had no jib and we were having great difficulty keeping on course, to head into the sea, by the wind. However, the worst was over.

With luck playing the larger part, we had made an almost impossible maneuver. Had we tried to wear around, we would have picked up terrific speed going with the wind. Then, at the moment of turning, if the ship had gone into a trough and simultaneously been hit by one of those huge waves, the water breaking over could have swept the length and breadth of the ship, with loss of every movable object on deck and possible loss of men besides. Tacking ship was the safer maneuver of the two and, fortunately, it had been accomplished with a minimum of loss and damage.

We had to replace the jib from the locker down in the sail loft where new sails were kept. The boat steerer on watch went down, but I helped bend it on. It wasn't actually a second mate's job, but the boat steerer and I were the nearest things to monkeys on board when it came to working on sails and in the rigging. One had to be half monkey anyway, to haul himself out on the jib boom in that kind of weather.

As we prepared to go, the mate ordered, "Put lines around your midships and as soon as you get out there tie yourselves to the stay. Then, if you get hurt you won't go overboard."

That was the only time I remember tying myself to a stay. The wind was about ten points on our port bow. That was as close as the *Greyhound* could go in heavy seas. Every little while, that jib boom would dive down into the water. We simply had to hang on and hold our breath until we came up again. The jib stay was about five feet out on the jib boom, but finally we got the jib bent on and the jib hoisted without getting hurt or washed off the jib boom.

Meanwhile, part of the crew had been busy taking the gear from the fourth mate's boat. When they replaced it the next day with the spare stern-boat and took it back to the stern, we could see how close we'd come to losing the gear, which by now was safely resting on top of the boards and canvas covering the try works. The bottom of the fourth mate's boat was in splinters, as though it had been pounded to pieces with a hammer.

The boat steerer and I were back on deck. I said we were not hurt. We did have bruises and Joe had a bad bump on his shoulder, but nothing that would show after a few days. How many times we'd been submerged, I had no idea. The tubnose of the old *Greyhound* didn't slice through the waves. It just hit them head-on and shoved them back into the ocean.

The storm subsided as fast as it had come up. By nightfall we were already in calm again—that is, in a light breeze, with the waves subsiding, and the usual good summer weather.

CHAPTER XXXV

FAILING FORTUNES

Three or four days later, we got more whales and we kept on getting them. By the middle of July we had a full ship. Every cask was filled except two that carried our supply of drinking water. The captain began putting casks together. We had about a dozen in shooks in the hold, some in smaller sizes, all packed separately. This time we couldn't call on coopers to do the job. It was up to us. The captain and Mr. Frates were both experts, and I'd had my initiation into the business. So, with some sailors for assistants, we made good progress.

We got two more catches of whales. So we finished up with all twelve casks put together and filled, with the cooling tanks and try pots also full, just as we'd done on the preceding trip, except that our deck load was thirty or forty barrels larger than before. We had to let go half a whale from alongside because we had no more room for oil. We put boards on top of the cooling tanks to act as splash boards so the oil couldn't spill over. Then we lashed the casks to the lash rail and wedged them with wedging blocks so they couldn't move in the slightest degree. Once a lashing loosened, even to the thousandth of an inch, there would be fast trouble on board. A freak wind, with a deck rolling twenty-five degrees either way—well, you can understand that we took no chances. In dry weather, which we had most of the time, we would keep checking the wedges and splashing water on the lashings. In a stiff breeze, flying spray would keep the lines moist enough to keep them tight.

Again, we were well ahead of time as we headed for the rendezvous. This time it was Las Palmas, in Grand Canary Islands, with the biggest load the bark *Greyhound* ever carried into port.

With a couple of weeks to spare, Captain Corvello decided to stop off at Flores, which was only a little off our course and only a couple of hundred miles away. Further, Captain Corvello had an idea my father might be in Flores, and he wanted to see him. If my father was there, the captain knew he would have firsthand information about the declining situation in the whaling industry. And, of course, Mary was eager to get home again for a visit with the family.

Three or four days later, we sighted Flores, and as soon as we were near enough, a boat was lowered and the captain, Mary and I went ashore. We made a landfall off Ponte Delgado and coasted over to Fajangrand. As we came from the northwest, no one in Fajanzinha sighted us, and we took everyone by surprise. Only a few people from Fajangrand were at the dock when we arrived.

We began walking toward Fajazinha while the ship kept going in a southerly direction right by Fajazinha. Lucy's home, situated as it was on a knoll, had the best view of passing ships. One of her brothers spied the *Greyhound* and immediately ran to tell my father, who was at home. Of course, he promptly grabbed the binoculars and positively identified the ship. When Lucy heard her brother announce the ship, she said, "It's the *Greyhound*. I know it's the *Greyhound*. I'm going down to meet them." She knew that if the *Greyhound* were cruising around, we would already be ashore. My father started off immediately to meet us, and soon quite a crowd was on the way.

Lucy was first. What a greeting! About a mile from her house, we met my father, followed by the rest of the gathering procession. The rest of the trip home followed the usual routine, with Lucy and me in the lead, arm in arm, as two kids pretty much in love would naturally be.

My father's news was discouraging. He had quit whaling, and he had sold his interest in the bark *Fairhaven*. He had come to the conclusion that the era of the whaling ships was very rapidly drawing to a close. The price of whale oil was dropping, and substitutes were taking its place in industry and commerce. He advised me to go to New Bedford and get into some new industry, or to go onto steamers.

My dream and my ambition was to be master of my own sailing ship, and now I felt sick and miserable. The future? According to my father, and I respected his opinion above all others, there was no future—not in sailing ships, anyway.

I went to see Captain Corvello and Mary to talk it over with them. The captain was out, but Mary told me, "Yes, we feel the same way about it. Tony is awfully downhearted since father told us he had quit the business."

"Heck," I said, "the captain shouldn't be downhearted because father quit and sold out. Father has worked hard long enough. It's time he quit, anyway. Even for captains, it is a hard life. I don't know yet what I'm going to do, but I'll be doggoned if I'm going to spend four or five years learning the business and then find that there isn't a ship left that I can be master on. That's what I wanted to talk over with the captain. Father has advised me to get into something else or to go on steamers. He says the sailing ships are done for, and that it will be all steamers from now on."

When Captain Corvello came in later, we continued the conversation. "Yes," he agreed, "the sailing ships are about finished. The price of oil is so low that the only thing that saves the *Greyhound* is the fact that she has no mortgage on her. If she had, I'd have to take her home now. As it is, this might be our last trip. We'll talk it over again when we get to Las Palmas in the Canary Islands. Captain Cory should know how things look. He can help you decide what to do."

Of course, I hadn't decided to quit at this time, but I was pretty well convinced that it was the thing to do if Captain Corvello agreed to let me go.

We stayed three days at Flores. Lucy and I were inseparable, as we had always been. I had begun to think pretty seriously about her, but the new turn of events put a crimp in my enthusiasm, so far as the future was concerned. She was as lovely, sweet and precious as ever—more so, if such were possible. Being at home, with her around, was a sort of heaven in its own way. But I realized that my ambition for bigger things than being second mate had to be satisfied before I thought seriously about anyone.

We left for Las Palmas on the morning of the fourth day. We sighted Pico's lofty crown in the far distance, the following day. There would be no stop at Fayal; no Josephine. I could only wonder what the past year had done for her, and when I might see her once more. For a moment, I was lost in dreams. Looking toward Pico, I could imagine myself again in Fayal, going down the by-paths and along the beach in the moonlight, hand-in-hand with a lovely girl who had come to mean much more to me than just a friend in another port. Slowly, Pico began to fade away, and its lofty crown became lost in the distance. I felt that something in my life was fading with it. Now, perhaps, it was lost forever.

As we approached the harbor at Las Palmas, about three weeks later, we could see the masts of the *Clark* and two or three other whalers, silhouetted against the contrasting lights and shadows of land and sky. We had hardly more than come to the anchorage before the captain and I were on our way to call on Captain Corey. The news he brought was even more disheartening than my father's. And his opinion was the same.

My mind was made up. Rather than lose valuable years of training, I decided to go at once to New Bedford and, if possible, get onto a steamer. Captain Corvello agreed to release me from my contract, and Captain Corey offered to check with the steamship companies to see what steamer I could take to get back to the United States.

CHAPTER XXXVI

NEW HORIZONS

We spent some little time visiting, but most of the time the two captains were consoling one another on the bad situation in the whaling industry. "Too bad, Tony." I remember Captain Corey saying to Captain Corvello. "Just when you bring in the two biggest catches the *Greyhound* ever made."

"Well," Captain Corvello replied, "at least we're a little better off than if the catches had been small." He turned to me and asked, "Are you going back aboard tonight?"

"Yes," I answered, with a grin, "if I don't find something better to do."

"Oh, I know what you mean, but Joe, you better get back to the ship and stay there. These women have been here before and they know a lot more than you do. Remember, you are not in Fayal. You'd better go back to the ship and stay out of trouble."

"What the heck?" I countered. "They talk Spanish, and I talk Spanish almost as well as they do."

"Joe, take my advice. Go back to the ship and tell Mr. Frates you are going home; that Captain Corey will talk to the agent for the steamship company and find out when there is one going to the United States."

I went back to the ship, considerably against my own personal inclination. Next day, Captain Corey came by on the motor launch to take me ashore with him. He located the agent, who was almost next door to the hotel where Captain Corvello was staying, and found that a passenger ship from Barcelona, Spain, would be in port in a few days, bound for Havana, Cuba, via Las Palmas, Tenerife Island and Porto Rico. From Cuba I could take a Ward Line ship to New York. It sounded mighty good to me.

"Joe, how much money do you have with you?" the captain queried.

"You've got it," I answered.

"That's right. You gave me your money to keep for you when we left New Bedford. We'll go aboard tomorrow and check to see how much it is." We found I had a little over two hundred dollars, so he advanced me another hundred and fifty. Cabin class fare to New York was close to two hundred dollars, American money. I wanted to go second class, but first class cabins were all they had.

When the steamer came in, I bade all my friends good-by. There were tears in my eyes as I left the old ship, the *Greyhound*. I'd learned a lot about men and ships, and I'd made good progress toward my goal of becoming a ship's captain.

I felt a good deal as I had when Pico had faded away in the distance, only this was a ship instead of a girl. My sister, the captain, Captain Mandley and Captain Corey went aboard the steamer and gave me a big send-off. They made me feel that the big things were all ahead and that the important thing in life was to look to the future and make the most of it. That was exactly what I resolved to do.

The steamer picked up anchor early in the afternoon and we arrived at Tenerife Island just as it was getting dark. At about midnight we headed for Porto Rico. The trip was one such as I had never imagined; nor have I ever seen the likes of it since. There were only a few young fellows going cabin class, but there were lots of young women—French and Spanish women. I have been on a lot of ships in my lifetime, passenger ships, trunk ships, freighters, whalers and tankers, but I have never seen so much free love as there was on that ship. Those girls were in and out of the cabins at all hours of the day and night. They certainly kept those boys awfully busy.

At Porto Rico there was a ship from the Red Star Line going to New York, so I tried to get on it. I had more than enough money for the extra fare, but, for some reason unknown to me, the authorities wouldn't let me get off the ship I was on. At Havana I had to wait four or five days for the Ward Line ship.

On the last night before going aboard, I was slugged while asleep and robbed of every cent I had, except twenty dollars that I had hidden in the toe of my left shoe. I'd broken the toe out while on the *Greyhound,* and it made a good place to stuff in those two bills. Then I had a couple of dollars that they had missed in one of my pockets. I had ten cents in my pocket when I got off at Pier 28, East River, in New York.

I asked a lot of questions about how to get to Pier 14, North River, to the Fall River Line ships, and finally got there. I found a fellow, Charlie Richards, who was from New Bedford and was visiting on one of the ships. He loaned me five dollars and went with me back to Pier 28 to pick up my clothes. Then we went to Pier 40, West Street, the New Bedford Line pier, and went aboard one of the boats that made the trip nightly to New Bedford. It was the steamer *Maine,* a beautiful, white passenger ship on which Charlie was quartermaster. He told me that a cousin of mine, John Henry, was second mate. We found him on the freight deck. Charlie introduced me, and I thought I had never seen anyone who looked more elegant in a fine, new uniform. We went up the stairway and found Captain Robinson on the second deck. I had seen him before, but had never met him, so Charlie introduced me.

Captain Robinson was a gentleman and a scholar. He had a smile and a greeting for everyone. He didn't care whether you were a pauper, a kid, or a millionaire with whiskers. He was the same to everyone. I never saw him any different, and I worked under him and with him for a long time.

When he heard my name, he said, "Gomes? Is that your father who was captain on the bark *Fairhaven?*"

"Yes, sir."

"Well, I knew him very well indeed. He's an old friend of mine." That pleased me immensely. "Your brother-in-law, Captain Corvello—?" he continued, questioningly.

"I just left him a few days ago."

"The *Greyhound?* Isn't that the ship he is on? How is he doing?"

"Oh, doing swell. We have had practically a full ship every season, and when I left him now, in the Canary Islands, we had just got in with a terrific deck load."

"Are you sick? What did you come home for?"

"I came home because the whaling industry is at an end. There is no future there. I got to be second mate, but that is as far as I could ever get."

"What are you going to do? Are you going to school?"

"Oh, no. I can't afford to go to school. I have to look for a job."

"What kind of a job are you looking for?"

"I don't know. I'd like to work on steamers, but I've never been on one. I may go to Boston, or come back to New York and look for a sailing ship."

"Ah," he said, "sailing ships are a thing of the past. Why don't you get onto a steamer?"

"That sounds very fine, sir, but—"

"Listen. We have a deck boy here named Handy who is going to the hospital day after tomorrow, which will leave an opening here."

"But I'm a sailor—"

"At least we'll have a good sailor on the *Maine,* and you'll be surprised what a good sailor can do on a ship like this. There is always line to be spliced and, well, you'd be surprised how handy you could be."

"Captain, do you mean it?"

"Listen, Joe, I very seldom say anything I don't mean."

CHAPTER XXXVII

FROM DUNGAREES TO UNIFORMS

I was pleased, beyond anything I can describe, to think that even before I got into New Bedford I had landed a job on a steamer.

Charlie took me to my stateroom, where I put my clothes down. I then went back to the freight deck to talk to John Henry. I felt very grateful to Charlie for doing so much for me.

New York was a big city and I was a stranger in it. He had loaned me five dollars and had practically led me to a new job just when I wanted most to get one. I was already dreaming of a brand new future on steamships.

On West Street, in those days, there were very few trucks. The place was literally lousy with horses—teams of two, four, six and eight—some coming, some going. They were loading or unloading at the piers. The freight was trucked aboard the steamers by human hand power. In due time, the freight and passengers were aboard and the captain called me up to the pilothouse so I could see the New York harbor. After we got outside Hell Gate Bridge —it was then under construction—he took me down to the coffee shop and treated me to a cup of coffee and a doughnut. More doughnuts if I wanted them, but I was too happy and excited to feel hungry, so one was all I had.

I was up before daylight the next morning. In fact, we had just come up to Hen and Chickens Lightship at the entrance to Buzzards Bay. I paraded around the decks and went up for a cup of coffee. I saw Mr. Farris, the first mate, whom I'd met the day before, and talked with him for a few minutes. I waited around for a while until Charlie could get away and go with me. While I was waiting, I got acquainted with the rest of the sailors, the other quartermaster, and the pilots and bow watchmen. When Charlie came in, he asked where I was going to go.

"I would like to go down to my aunt's house because that is where I'll sleep." He said, "Okay. Let's go. You have only two bags. We'll carry them and take the street car." We walked up Union Street, and I stopped at the whaling outfitters and talked to Captain Mandley's father and another retired captain named Rodman, and went on to my Aunt Emily's.

She wasn't expecting me. When she saw me come through the kitchen door, she was so startled that she dropped the plate she had in her hand. She was drying dishes at the kitchen sink. "Well, Joe. What's the matter with you? What are you doing here? I thought you were out at sea. Look at you—you cost me a plate!"

After I had explained to her, she said, "I'll tell you what. Don't go on a steamer. Why don't you go with Joe, my husband?"

"Why? What do you mean?"

"Go with Joe. Learn the fishing business. He's thinking of buying another boat and as soon as you know how to handle a boat he'll give you one."

"Me, a fisherman? No, ma'am, not on your life. I already have a job to go to."

"You haven't got in yet, and you already have a job?"

"That's right."

I stayed there that night. I saw the old boarders, those who were still there from two years before, and the next day I walked around, saw some old friends, and went to Mount Carmel Church, where I used to go every Sunday when I was in New Bedford. I talked for a while with the pastor, a very old but a very brilliant man. Then I visited with some families I'd gotten acquainted with two years before. I thought I'd go to a movie afterward but changed my mind and went home to spend the rest of the evening with my aunt and her husband's niece.

Next day I got up early and got my clothes ready for the trip down to New York to the steamer. I bought a suitcase—the first one I'd ever owned—at the whaling outfitters. Eleanor and Aunt Emily put the finishing touches on my clothes, and as soon as I heard the steamer's whistle I bade them good-by, took a streetcar and went down to board the ship. Everyone greeted me and I felt that it was a genuine welcome. I wasn't a passenger, and I wasn't yet a member of the crew, but it felt good to be greeted as though I belonged.

I walked around and visited with the sailors around the fo'c's'le, with my cousin (the second mate), and with some of the passengers. I kept walking around, admiring the ship. It was all white and beautiful. The cabins and dining room were all nice and clean, just as in a first class restaurant. I went to bed late in the evening but I was up before daylight, too excited to sleep. I saw a flashing white light when I looked out the porthole, and as soon as I'd dressed, I went up on "B" deck and asked the bow watchman what it was. "That's Sandy Point on Long Island."

"What's the other one ahead?"

"That's Stepping Stone." It was just ahead, a little off the port bow. The steamer *Maine* was going full speed ahead, about eighteen or twenty knots. I noticed still another light off to port beyond Stepping Stone. That proved to be Port Schuyler. As we approached Stepping Stone, the light revolved and threw a glow on deck. The pilot, Captain George Peterson from New Bedford, recognized me and called me up.

"Joe, would you like to come up to the pilothouse?"

"Yes, sir. With pleasure." He asked all sorts of questions about whaling and about Captain Corvello. Captain Robinson came in as we approached Hell Gate. We went through the East River, around the Battery, and up to Pier 40, North River. As we came up to the dock, I left the pilothouse and went down to give the sailors a hand with the line. I was going to work that night, and figured there was no better time to start learning. After the ship was tied up, we all went to breakfast. Handy, the fellow who was going to the hospital, stuck out his hand. "Good luck, Joe. You're on a good ship with a good gang. They're aces high and the captain is very good and he's democratic. The first mate is a little cranky, but he doesn't mean it. He's old and his feet and legs bother him a lot. He walks around with a stick a good deal. He means all right, so don't get discouraged."

Handy bade us good-by, and I was at work on a new job.

Handy was head deck boy—in other words, boss of the sailors, or bo's'n. A Norwegian fellow took his place but proved to be a poor boss. Most of the time, only two or three of the fellows would be working and the rest would be smoking or hiding out. He was young, about twenty-two years old, and a pretty good sailor, but too lax. He just couldn't run a gang of men.

I had been on the job about two weeks when Mr. Farris sent for me. I had organized a regular gym the first week on board, and had interested a lot of fellows in boxing. I thought I was in for some kind of reprimand, but Mr. Farris came right to the point with, "Joe, how would you like to go bo's'n?"

"I'd love it when the time comes."

"Well, the time is here."

"No, sir. Not yet, certainly."

"Oh, yes. If you want to go bo's'n you can start today. I've got to let the bo's'n go. He's a good sailor but he can't handle men."

"But this is all the experience I've had on a steamer."

"I know you can handle men, and I know you're a good sailor, so if it's agreeable with you, you can go bo's'n right now."

I thanked him a couple of times. I really liked the idea. I went down immediately to John Henry, my second mate cousin, and told him the good tidings. "Well," he said, "I could have told you that a week ago, but I figured it was better to wait."

The first thing to do was to put the twelve sailors to work. The ship had begun to look a bit dirty since Handy had left, so I put everyone to work with rags, soap and water. I didn't find it difficult to keep them busy, and before long everything was clean and bright again. I reflected that I'd been on the steamer two weeks lacking a day and already had my first promotion—made my first step up the ladder.

The more I saw of the life on the steamer, the more determined I was to become the captain of my own ship. With this in mind, I became rather a pest whenever I was off duty, asking questions and learning from whoever I thought could give me the answers—sailors, deck hands, quartermasters, bow watchmen, even stewards and passengers. The stewards were mostly colored, well-educated and intelligent people, and capable of giving first class service to first class passengers. They were always obliging, and helped me with new words and unfamiliar expressions.

I began to analyze the difference between working and living on a steamer as compared to a whaler. To begin with, we had very good meals—fresh meat and vegetables, and fresh running water. That fresh cool water was wonderful compared to the water out of the whale oil casks. It was delicious—and then to be able to turn a faucet and have fresh, cool water for washing one's face as often as one liked! No cockroaches or bedbugs, no hardtack, no salt pork, no salt meat. There were no "donkey breakfasts," that is, no straw mattresses, as on whalers. Here there was a good bed to sleep on. I felt as though I'd suddenly stepped through a gate right into heaven. Nothing would ever satisfy me now until I'd made captain—become master of my own ship.

After a few weeks, we changed from summer boats to winter boats. Winter steamers simply carry cargo—no passengers. One day they are in New York and the next day in New Bedford, usually making the run at night. They have no special time of departure, and, of course, the winter steamers stay on the run until spring.

Some little time after we'd become accustomed to the routine of traders (one day in January or February, I think it was), Captain Robinson surprised me by coming up to me and greeting me with, "Joe, how would you like to go bow watchman?"

"What! Bow watchman! Oh, God, that would be wonderful, perfect, but I'm not ready for it yet, am I?"

"Yes, you are, Joe. I've been in the office and spoken to the general manager. I want you for bow watchman, and from there I want you to go quartermaster. A fellow like you, who is always busy, is the kind who helps the ship make money. I've noticed also that when you don't have work to do, you always have a book stuck under your nose. I like your style. I told the manager there was a chance for you to go bow watchman and I wanted you to have it. I think you know that one of our bow watchmen, Arthur Manchester, who lives in Providence, is going quartermaster on the Providence Line. He is being transferred today, so you will be starting out as bow watchman tonight."

I could only thank Captain Robinson as I had done before, on my first promotion. I had never expected another so soon. I had to share the news of my good fortune with someone, so I immediately ran down to Mr. Farris and John Henry, who happened to be talking together.

"Do you know what happened?" I broke in.

"Yes, we know all about it." Apparently everyone on board had known about it except me. Anyway, I sailed out of there that night on the bow. It is the bow watchman's duty to stand watch outside as the ship leaves the harbor, to walk back and forth on the bow and report anything unusual to the pilot who is in the pilothouse, but the bow watchman stands no regular watch outside, except under unusual conditions.

Everyone treated me superbly. The captain and both the first and second pilots and, yes, the quartermaster too, all told me to ask them any questions any time about anything I needed information on. It was a white-collar job with a lot of opportunity for studying. It didn't pay much, but to me it spelled opportunity, and I was very glad.

In later years, because of the work and the fine treatment I had experienced on those inland steamers, I always thought of them and frequently referred to them as the "Gentlemen's Lines."

CHAPTER XXXVIII

NAVIGATION AND KNOCKOUTS

After going into the pilothouse, a bow watchman would relieve the quartermaster at the wheel, or after a while, go down to the galley and get coffee and sandwiches for the pilothouse—for the pilot on watch, the quartermaster, the bow watchman, and an extra or two with sandwiches for the captain, if he so desired. In going by the captain's door, the bow watchman would rap, and say, "Coffee Captain?" and Captain Robinson would usually come up and have coffee and sandwiches or a cigarette with us. The ship would be going full speed through Long Island Sound out of New York, for instance, so there was no relaxation. The pilot would be at the midship window, which was open or partly so, and the quartermaster or bow watchman would be looking out and around for small boats or anything that might be in front, while the other was at the wheel. It took but a couple of minutes to fetch the coffee and sandwiches. Going out of the harbor, though, the bow watchman never left the bow.

We would be relieved by the second watch when we got to Cornfield Lightship, which was just about midway on the run. Then we would go to bed until we reached port again—New Bedford, in this instance, and there would be no more duty until evening, when the ship left the dock. That would leave me the entire day to sleep, rest, walk around, or sit in my room or in the pilothouse, and study. With all this time on my hands, I felt like a millionaire, without money. In my own language, I was feeling like a "rich bitch."

On this first trip, I stayed on the ship and studied until about ten o'clock, then I walked down to Aunt Emily's to give her the good news.

When I was bo's'n, I went to see Aunt Emily about once a week.

Now I could go every other day except Saturday, when we lay over wherever we happened to be. So, of course, if we happened to be in New York, the routine would change somewhat. I kept up my gym work and boxing with the crew. I liked fighting as much as ever, if not more. The only officer who would box with us was John Henry, who could hold his own with anyone. With the crew there was no deference as to size or weight. The gym work also helped me keep my resolution neither to drink nor smoke.

The longer I remained bow watchman the better I liked it. There wasn't a heck of a lot to do. Up to now I hadn't known that I had a lazy bone in my body, but the lazy bones began to show up. However, the gym work helped keep me fit, and one Saturday night in New Bedford I went down to see some fights. The arena was absolutely filled. I had a seat in the bleachers. In one of the preliminary six-round bouts, someone called out from the ring, "Is there a volunteer in the house about a hundred forty pounds? One of our boys is sick and couldn't come."

"Here," I yelled, jumping up and waving my arm. "I'll take it." I ran down into the ring. The promoter met me just below the ring.

"Here," he said. "I'll take you to a dressing room." He took me to one and started looking for a pair of trunks. He couldn't find any, but Jack Doyle, a policeman who acted as agent for the local talent, came in with a pair several sizes too big. He took them up on the sides with safety pins.

"Who's your second?" he asked.

"I haven't any. I just volunteered."

"I'll act as second for you."

"That's okay with me." And we headed for the ring. Once in it, I forgot about the crowd—about everything except that I was getting into a match. I started sparring, feeling out my opponent. He barely got to me with a couple of jabs, and before the first round was over I was sure that I was the better boxer. Between rounds, Doyle asked, "Can you switch to southpaw?"

"Just as good as my right," I answered. "For anything else my left is no good, but for fighting, my left is as good as my right."

"Good. Feel him out on this round and then if you think you can handle him, let him have it in the third."

I switched, and before the round was over I was sure of myself.

I continued sparring. As the third round began, I settled down to serious work. Suddenly I found an opening and came in with a left hook and a right cross. He went down for the count. I had won my first professional fight, and in a matter of minutes I was being paid off. Thirty-five dollars—the easiest money I had ever made. Jack Doyle came into the dressing room with me. "What gym do you work in?" he wanted to know.

"I have my own gym."

"Where's that?"

"I'm bow watchman on a New Bedford Line ship, the *Mohican,* and I set up my own gym on it."

"I'd like to sign you up as one of my boys."

"No, thank you, but I'd rather keep on just as I am right now." Just then the promoter came in and announced that there was an opening in a fight two weeks later. He asked whether I would like to sign up. I did, and I won that fight with a "K.O." in the second round. Without realizing it, I had picked up a side line as a professional fighter. Except for a few bouts, however, I didn't go into it seriously until considerably later on. But each fight gave me better money, and I liked that as well as the fighting. The last of the series at New Bedford paid me ninety-five dollars. I did a lot of fighting later on, but that belongs in another story.

With my job as bow watchman I had a good deal of time on my hands. I was sure that my English was getting much better. I could both read and write with much more facility. On my days in New York I would spend a good deal of time learning my way about the city. And with all the time I had at my disposal, I decided to enter a navigation college that would be easy to get to.

I found that college. It was one of the very best, and was located in Brooklyn, a five-cent ride from Bowling Green. I could take a West Street car to Bowling Green and go from there to Brooklyn on the subway. The next consideration was money. The navigation college required one hundred and fifty dollars tuition, payable in advance, for the first six months. My bow watchman's pay wouldn't go very far on that. It took a good deal of my weekly pay to meet the cost of my new uniforms, white shirts and black ties, and other necessities.

As with most white-collar jobs, the wages were low and it took a lot more to keep up appearances. But I liked it. It was a new world and it was good. It was a step on the way toward a captaincy, and like the navigation school, it was one of the essentials —only, navigation, so far as knowledge was concerned, was much more fundamental. I was sure that the only way to a steamship captaincy was through hard work and study, and while I knew enough about celestial navigation to bring a sailing ship into port, I felt that proficiency on a steamer demanded a thorough knowledge of astronomy—the heart of navigation.

I went to my cousin, John Henry, and explained what I wanted to do. I told him that I had a few hundred dollars coming from the *Greyhound*, but that it might be a year before she came home and her ship's business was settled.

"I'll lend you the money, Joe. I'll go to the bank and get it, as soon as we get back to New York." I was very pleased with his offer.

Next morning, we arrived in New Bedford and I went to the whalers' outfitting store and asked for Captain Smith, the agent for the *Greyhound*. Mr. Harwitz, the owner of the store, told me where he lived. I took the streetcar to his house and arrived just before lunch time. The captain and his wife invited me to stay, and we had a nice visit. Captain Smith wanted to know how things had gone with me on the *Greyhound*. After relating some of my experiences, I told him of my present plans and the predicament I was in; that I needed the hundred and fifty dollars for tuition, and that John Henry had offered to make me a loan.

"Well, no, Joe. That isn't necessary. Although the ship's business won't be settled until after the ship comes in, I know you have several hundred dollars coming, and I know you and your family and Captain Corvello, and I can advance you a couple of hundred dollars. That will take care of your tuition and leave a little for other expenses until you get your new uniforms and things paid for. It's your own money and you're entitled to it."

I felt like kissing the old gentleman, and thanked them for the nice lunch they had given me.

I returned to the *Mohican* and told John Henry of my good fortune. "That's fine, Joe. Of course, it's your own money. But I'd have let you have it," he said, almost as though he was sorry. Of course, I thanked him. I appreciated it as much as though he'd actually lent me the money. One thing I discovered: that when people knew I was sincerely trying to accomplish something or that I was working hard to achieve some particular goal, there was always someone willing—even eager—to help.

When we arrived in New York the next day, I went to Brooklyn and paid the hundred and fifty dollars for the first six months at navigation school. When I asked how long the course would take, I was told that since I would be coming only three days a week, it would take over two years. "That's all right," I said. "I expect to be around here for more than two years, anyway." Then the man to whom I had paid the fee began questioning me on navigation. After a few minutes of questions, he remarked, "No. It won't take two years. It will probably take less than a year for you to get the full course, because you are pretty well advanced." The more I talked with him the happier I began to feel. I went back to the *Mohican* in high spirits.

We soon resumed the regular summer runs, and I kept busy. I studied much of the time, kept up with my gym work, and got an occasional fight. After I had my uniforms paid for, the fights kept me in pretty good financial shape, considering my few needs.

There was no chance to get any assistance from any of the officers on my navigational studies. Navigation on the high seas is an entirely different thing from navigation on inland waters. Suffice it to say here that I studied very hard. I finished the course in navigation in less than a year. At the time of my graduation, I took the examination for second-mate's license on ocean-going steamships of any gross tonnage, and passed it. I presented the necessary letter from Captain Corvello covering my experience on the *Pedro Varella* and the *Greyhound,* to the United States Bureau of Steamboat Inspection. I felt that it was a great day indeed when I received my second-mate's license and signed it before the U.S. Inspector.

I began at once to study for first class pilot's license on New York bays and rivers, and obtained it. Within the next six months I passed examinations for Long Island Sound to Bridgeport, Connecticut; New Haven, Connecticut; New London, Connecticut; also through the Race and Block Island Sound; to Providence,

Rhode Island; Fall River, Massachusetts; and through Buzzards Bay to New Bedford, Massachusetts. During this time I had been bow watchman and quartermaster. Then I began to relieve the second pilots on various runs to the above-named harbors. Some time before I obtained my pilot's license, Captain Corvello and Mary had come home to New Bedford and remained for the winter. With them came a beautiful little bundle of joy, just learning to talk. My vacations had accumulated so that I had three weeks due. I took them all together and spent them with Captain Corvello, Mary, and my new little niece.

CHAPTER XXXIX

YOUNG CAPTAIN

Much more could be told of my experiences during this initial period of my life on steamships, but I feel that it belongs more properly in another story, since this book was designed to cover that period of my life spent on sailing ships. Of this there remains one chapter to be written—the one in which I first realized my ambition to become captain on a sea-going ship.

Shortly after my vacation, I was sent second pilot on the Providence Line. We had just completed the run to New York. I left the ship, and as I was walking on the dock, the captain of the ship, Tom Rawlin, who was coming out of the company office, saw me and called out, "Joe, the boss wants to talk to you in his office." The "boss" was Tom Elliott, whom I had known for some time.

"Oh, oh," I said to myself. "What the hell have I done now?" I walked over to Mr. Elliott and saw he had a pleasant smile, so I consoled myself that nothing was wrong. He shook hands warmly. "Joe, I was just looking for you to come by. How long have you been with us now? Over two years?"

"That's right."

"You were for a long time on ocean-going sailing ships, and you are a celestial navigator, isn't that right?"

"Yes, sir. I think I can handle any kind of sailing ship anywhere."

"Well, Joe, that's what I want to talk to you about. My brother Frank is representative in this country for the Barcelona Navigation Company. He has a four-masted schooner anchored off Bay Ridge Flats. You know where that is. It's fully loaded, with a crew on board, but they've been unable to locate a captain—a navigator with sailing ship experience who speaks Spanish."

"Wait a minute, Mr. Elliott. I don't follow you."

"Well, Joe, from what our captains have told me, you are just the man Frank needs."

"What is this all about?" I asked.

"They want this ship to be taken to Barcelona and turned over to the Barcelona Navigation Company. You don't have to stay there. You just turn the ship over to the company, under the supervision of the American Consul, and bring the crew back."

"Mr. Elliott, does the fact that a war has just broken out have anything to do with the difficulty of getting a captain?"

"That could be partly the reason. The ship and cargo have just been sold to the Barcelona Navigation Company and put under the Spanish flag, so the most important factor seems to be the need for a captain who can speak Spanish fluently. Neither this country nor Spain is involved in the war, so even if you are boarded, there should be no difficulty. Are you willing to take it?"

"Well, yes, if my job will still be here for me when I get back."

Frankly, the proposition intrigued me immensely. Here was a chance to see how it would feel to be a captain with the deck of a big four-master under my feet. It wouldn't be for long, but it would be the real thing while it lasted.

"Joe," Mr. Elliott assured me, "regardless of who has your job while you are gone, it will be waiting for you the day you return."

"That's good enough for me."

"I'll call Frank and tell him to come over." He telephoned his brother, and we waited for a few minutes. He offered me a cigarette but I refused, saying that I didn't smoke. In a few minutes, a tall, young fellow walked in. They exchanged greetings and Tom introduced us. Frank Elliott then explained that they had been held up for over a week with a ship and full crew at anchor off Bay

Ridge Flats, unsuccessfully looking for a captain. They had even called Norfolk and Boston, among others. Frank had told Tom of his predicament and Tom had talked to Captain Robinson. "Wait a minute," Captain Robinson had said. "Joe Gomes is the only man employed by our company who can handle this kind of a job." Mr. Elliott had spoken to Captain Rawlin, and here I was—going captain on a four-master, which I soon discovered was even bigger than the *Richard W. Clark,* which, to me, had been the ultimate in sailing ships.

Frank explained to me that everything was ready. All I had to do was to get under way and take the ship to Barcelona.

"Just a minute," I broke in. "That's in the Mediterranean. I've never been in the Mediterranean Sea and I don't know a thing about the winds or the currents. Will you get me an ocean-going pilot book so I can study the currents and weather conditions in the Mediterranean on the way over and know what to expect when I approach the Rock of Gibraltar?"

"I'll have it in the next hour," he said. "How soon can you go?"

"I'm ready, but I don't have a sextant."

"There's one on the ship. It may not be correct."

"I know how to adjust it. What about a chronometer? How many are there? One, or three?"

"One, I think."

"We will have to check it. I want the date when it was adjusted and the rate on it."

"I am pretty sure that everything is there on it. Are you ready?"

"Just give me time to get on board, get my clothes, tell the gang the news, and say good-by to them. But don't figure on sailing today, because there are lots of things to check. I haven't met the mates, and I have to check the equipment, and I've got to know a little more about what goes on, before going out to sea, but if everything is as ready as you say, you can figure on sailing tomorrow morning at daylight."

"Okay, Joe. I'll wait here while you get your gear."

The gang on board was really surprised at the news, and they all wished me good luck and a safe voyage.

Wages hadn't been discussed as yet. I didn't know what to ask, and they didn't know what to expect from me. I wanted a little time to think. By the time I got back to where Frank Elliott was waiting, I thought I had it pretty well figured out.

He called a cab and we went to his office. He introduced me to his secretary as Captain Gomes. You can imagine how straight I stood and how my chest stuck out when I was introduced as Captain Gomes. He introduced me to everyone in the office as Captain.

"Well now, captain, how about wages?"

"Frankly, I don't know what sailing ship captains get on freighters or cargo vessels. I have been waiting for you to suggest something."

"What do you think of two-hundred-fifty dollars a month?"

"Until we get to Barcelona, or back to New York?"

"Back to New York. We have discussed that. If it were only to Barcelona, we would have offered more."

"That seems fair enough. I'll accept the two-fifty to run until the day we get back to New York. Now that wages are settled, the next thing I want to do is get on board and check the chronometer."

"I can't go," Frank said. "I've got too much to do. But I'll send one of my boys with you."

He called a fellow to go with us, and we took a cab over to South Ferry, where we got a motorboat to take us to the ship. I was really surprised at the size of the ship. I had compared all sailing ships, more or less unconsciously, to the *Clark*. As I looked at it, I realized for the first time that I was master of a ship bigger than the one under Captain Corey. And, as the reader may well deduce, Captain Corey was my idol. Even in the two years or more that I'd been on inland steamers, I still thought of Captain Corey as the one to judge other captains by. Now I was comparing myself and I felt sort of amazed and a little shaken at the thought. But there was no time for daydreaming.

Jack, the fellow with me, and I, climbed aboard. He introduced me to the mate and second mate. "This is Captain Gomes who is taking the ship to Barcelona."

The mate frowned a little. I could see by the expression on his face that he thought I was too young for the job. I began asking him questions. "Have you ever had the sails set?"

"Yes. We set the sails one by one and everything seems to be in good working order."

"Seems to be, or is?"

"Everything *is* in working order."

"How about the sheaves on the heavy sails? The mainsails? Are they all working?"

"Yes, sir."

"How are the halyards? Are they in good condition?"

"Yes, sir. They are practically new."

We went down to the cabin. I asked the mate, "When was the last time you wound the chronometer?"

"I wound the chronometer at eight o'clock this morning."

"Is that the usual time?"

"Yes, sir."

I checked on the rate of the chronometer. The date it had been adjusted was there, and the rate showed very plainly. I then inquired about the taffrail log and the adjustment of the compass, which were both satisfactory. I went to the captain's room—my room—and opened the sextant box. I saw that the sextant, either new or nearly so, was in very good condition. I checked on the water and provisions, making sure that we had enough for more than seventy days.

"How are the bilge pumps?" I asked the mate. "Have they been tried?"

"Yes, I try all three every morning and they are water-free."

"There are no leaks of any sort?"

"No, sir."

"How are the anchors, windlass and chains?"

"Very good, sir."

"Have you been down on the fish strike?"

"I have examined everything out there. I have also examined the jib boom and foremasts. The riggings are in good condition."

We came up on deck and we talked and walked around the quarter-deck and I looked at the motorboat. I asked the mate about it. "It is practically a new boat," he said. "It seems that on the last trip they had an accident coming alongside with the old one, so they junked it and got this new one. The motor is excellent."

"How about the equipment?"

"It is fully equipped with mast and sails and it is fully provisioned."

"Have you checked the water?"

"No, sir. I haven't."

"Tomorrow, after we get outside of Ambrose Channel, check the water and provisions. Be sure we have enough in case we should have to abandon ship. Also, I presume the galley is fully equipped."

"Yes, sir."

"What type of cargo below decks?"

"I don't know. The vessel was loaded before I boarded, sir."

I looked at Jack, the fellow from the office, and he said, "Mr. Elliott will give you the manifest when we get to the office."

I turned to the mate and ordered, "Have all hands on board at five in the morning. I will return this afternoon with the ship's papers, ready to sail."

Jack and I left and went back to Frank Elliott's office. I informed Mr. Elliott that everything was satisfactory, and asked him to order the tug for daylight in the morning. I asked for the cargo manifest and the articles and, taking Jack with me, went to the Spanish Consul's office where I signed all necessary papers. I received my clearance together with all required official papers, and bade the Consul good-by.

We returned again to Mr. Elliott's office to get my final orders, and to pick up my personal gear which I had left there. It was then past noon, and Mr. Elliott was waiting to take me to lunch.

Over a luncheon of excellent steaks, he gave me my final instructions and informed me that he was sending a letter to the owners by registered mail. He also informed me he had that day received a letter saying that the owners were anxious to receive some of the cargo. Our business finished, I bade Mr. Elliott good-by, and Jack took me back to the ship in the motorboat. It was about four o'clock when I arrived on board, and the mates took my gear to the cabin. We sat down and talked, as it was the first opportunity we had to get acquainted. After a little while, the dinner bell rang and I told the cook that a piece of pie and a cup of coffee would do for me as I'd just had a hearty lunch. He looked at me and said, "Oh, my God! What a young Captain!" I just grinned and went and sat down with the mates.

I checked around through the galley. It was the most elaborate one I had ever seen on a sailing ship and everything was spotless.

From my brief observation, it seemed that we had a very good cook, also. On a freighter, only one man served in the galley. Some referred to him as cook, others as steward.

I went out on deck to do a little more checking on the ship in general. I was still amazed at the size of this four-master. The quarter-deck was huge. I hadn't had time to go over the manifest to discuss what type of cargo we had below decks, but we had a very large deck cargo of new lumber. The fo'c's'le and the galley were both on one house, amidships beyond the main mast, with lumber on both wings, stacked just as high as the midship house.

I took the mates with me to have a look at the windlass and the donkey boiler. I asked the mate if the donkey boiler was all right, and he said that everything was in perfect shape. Of course, ever since coming aboard I had been keeping a critical eye on the two mates. After my first round of inspection and questioning, the first mate seemed to be satisfied that I knew how to handle my job, and he seemed to know his job satisfactorily. His manner was respectful, though a bit reserved, which I would expect of a good chief mate of his age—fifty-one, according to the Articles. The second mate didn't impress me very favorably. He was a younger man of about thirty-five, and his attitude toward the first mate was one I would describe as of sneering tolerance. Time, very shortly, would help to set everything in place, I told myself—if I did my part. Another thing I learned out of my experiences (and I believe it to be particularly true at sea) is that there always seems to be a time of testing in every new job; and a man either comes through satisfactorily, or falls miserably by the wayside if he is found wanting in any important respect. I had a goodly measure of confidence in myself. Of one thing I was sure—if I ever did fall short in any way, I would at least go down fighting. So, while I felt a little inadequate when I considered the size of this ship and saw myself in comparison to Captain Corcy, I was still confident that I would pass the test, even though I was very young to be the master of a big ship.

CHAPTER XL

OFFICER OR SAILOR?

Besides the two mates, the crew consisted of the cook and eight sailors before the mast—a small but adequate crew. I blessed myself and prayed that I might bring that ship, the cargo, and those lives into port in good condition. After I had checked everything aboard that could bear any importance in relation to our passage, it was dark. There was nothing in particular to do, and I had a busy day. I went to my cabin, said a prayer to the Blessed Virgin, and went to bed. I thought I couldn't go to sleep for thinking what was ahead of me the next day, but when I lighted a match to see what time it was, I was amazed to see the hands of the clock standing at four-thirty. I lighted the lamp and lay back in bed to do some more thinking. If I'd had cigarettes, I would have smoked, or if there had been some Scotch handy, I might have taken a tiny nip! I wasn't myself. I felt so big and strong and powerful that the Lord only knows how I really felt.

I dressed and went up on deck. It was pretty chilly. I found myself shivering a bit, so I went down and put on a sweater. The mate was up, talking to the man on watch. I joined them. It was about five o'clock, and a few minutes later we saw the dim form of the tug, with its lights, moving out from the pier and starting toward us. The mate called for all hands on deck. The tug came alongside. I can still close my eyes and see the name of that tug as the letters became visible in the growing light—big, white letters spelling out the name *Dell-Zell*. I smiled as I thought of some other white letters I had once made—*Kipp ovv dis boat!* The captain of the tug asked me if we were ready.

"All we have to do is heave up anchor!"

The mate who had been working the donkey boiler came up and said, "Captain, we are ready."

"All right," I answered, "go forward and heave up short."

As soon as the chain was straight up and down, he called out, "The chain is up and down!" I relayed the message to the captain of the tug boat, who gave the man on the bow his towing hawser, after which he came on board the ship.

"Captain," he questioned, "do you want me to bring my mate on board to handle the vessel going down the stream, or do you want one of your own men at the wheel to follow the tug?"

"What is the usual procedure?"

"Well, Captain, different ships differ on long splices." I just smiled, and he continued:

"Okay. Just put one of your mates at the wheel and follow me."

"All right," I answered, and ordered the second mate to take the wheel. We hove up the anchor and the mate secured it while we were going down New York Harbor.

Except for a couple of trips to Staten Island to see the bay, I had never sailed this part of New York Harbor on the lower bay. As we got into Ambrose Channel, I told the mate to unfurl sails and have them ready to hoist. After that was done, he said, "Captain, it will take awhile before we get out to Ambrose Lightship. Will it be all right to let the men have coffee?" "Oh, yes, of course," I responded. He ordered the men to have coffee, and brought one out for me and one for himself, and told the cook to bring one to the second mate. We stood there, drinking the coffee and talking, occasionally addressing the second mate. My opinion of him hadn't changed. I took a distinct dislike to the sneering way he looked at the first mate when the latter's back was turned.

When we got down to the end of Ambrose Channel, going toward the sea buoy, I gave orders to set the forestaysails, jib, foresail, and the spanker. We still had booms and gaffs amidships. I didn't know just how far out the tug would take us, but just after we passed Ambrose Lightship, the captain gave us the signal (two short blasts) to stand by. To the mate I said, "You might as well hoist the mainsail and the flying jib." The tug blew one blast and I yelled to the men on the fo'c's'le head, "Let go the tow line!" We put the wheel over and headed out to sea on the starboard tack. We began to make headway, so I told the mate to set watches and send a man to relieve the second mate; then set all sails. We had a moderate breeze, close to twenty miles an hour, about N.NE.—just enough to heel the ship over and give her good steering way.

It was about time to eat, so we all had breakfast. The mate turned the first watch over to the second mate and I set the course toward Nantucket Lightship. The second mate suggested that we were going too far off shore. "Mr. Second Mate," I said with all the authority that I felt my position gave me, "you will stand your watch under my orders. I have set the course." He walked away, and I let it go. I wanted to pass five or six miles off Nantucket Lightship, steering clear of the steamship lanes. By ten or eleven o'clock the breeze had come up quite a bit. We picked up the lightship in the evening—about four points on the port bow. The second mate was again on watch and the wind was about N.NW. We were sailing on course, making good speed—about ten knots. Everything was satisfactory except for the fact that I didn't feel I could place much trust in the second mate. He went off watch, and I talked to the first mate for a while, then went below to bed.

I felt my responsibility a little too much to sleep well, and at about midnight I came up on deck. The barometer was steady but had dropped a bit. The mate said the breeze was getting stronger, but there was nothing to be alarmed about. I went below again and slept until about five. I knew the second mate was on watch, but reminded myself that he should be capable, so I lay back for a while, thinking. An hour later I came up on deck and found the second mate sitting down, drinking coffee and smoking a cigarette. I didn't like it. In fact, I guess the reason I came up on deck early was that I couldn't hear him walking overhead. I bade him good morning and asked him if all sails were still out.

We were practically making steamboat time, and the vessel

was laboring quite a bit. The wind was off the port quarter. We were sailing full and by, but I was a little skeptical, not knowing just how good the riggings were. I walked about the quarter-deck for a while, and between seven and eight o'clock I ordered the second mate to take in the topsails and furl them, as I expected more wind when the sun got higher. It was going more to the left and I was pretty sure we were in for a heavy blow. Coming from that direction, however, it wouldn't do us any harm. We had breakfast at the usual time, and the mate took over the watch.

We went all day with lower sails, making really good time. I had the taffrail log out and we were logging twelve knots, but in the middle of the afternoon I had to take in the driver as it was too heavy on the wheel—one man couldn't handle it. Before dark I ordered the spanker taken in, and put out the trysail, and we sailed all night that way. At midnight the wind was dead astern. At about two o'clock I heard a noise overhead, with the ship heeling over to port, so I knew they had jibed over, going on the port tack, the wind W.SW. I had decided to travel on the semicircle, which is the shortest route, keeping toward the grand banks, outside of the steamship lanes, where there is a better chance for wind.

About fifteen days later we were coming abreast of the Azores, about 200 miles north. How magnificent it would be, I thought, if I could sail into Flores, take the motorboat to the dock at Fajangrand, and let my family see me, a full-fledged captain in a big four-master! Wouldn't that be something for the village to talk about! And Lucy—how I would love to see that sweet girl again! It was going on three years since I had last held her in my arms and felt her loving kisses! And so I dreamed for a while, but, though I was master of a ship, I had a course set for Barcelona, with no stopovers provided for, along the way. I have often wondered how my life might have changed if that detour could have been taken then!

Things went along nicely on board ship except for one thing—the second mate. From the day we left New York, he never had one good word to say about the mate.

I discouraged any gossip whenever he tried to say anything, knowing that if I let him talk to me about the mate, he would be talking to the mate about me. I liked him less, day by day. I never could tolerate a back-biter, anyway, and this fellow was one for sure. We had sailed a couple hundred miles eastward of the Azores, the wind had died down and we were practically in a calm. We'd had dinner and were all sitting in deck chairs on the starboard, or weather side, when the second mate began ridiculing the chief mate to his face. I corrected him: "You ought to be ashamed of yourself—the mate is your superior officer—how can you be so disrespectful?"

I believe he must have had some liquor hidden away somewhere; I was sure he'd had a drink, else he wouldn't have been so brazen. I had looked in his room for liquor—searched everything but his seabag, but had found nothing. Anyway, he turned on me just as sneeringly as he had on the mate. I don't remember what he said, but I decided the time was exactly right to teach him a lesson. I gave him the first judo before he knew anything was going to happen. He found himself stretched out on deck, but jumped to his feet, clearly in a fighting mood. I didn't wait for courtesy. I sailed into him again and gave him another judo, throwing him over my head to sit solidly on deck. He landed on his head and shoulders—pretty well shaken up and a bit dazed.

As he started to get up, I said angrily, "Now, are you going to be an officer, or are you going to play sailor? I can take very little more of it, so if you aren't going to be an officer, sing out!" And I started for him. He said, "Yes, sir, I'll try to be an officer!" That was the best thing I ever did for that man. From that day on, he was obedient and respectful, both to the mate and to me. A few days later even the sailors on his watch said he had changed a lot; he was a good man, and he didn't insult them any more. The mate told me that the men had just about decided to gang up on him and throw him overboard. The mate's remark was, "Captain, I think the incident came at just the right time. I am glad you did it, and I think maybe you saved the poor fool's life." "Well," I answered, "at least he is more obedient to me and respectful to you, and I think we have a peaceful ship, after all."

CHAPTER XLI

COUNT FELIX VON LUCKNER

My remark was, in a way, a bit premature, but for a very different reason. We had all forgotten that a war had started. Only a day or so later after my comment to the mate, we sighted a very large bald-headed three-master coming toward us. We were doing no more than three knots, with all sails set, and as she hove into plain view we were at once impressed and amazed to see her bow cutting quite a crest of water. As she came nearer, she slowed. I had my glasses and was trying to determine what she was and how she was making such speed. "She must have a propeller and a powerful engine," I told myself. There was some activity on deck, and while I was trying to make it out, there was a sudden "BOOM!" and a shot went over our bow. I immediately ordered: "Run up the Spanish flag!"

"Stop the ship! Clew up the topsails! Lower the picks! Haul the forestaysail to windward!"

The three-master lowered a motorboat with an officer and three men; they came alongside to the Jacob's ladder which I had ordered dropped over the side. The officer came up on deck and told me to pick up the manifest and ship's papers and come with him in the boat. The officer, who spoke good Spanish, went with me to my cabin. When we returned to the deck, the mate was waiting for me at the companionway, almost crying, and he said,

"Oh, Captain, what are they going to do with you?" The officer answered for me: "My commanding officer wants to talk with your captain." I told the mate to hold the ship just as it was. As I was leaving, the second mate said, "Oh, Captain, how in hell can you be so calm?" I answered, "What the hell—I'm no particular good to anyone!" I glanced forward. The crew were all sitting on the deck cargo waiting to see what was coming.

On the way over, I asked the officer, my escort, "What type of ship is that?" "That," he answered, "is a frigate of the German *Reich*."

"What," I asked, "are those two men doing at the foremast-head?" Short and brisk came the reply—"You are not to ask questions."

I climbed aboard the frigate to stand before a big officer in uniform who had come forward to meet me. He had a pair of binoculars hanging from his neck. He extended his hand, and when he gripped my hand, I felt as though mine was the hand of a child, caught in the hand of an adult. I stared for a second, in amazement, and I think I blushed, realizing the discourtesy, but in all my life I have never seen a human hand the size of that one. He was a tall, slender man, not huge but still pretty big. He greeted me with: "You are rather young, Captain, to be master of such a large sailing ship, are you not?"

He immediately wheeled around, ordering, "Follow me." I followed him down to the cabin. He sat down at the table, motioning me to a chair and extending his hand for the manifest. He then asked, "Is this a true manifest of the cargo?"

"I do not know," I answered, "the vessel was fully loaded when I shipped."

"Did you tell my lieutenant that you were from New York to Barcelona?"

"Yes, sir, that is correct."

"You are not a Spaniard, are you?"

"No, sir. I am Portuguese—born in the Azores—brought up on American whalers. My father was captain on a whaler and so was my brother-in-law."

"All right, Captain, I can tell that you are telling the truth. Anyway, we are not at war with you. Follow me to the deck; I will send you back to your ship."

On the way up, I said, "Commander, I didn't get your name." "My name is Von Luckner."

When I got to the rail, I bade the commander good-by, observing that the deck was full of officers and men in uniform. We went down to the motorboat, and the same lieutenant took me back to my ship, the *Leonora*. The mate grabbed my shoulder as I came up on board, and said, "Thank the Lord you are back; I've been pretty scared." I turned around to look at the frigate. They were already hoisting the boat out of the water. They blew three blasts and disappeared over the horizon as quickly as they had come.

In later years, when I was master of a passenger ship out of New York, I had the honor of meeting Count Von Luckner again. I reminded him of the incident and he remarked, "I remember it perfectly."

CHAPTER XLII

AQUI NOS ESTAMOS, BARCELONA!

After the boarding incident, everything settled down to a pleasant routine. The cook did very well, serving good meals and coffee. We were becalmed a couple of times but never lost our steerage way; never got off course. Every day I spent considerable time studying the ocean currents and charts around the entrance to Barcelona. By the time we got to the Big Rock I had familiarized myself with the ocean currents and weather of the Mediterranean. I knew the location of the islands and the proper course to follow to the entrance of Barcelona. Once in the Mediterranean, I gave both the islands and the coast a wide berth, taking the topsails in at night. In the middle of the afternoon of the forty-third day out of New York, we dropped anchor outside the entrance to Barcelona Harbor.

My Spanish stood me in good stead. The captain of the tug told me the doctor would not come so far out; that he would have to take me into the quarantine station where we would have to anchor again. He asked me if I was willing to pay the towing fees and I said I would pay all necessary fees to get my men ashore. I gave him the order to take us in to the station, instructing him to give us two short blasts for the usual stand-by signal, and to slow down, as I didn't want to take any chance of breaking the anchor on such a heavily laden vessel. "Yes," he answered, "I am well aware that the vessel is very heavy." I instructed the mate to stand by with the second anchor in case we made too much headway for one, and to be sure we wouldn't foul any other craft. The tug handled us nicely and we dropped anchor; the doctor came aboard and agreed that everything was okay. I gave him the owners' names and he told me he would call them and find out what to do with the ship.

The same tug returned in the afternoon with the owners' representative, who introduced himself and said he had a berth ready for the ship. "Would you be kind enough—" Oh, how polite he was—! "Would you be kind enough to give orders to heave up the anchor and stand by to tie the vessel up to the dock, port side to?" He had everything mapped out. Believe me, it was just about the happiest moment in my life when, just as it was getting dark, we were tied up and secure. My first voyage as captain was completed. Ever after, anyone could call me "Captain Joe," and I would pick it up with both ears!

I had checked the medicine chest before leaving New York, and knew that there were two bottles of Scotch and three of American whiskey in it. According to the tradition of the sea, there was no more proper or fitting occasion than that final triumphant moment, to "Splice the Main Brace!" I bellowed the order, and everyone heard it. While the two mates were walking toward me, I poured a couple tablespoons of whiskey in my glass and filled it up with water. I made a face as I drank it, and of course they couldn't tell how much I had. I poured a half-tumbler for each of them and for the rest of the crew who came up a moment later. Only then did I find that one member of the crew didn't drink at all. Everybody was happy. The cook asked if he might have a little bit more, so I poured in another half-shot. The first mate had enough, but the second mate took a little extra, too.

I sat down in my desk chair. There was very little activity around the dock. I saw a few women and girls walking toward the ship and I asked the mate if there were many skirts around the water front in Barcelona. "Yes, Captain, just like in any other port, there are plenty. Do you want me to stop them from coming aboard?"

"Well, I don't like to be different from any other skipper. What do you think?"

"They don't do a ship any good. They get aboard and they bring liquor and they get the boys drunk."

"Well, they don't get much benefit from the boys, because I don't believe they have much money." The second mate spoke up, "A few of them have a few dollars, but not much."

"Let's make sure we are not going to have any fire with all this lumber on board." Then I informed the crew that I would advance money the next afternoon as soon as I got it. I had been assured that there would be someone down from the office in the morning.

I didn't go ashore. I was so exhausted, and at the same time so contented that I felt like thanking my guardian angel for such a good passage. I read and studied. At about ten I walked around deck, finding everything serene and peaceful. The mate hadn't gone ashore either, so we talked for a while and I went to bed. I awoke before daylight, as usual, dressed, and came up on deck.

The weather was dry and pleasant. As soon as the cook got up, I had some coffee. The mates came in very shortly, the second mate apparently suffering a trifle from one too many the night before. We had breakfast at 7:30, the usual time, and I told the cook I would let him know what the procedure was going to be. "I don't know whether the agents will want us to remain on board until the ship is unloaded," I told him. "They told me I would get my instructions after I got here, so here we are and here we shall have to wait patiently until we get them."

I noticed there was a cathedral not far away, so I promised myself that would be my first stop. I decked myself out in a white shirt and tie but I had no presentable hat—mine had seen a lot of hard wear. But I had a brand new uniform cap in my gear, so I used that. A young fellow from the office came aboard and introduced himself, telling me he was to take me to the company office.

"How far," I asked, "is it from the American Consul's office?"

"It's just a block before we get there."

"That's just fine. I want some money to advance to the crew and I want some, myself. I want American money because American money is good anywhere in Spain."

"Oh, yes, I agree with that, but due to the rate of exchange you always lose. You want Spanish money." We were almost opposite the cathedral, so I asked, "Is that a Catholic church?"

"Oh, yes, indeed. Spain is Catholic."

"I presumed so. Would you wait a moment for me?" So I went in and said a little prayer, after which we resumed our journey in the horse-drawn buggy.

We stopped at the American Consulate, where I introduced myself. I told the Consul that I had to go to the company's office. He said they were expecting me; that he had talked to them a while ago and would go to the company office with me. There were the usual introductions in the company office, where a Señor Gonzales seemed to be the big wheel. I tried to ask questions but the señor informed me that first things came first.

"This," he announced, "is lunch time, and we shall have plenty of time to talk business tomorrow. You Americans are always too much in a hurry." I thanked him for calling me an American.

"By the way," he queried, "how is it that you talk such good Spanish? You speak it almost like a native." I responded that I had grown up speaking Portuguese and on the way over had spent a good deal of time improving my Spanish vocabulary. He took the American Consul and me to a lunch which lasted from about 12:30 until almost 3 o'clock. And all the stuff that man ordered—and ate! I'm sure it was enough for three average appetites. The American Consul didn't seem to be surprised—in fact, I'm sure he expected it. So, between smokes and liquors, he called his office twice. Back at the señor's office, I gave him a list of the amounts of money each man wanted, and he sent to the bank and got it for me. He asked if I was going back to the ship. "Yes," I answered, "I promised the boys I would bring money so they could go ashore and enjoy themselves."

The American Consul went with me to the ship, via horse and

buggy, and I advanced the money to the crew. During the drive back to the ship I spent most of the time answering questions.

How in hell could such a young fellow be captain and bring such a ship from New York to Barcelona. So I told him that I might be young in age but I was old in experience; that I went to sea on windjammers when I was fifteen years old. He stayed around, talking. I asked if he cared for a drink. He did. I asked him later how they were going to work the cargo. Would they want to keep me and the crew on the ship until the cargo was off?

"I rather think so," he replied. "You see, the Spaniards are not used to the American methods of handling donkey engines, and I'm pretty sure you'll have to hang around for two or three weeks at least. I'm not sure when they are going to start unloading, and when they do they won't be working as you do back home. They take time about it. By the way, Captain, what are you going to do tonight? I'm going back to the office, and at about five o'clock" (he glanced at his watch) "which will be almost right away, I'll be going home. Why don't you come with me?"

"Well, Mr. Dobson, I haven't anything to stay on the ship for, and I might as well go somewhere. It sounds like a nice thing to do."

"Well then, come along with me. My wife's niece from Madrid is visiting us and I'm sure you will find her to be good company. You see, when I was a young fellow I fell in love with a Spanish girl and married her. Her family lives in Madrid."

CHAPTER XLIII

FLOWER OF MADRID

Although we stopped at the office, and there were more introductions, my interest had suddenly been projected into the immediate future. At Mr. Dobson's home I was, of course, shortly introduced to the niece, Louisa. She was one of the classiest-looking girls I've ever seen. She was not only beautiful, but she was elegantly dressed. She was like a dream boat—in my language. My first thought—and most of the succeeding ones were the same—was that I'd like to dance with her. After all, what better way was there to get a little closer?

I told Mrs. Dobson, who spoke fairly good English, that her niece was beautiful. Then, in Spanish, I suggested that we go out for dinner and dancing.

"Oh," she replied, "it will be fine to go dancing, but I have dinner almost ready. We might as well have dinner at home and then go out. I know a nice place, not far from here." By then she could probably see that I was goggle-eyed over her niece, so she left us to get better acquainted. We had an excellent dinner, leisurely eaten, and afterward walked up to a dance hall about three blocks away.

Louisa danced like a dream. I wasn't such a good dancer, but she carried me around like nobody's business. She was gorgeous to look at, lovely to hold, and she had beautiful sparkling eyes, just like my favorite movie star's (whom I shan't name because she might not like it), and how she danced! I danced with her aunt, Mrs. Dobson, but didn't get on quite so well. I guess the enthusiasm was lost somewhere between the two.

It ended all too soon. Mr. and Mrs. Dobson left Louisa on the front porch with me. We were holding hands. I tried to kiss her but unh, unh. She wouldn't allow it, but she gave me a little good-night hug and that was it—except that we made a date for the next afternoon.

The date was to go aboard the *Leonora* and show Louisa the ship. She had never been aboard a sailing ship, and asked if it would be permissible. "By all means," I answered.

"All right, I'll be at my uncle's office when you get through at the company office and you can pick me up on your way down to the ship. I'll be there any time after one o'clock."

"Good. I'll be there as soon after one as I can make it." That's how the date was made.

I went back to the ship and asked the watchman if there had been anyone looking at the cargo. There hadn't, and I had not yet received any letters of instruction, so I went to bed with no worries or responsibilities and slept like a log.

I was at the company office at nine the next morning, but I found that in Spain there is no emphasis on punctuality. Finally, about eleven o'clock, Mr. Gonzales came in. I asked if there were any letters for me. "Yes," he answered, "there is a letter from your Mr. Elliott in New York. It is addressed to you, so we didn't open it. Come into my office." Mr. Gonzales asked me to read the letter and tell him what my instructions were. After studying it for a moment, all I could find in the way of orders was to do whatever Mr. Gonzales wished. Mr. Gonzales' reply was, "Well, if your Mr. Elliott left you to my discretion, my wishes are that you and your crew remain on the ship and unload it, because I believe we can make better progress with your crew, particularly with the deck cargo. We are not familiar with your winches and donkey boilers, and your crew works faster and more efficiently than one of ours could possibly do. If you don't mind, I wish you and your crew would stay."

That pleased me immensely. If it had been before I had met Louisa, I should probably have objected a little, but it was better pay than I had ever had before, and I was still captain of my own ship. It would be ridiculous even to suggest that I did not enjoy the prestige it gave me, and now that Louisa had come into the picture, I would have been happy to have the job—my first command—last another six months. I had nothing to lose and a good deal to gain. I agreed to his propositions and he immediately offered to take me to lunch. After my first experience at lunch with him, I declined, knowing that I'd never keep even a three o'clock date with Louisa if I accepted. I thanked him, and excused myself, explaining that I had a date for the afternoon and it was almost time to go.

Louisa was waiting at the Consulate, so we walked down to the square, got a horse and buggy (with a driver) and went down to the ship. She was amazed and intensely interested. I showed her everything—the deck cargo, the galley, the fo'c's'le, the windlass and the winches, and then walked back to the quarter-deck and the cabin. She was further amazed to see that I even had a private bathroom. There were never any bathrooms on Spanish ships until steamers came along. I showed her the chronometer, barometer, and sextant, and explained their importance on a ship, and that I had to keep my cabin locked on account of them.

We spent a most pleasant afternoon. We made some tea, into which she put a little gin, and when I started to make a little love, she didn't object. I kissed her and she kissed me back, and I felt I'd made pretty good progress. A little before dark, we left the ship. She didn't think it would be quite discreet to stay any later.

We got a horse and buggy and went back to town. The Dobsons didn't care to go out, so Louisa and I went out for dinner and dancing and had a wonderful time. I took her home around eleven, and went back to the ship. It occurred to me that it would be nice to have a room at the hotel, but on second thought, I asked myself, "Am I crazy? Here I have private quarters, a cook to serve dinner right in my cabin if I want it. I am completely master of my own ship, and Louisa apparently enjoys coming here and feels perfectly at ease in doing so. No. I'll stay with my ship."

The fourth day I was in port, Louisa came down with me again. We were hitting it off very well by now. We were much more like a pair of lovers. I was even more goggle-eyed than ever over her, and she liked me well enough, I thought. I asked the cook to serve tea, which he did very nicely. When he cleared the table I suggested to him that I didn't want to be disturbed. Louisa was quite the loveliest thing I'd ever seen, and she was as loving as could be. We stayed until well after dark, with no objections this time. The cook asked if I wanted dinner served but I said we would go up town. There was a good restaurant about three blocks from the dock, where we had a good dinner, taking our time about eating. It was after twelve by the time we got back to the Dobsons, but that was early enough for me with a girl like Louisa. I was liking her more every day.

We made a date with the Dobsons for an evening of dining and dancing on Saturday, and Mrs. Dobson invited me to come in at three o'clock for tea. I hung around the ship all morning. No one had yet been aboard to look at the cargo or make any plans for unloading. It worried me a little, but I reminded myself that I was in Spain and nobody ever got in a hurry when it came to work.

I left the ship at about two and arrived at the Dobsons' a little early. We visited, and Mrs. Dobson told me she had spent about three months in the United States, mostly at Baltimore, her husband's home town. Louisa had been born in Madrid and had lived there most of her twenty young years. It was almost four when Mr. Dobson came in. Mrs. Dobson excused the servants for the rest of the day, and then she and Mr. Dobson went out to see some friends for about an hour. Most of the time Louisa and I spent in the drawing room where Louisa was comfortably resting, sitting on my lap with her head on my shoulder and those lovely lips and beautiful eyes very close to mine.

The Dobsons returned somewhat later than they had intended, but still rather early for going out to dinner. We visited some more, and at about seven thirty we all went to the place where Louisa and I had dined and danced previously. We were sitting at our table, having already ordered dinner, when a young fellow, pretty well built and fairly good looking, came over to talk to Louisa. He got quite angry at her, and I didn't like his attitude. After all, though I had no strings on Louisa, I was still her escort. I asked Mr. Dobson if I should interfere. "Oh, no, Captain, Louisa can handle him." Louisa excused him after a couple more minutes and he went away, glancing back a couple of times as he did so. He was with two other fellows at another table, but paid us little further attention. We had dinner and danced all evening, and I expected the fellow to come and ask for a dance with Louisa, but he didn't. Some time later, between eleven and twelve, Mr. Dobson said he was a little tired and suggested that we leave. At the house, they invited me in, but I excused myself, saying, "It is late and you are tired and no doubt we shall all want to go to church in the morning."

Louisa said she would be glad to go with me if I would come by before ten o'clock. We kissed and said good night, and I got a coach and went back to the ship. When I left it, just a short distance from the ship, I noticed a fellow over by a railroad car, twenty feet or so away, on the dock, but I paid no particular attention—probably a wino, I thought.

I paid the driver, who wheeled around and left, and I started to walk toward the ship. I saw this fellow come out of the shadow with his hand raised, something shiny glinting in the dock-light. I knew that if I ran he could catch up and stick me in the back if it was a knife that he had in his hand, so I stood and faced him. I grabbed at his hand in an attempt to give him a judo, but I missed and the knife came down on the back of my shoulder. My arm was under his, however, so I didn't take a serious cut, although it stung enough, at that.

I shifted, grabbed his arm, gave him a judo. He landed, hard, on the railroad tracks and the knife flew out of his hand. He started to get up, but I pumped both fists into his face and he sagged back onto the rails. I picked up the knife and, leaving him half lying, half sitting, and pretty well dazed, I went back to the ship.

I asked the watchman if the mate was aboard and when he said that he was, I went to the mate's cabin and woke him up to see how bad a cut I had on my shoulder. I took off my shirt, and he said, "Captain, I can't tell how bad it is, but I don't think it is very deep, and it isn't very long."

I pulled out the knife and said, "This is what he stabbed me with." The cut was a little wider than the blade of the knife. "I can't tell how deep the cut is, but I think you had better see a doctor. I'll ask the watchman where we can find one." We debated about putting iodine on it, but I didn't want it if there was anything else. I hated the stuff on a raw cut.

The watchman, who had been hired by the ship's owners, told us that there was a doctor on duty twenty-four hours a day on the next dock; that he took care of all cases of the five warehouses and docks. "Will you please walk over with me? I'll have the mate stand watch while you're gone. I might not find him, myself," I stated.

He agreed, and in a few minutes we had found the doctor. He said, "It isn't very bad, but it will be pretty sore tomorrow. You'll have to put your arm in a sling so as not to damage the muscle. I'll put some medicine on it so it won't get infected." I showed him the knife, which was clean, with no rust. He bandaged my shoulder, fixed a sling, and told me to come back on Monday.

You should have seen the surprised look on Louisa's and the Dobsons' faces the next morning when I went to church with them.

"Now what is it?" they asked.

"A funny thing happened last night. You remember the fellow who was talking to you in the restaurant, Louisa?"

"Yes."

"Well, he was waiting for me when I got out of the coach, and he stuck a knife in my shoulder."

"That big coward! He is twice as big as you!"

"I saw him coming with the knife and I tried to stop him, but I missed his arm and he got me anyway."

"Are you sure he was the one?"

"Yes, I am positive."

We went to church and when we got back to the Dobsons', there was the mate from my ship with two policemen, waiting for me. The mate introduced me to the policemen in the best Spanish he could muster, which wasn't much, but we understood. The police explained that the fellow had been taken to the hospital and placed under arrest and that they wanted me to go and prefer charges against him. I looked at Mr. Dobson and asked if I had to.

"No, you don't have to, Captain. It is entirely up to you."

"I don't want to prefer charges. He got the worst of it."

"What do you mean he got the worst of it? You've got your arm in a sling."

One of the policemen smiled, and said, "Yes, I think he did. His nose is broken. He has three front teeth missing, and he has one very black eye. He is in bed in the hospital."

"How is that?" the Consul wanted to know. "Did you do that by yourself?"

"I sure did. I'm a fairly good boxer and I'm pretty good at judo. At least it is very effective against someone who doesn't know anything about it."

So then I had to explain what judo was. When they thought they understood it and the conversation ended, Mr. Dobson said to the policeman, "This involves an American skipper, so I'll have to go with you."

The policemen, Mr. Dobson, and I went over to the hospital. The fellow was pretty well bandaged, with his nose and left eye covered. His mouth was pretty badly swollen too. Mr. Dobson introduced him as Joe Zephyr. I'll never forget the name of that miserable guy. I asked him what was the idea? Was he trying to rob me?

"No," he grimaced. "Why should you try to steal Louisa from me?"

"I didn't steal her. She came with me because she wanted to." I didn't feel like arguing, so I said to him, "You are on your own, mister. When you see an American on the street, bless yourself and cross to the other sidewalk." We went back to the Dobsons.

Next day, two policemen, one in uniform and one in street clothes, came again to the ship and insisted that I prefer charges. Mr. Dobson had assured me that I was within my rights to refuse, so they finally left.

By Tuesday, the cargo had not yet been touched, so I went over to the office. Mr. Gonzales, I was informed, had gone to Valencia on business and would be back in one week, or possibly in two.

"What about the cargo?" I asked.

"The cargo won't be touched—nothing will be done until he comes back, so go and have a good time, Captain! You Americans know how to enjoy yourselves!"

I was very proud and happy that they were taking me for an American. I went to the American Consul's office and told Mr. Dobson. His advice was: "Enjoy yourself. You may not come back to Spain for a long time, so take a few trips around the country."

"That's a wonderful idea," I agreed enthusiastically. I hired a vehicle to go over to his house and asked Louisa if she would take a trip to Valencia with me. She threw her arms around me and kissed me and said, "When can we start?"

"As soon as I can get my clothes from the ship."

"I'll be ready when you get back."

I went down to the ship and, deviating slightly from the truth, told the mate I'd have to go to Valencia on ship's business. I told the mate that either he or the second mate must be on board at all times. We had clothes and navigation instruments to be responsible for, but that the watchman was responsible for the cargo. "Don't trust any strangers or let them on board."

"Don't worry, Captain, I'll take care of everything."

I asked the mates and sailors if they had enough money to last a week. They all said they had, but the cook needed a little so I gave him some out of my pocket. Things were pretty cheap in Spain and converted American dollars lasted pretty well. Apparently, the boys were all having a good time, at least nobody complained. I packed my suitcase and left for Dobson's house. Louisa was ready, so we went to the station and took the train to Valencia. Louisa was well acquainted in Valencia. We stayed there for two days, and I had one of the best times of my whole life. Then Louisa said, "Joe, why don't we go to Madrid? I'll take you to my house and you can meet my people."

"Wait a minute," I said, "is that quite nice? You are a nice young woman and I am a rascal, and do you think that is a nice idea? What about your mother and father?"

"Oh, my pa-pa. My pa-pa is an angel, and my mother—I lost her when I was a baby. I've been brought up by my aunt and, of course, the servants."

"Well, if you think it is all right, it is okay with me. All your father has to do is to tell me to get out and I'll take the train back to Barcelona. The only trouble is, I won't see you any more, but if that is the way you want it, that's how it'll be!"

The next morning we left Valencia for Madrid and when we got there I suggested that I should get a hotel room and then go over to her house. "No," she insisted, "my father's house is very large—it has seventeen rooms—you come to my house." Apparently she was in command, so I went along with her. She introduced me to her aunt, Señora Isabela Cabrillo, a rather youngish, good looking, and very pleasant person of about thirty-five, and to three servants, a man and two women. She kissed her aunt and the two women, all of whom seemed to be very fond of her. Her aunt was very cordial toward me. Louisa asked for her father and was told that Mr. Chavez would be in soon.

Mr. Chavez entered shortly afterward—a regular Spaniard with a very well trained goatee and mustache, long, curly hair, graying at the temples, white vest with a heavy gold watch-chain, white high collar, and an elegant cane. Louisa made a dive for him, almost screaming, "Oh, pa-pa," and throwing her arms around his neck, she kissed him, first on both cheeks and then on his nose. She then introduced me to him. I felt rather awkward in front of one with such a dignified bearing, but in my language he was either a duke or a prince, or both.

"A friend of my little Lisa is a friend of mine," he said, and made me welcome. He excused himself for a few minutes and came back dressed comfortably in an elegant silk lounging jacket, or perhaps it was a sort of dinner jacket. He wanted to know all about me, my father, and the United States. He was genuinely interested, and I was surprised at the interest he took in me.

We had a fine dinner, and afterward went to the library, which was filled with shelves of fine books. He asked if I had ever been in Madrid before. "No, I never have—in fact, I've never before been in Spain."

"There are lots of historical places in Madrid," he went on, "how long are you going to stay?"

"Oh, a couple of days."

"No, you should stay at least three or four days. It will take Louisa that long to show you around. Tomorrow, I'll turn my car and chauffeur over to Louisa, and you two can see Madrid as it should be seen. I'll get off at my office and you can go wherever you want to."

I had an excellent night's rest in a perfectly beautiful bedroom and came to breakfast the next morning feeling like a prince in a foreign country. Louisa had requested of her aunt that we all have breakfast in the dining room together. At about nine o'clock, the three of us left in her father's car. He got off at the office and we spent the day seeing old castles and cathedrals, including the one which was built by Charlemagne in the ninth century. I had read the story of it and enjoyed it immensely. I was particularly interested in the museum, which was added later with his statue at the entrance, along with those of Roland and Oliver, two of his generals.

On the third day I decided it was time to go back to Barcelona, so I asked Louisa if she was staying. "Oh, no. I'm going to the Dobsons'. I am going back with you. You don't think I'm going to leave you to play around with other señoritas? Oh, no. I'm going to stick close by while you are here. Anyway, I have a proposition to make to you. We can talk about it on the train."

We said good-by to her father and to her aunt and left for Barcelona. I didn't know what the proposition was going to be, and when it came, it was as unexpected as it was direct. "Joe," she said, breaking the silence of a thoughtful interval, "I'm in love with you and I want you to marry me. How do you feel about me?"

"Louisa honey, I love you very much, but about the worst thing you could do for yourself would be to marry me. You'd just about starve to death for the next few years. Just the fact that I'm captain on this sailing ship doesn't mean that I'll keep on being a captain. It may be years before I'm captain again. The days of sailing ships are nearly over. I have a second-mate's license for steamers, but it may be quite a while before I get a job as second mate. I could never even come close to giving you the kind of home or the kind of life you are used to. It just wouldn't do. It would be a long, long time before I would be able to come back and feel that I could give you what you deserve. No. It just wouldn't work." I made it as plain as I could. I had never been proposed to before, or ever made a proposal, and I was so taken by surprise that I didn't really know what to think.

"All right, Joe. After you get through with the ship, we will go back to Madrid. My father likes you very much, and we have a lot of land. We have one rancho of two or three thousand acres." She mentioned how many sheep and cattle they had and how many people there were working for them. "And Joe, you don't have to work. My father will teach you the business."

She continued the argument somewhat further, but it didn't appeal to me. Louisa appealed—oh, yes, but the cart was ahead of the horse. I preferred to make my own proposal, but more than that, and vastly more important, I felt I had to be on my own and make my own way, just as I had done since I blacked my skin at Fayal the day I went to sea. No silver-platter, ready-made destiny would ever do—not for me. This I tried to explain, but not too successfully, I'm afraid. She was sweet and beautiful and I wanted her for my very dear friend. But as a wife—well, I just wasn't ready.

"We will talk some more, Joe. I'm going to convince you that we are the right family for you."

In due time we arrived in Barcelona to find that Mr. Gonzales had not yet returned. Louisa said, "Let's go for a little trip. How about the Riviera?"

"Oh, no. That's too far away. Suggest something for two or three days, maybe four, and I'll go, but not there." So we went on some short trips to different places and had a wonderful time. She brought up the marriage idea again, but I couldn't be convinced that it was the right thing for either of us. The thing that Louisa couldn't understand was that I would rather be a pauper in the United States than a millionaire in Spain, and that I would never give up my recently-acquired American citizenship for any other prize in the world.

CHAPTER XLIV

EMPTY SHIP — HOMEWARD BOUND

In the United States it would have taken seven or eight days to unload the *Leonora*. In Barcelona, it took two and a half weeks. The winches were both handled by my sailors, but the crew on the dock and the men working on cargo and the after gang were native longshoremen. The forward gang was made up of my crew only. The natives talked too much to get anything done, and when they got tired of working they just walked off. So, even with my mates as deck bosses, we could work cargo only as fast as the dock gang would put it away.

We had been in Barcelona forty-nine days when the cargo was finished, and when I signed the ship over to the Barcelona Navigation Company. In the meantime Louisa hadn't given up, and I still kept trying to explain how I felt. I said that if she would give me all of Barcelona, with Madrid thrown in, and a first mortgage on all of Spain, it still wouldn't buy the rights given to me with my citizenship papers. To me, the U.S.A. was heaven, and there I would live until God took me somewhere else.

Soon after the cargo was off the ship, Mr. Gonzales told me there was an Italian passenger steamer for which his company was agent, that would be going from Barcelona straight to New York. That suited me perfectly. I took my crew and moved to a hotel until we could be ready to sail.

I lost no opportunity to spend my leisure time with Louisa.

She was intelligent, well educated, and beautiful, and if that were not enough, she had a wonderful disposition and a warm and loving heart. But as at all other ports, the time of parting was drawing hourly nearer.

A couple of days later, Mr. Gonzales took me aboard the steamer and introduced me to the captain. Unbeknown to me, he gave orders that I should be seated at his table. I was given a stateroom all to myself, first class. The marine law is that captain and mates must sail first class and the crew (my crew, in this case) second class. The steamer was to sail at ten the next morning. I went ashore and over to the American Consul's office, and later in the afternoon went with Mr. Dobson to his house. In the evening we went to the usual place to dine and dance.

Louisa was pretty quiet, and every time I looked at her I could see a sort of hurt look in her eyes. Occasionally, I saw her brush away a tear. I had spent last nights ashore in other places, but this one was the saddest of all, I think, because Louisa had tried so hard to get me to stay, and I truly adored her. But I was sure that I knew myself well enough to know that I would never be happy or satisfied on any course set by someone else.

Next morning I went to bid Louisa and the Dobsons good-by, and they went with me down to the ship. We walked around the decks and I showed them my stateroom. About ten o'clock we heard the first whistle and the usual cry, "All ashore that's going ashore!" It hurt to say good-by to Louisa. Her final plea was, "Joe, my father is getting old, and we need you. We could be so happy together!" I could only promise that I would come back as soon as possible. Then the last whistle blew. The gangplank went up and they were waving good-by from the dock, which receded rapidly into the distance.

The ship was pretty well filled. The best chance to look over the passengers came at dinner time. There were a lot of attractive Spanish and Italian ladies at the captain's table, but my heart was dull and heavy. Louisa had become a big part of my life.

We had good weather—just a couple of modest blows. Three days before we reached New York, I sent a wire to Frank Elliott telling him when we would arrive and asking him to call his brother so that my job would be ready the day I got there.

In New York we had no trouble, of course. There were lots of taxicabs and we hired two to take us over to Frank Elliott's office. Mr. Elliott was pleased with my part in the *Leonora* affair, and when he handed me my check he also presented me with a letter of recommendation.

Frank Elliott called his brother, and Tom Elliott told me to get a cab and come to his office. When I got there he was really glad to see me. His greeting was, "Well, well, Captain Joe! How did you make out? Did you get swell-headed?"

"No, sir. I don't think so."

"Do you want your job back?"

"Yes, I do. I'm ready to start right now."

"You're on the payroll but we've decided to send you home for a week's vacation for helping us out on this Barcelona affair."

He gave me a pass on the New Bedford line as a passenger, and told me to report to Captain Robinson a week later on my old ship, the steamer *Maine*. "I'll try to have you going second pilot. If not, you'll have to go quartermaster until I can get you some relief jobs as second pilot."

I felt kind of guilty as I had it in my mind to look for a second or third mate's berth on an ocean-going steamer, since I had the second mate's license that I had worked so hard to get. I had to tell him what was in my heart. He agreed that I had a perfect right to do so, and promised, "If there is anything we can do in lining up an outside berth for you, we will do so."

I bade him good-by and went on board the steamer *New Hampshire,* which was in New York that day, leaving for New Bedford that evening.

I greeted everyone whom I knew on the *New Hampshire,* especially the mates and pilots. Next morning we arrived in New Bedford. All the foremen on the dock were glad to see me, and asked what kind of a trip I'd had, for word had gotten around very quickly after I left that I had taken a big ship to Spain, acting as captain. I left my clothes with the mate, John Asklund, and walked up to Harwitz' whalers' outfitting store. They informed me that the *Greyhound* had left three weeks before with the captain and Mary and the baby, all of whom I was most eager to see. Everyone wanted to know about my trip to Barcelona, and they also told me that Captain Mandley of the *Margaret* had left the sea and bought himself a business. Would I like to talk to him? "Yes," I said, "by all means. He is a good friend of mine." They called a number, and called me to the telephone. When I heard Captain Mandley's voice on the other end of the line, I was very happy. His first words were, "Well—Captain Joe! How are you? Wait right there. I'll pick you up in my automobile in about five minutes." He came rushing through the door, leaving his auto with the motor running and the door open, just as though I were a long-lost brother.

"Joe," he said, "you got a nice reward for working hard. Was it a successful trip?" In the same breath he asked, "Where are you going and where are your clothes?"

He drove me down to the pier. I picked up my clothes, and on the way to his garage we stopped at the bank, where I deposited my money (except for a hundred dollars which I kept out for a good time and some new clothes). We went down to Captain Mandley's garage. It was a pretty big deal—covered a square block—and he had six rental U-Drive cars, a couple of full time mechanics and a good business. He, too, wanted to know all about the trip, so we kept on talking while he took me down to my Aunt Emily's where I left my clothes. I arranged to board with her for the week, though I confess she didn't see much of me. I slept there and had breakfast, but the rest of the time I stuck to my idol, Captain Mandley, like a leech.